Everglades Patrol

UNIVERSITY PRESS OF FLORIDA

Florida A&M University, Tallahassee
Florida Atlantic University, Boca Raton
Florida Gulf Coast University, Ft. Myers
Florida International University, Miami
Florida State University, Tallahassee
New College of Florida, Sarasota
University of Central Florida, Orlando
University of Florida, Gainesville
University of North Florida, Jacksonville
University of South Florida, Tampa
University of West Florida, Pensacola

EVERGLADES PATROL

TOM SHIRLEY

Foreword by Patsy West

University Press of Florida

Gainesville · Tallahassee · Tampa · Boca Raton

Pensacola · Orlando · Miami · Jacksonville · Ft. Myers · Sarasota

Library of Congress Cataloging-in-Publication Data
Shirley, Tom, 1930–
Everglades patrol / Tom Shirley ; foreword by Patsy West.
p. cm.
Includes bibliographical references and index.
ISBN 978-0-8130-4191-9 (alk. paper) — ISBN 0-8130-4191-0 (alk. paper)
    1. Shirley, Tom, 1930– 2. Park rangers—Florida—Biography.
3. United States. National Park Service. 4. Everglades National Park (Fla.)
I. West, Patsy, 1947– II. Title.
SB482.F6S44 2012
363.6'80975939092—dc23
[B]
2012009923

University Press of Florida
15 Northwest 15th Street
Gainesville, FL 32611-2079
http://www.upf.com

For my children, grandchildren, and all the people of Florida, and
to Peter Gonzalez, Lee Chamberlain, Freddy Fisikelli, and Jack Moller

Contents

Foreword

Few people have the collected knowledge of the Everglades wetlands as does Tom Shirley. Raised in Miami, a wildlife enthusiast, and a legend in his own time, he has been captivated by the Everglades wetlands since he was a child in the 1930s. As a result of his long association, he commands the introspective view of the serious chronicler, an acute observer, a poet, a storyteller, a man in love. Knowing his subject intimately, biologically and seasonally, he has created for us in *Everglades Patrol* a page-turning personal memoir that affords us flashbacks to an Everglades that, unfortunately, we will never experience. Hopefully it will give us the determination to be more aware of the famous site in our backyards and show some real concern for its future.

Indeed, most of us are very proud of our world-famous, unique Everglades wetlands, but few have more than a basic "newspaper-headlines" knowledge of the results of the political agendas that have (and are still) destroying the Everglades' islands and wildlife, from man-made floods, droughts that cause fires, stagnant retention ponds—all created in the name of flood prevention and adequate drinking water—to the runoff of pollutants and deadly toxins that are by-products of intrusive agriculture. *Everglades Patrol* emerges as a most sensitive and realistic assessment of the impact of these invasive programs of the twentieth and twenty-first centuries on one of the most vital, threatened, and beleaguered ecosystems in the world.

As a lieutenant in charge of the Everglades District for the Florida Game and Fresh Water Fish Commission, 1955–85, Tom Shirley had a 24/7 beat that placed him in the unenviable position of witnessing the ditching, diking, and pumping of, and the disastrous effects of water conservation areas on, the Everglades wetlands and the wildlife he had sworn to protect "so help me God!" His frustration is tempered by a narrative that provides vivid imagery of wood ibises flying high, spoonbills sieving in shallows, hundreds of egrets rising up like clouds, herds of deer, and sloughs full of alligators . . . before the muck fires from the drained, smoldering Everglades wetlands clouded our vision. Next, we see Tom Shirley retired, with his advocate hat on, working tirelessly to gather data from his own records and the Everglades itself to fight environmental ignorance and big-time Everglades politics.

Join Tom Shirley for a romp through the Everglades wetlands, swat a mosquito or two, hear the bellow of alligators, soar up over the saw grass on a dark night in your aerodynamically designed airboat, chase after a few poachers who ran for it, sleep by an Everglades campfire on a three-thousand-year-old island with one ear cocked for the sound of airboat activity, and you'll have some idea what it was like to be Lieutenant Tom Shirley on Everglades patrol.

This publication is a tutorial that every South Floridian, every transplant, every tourist, and every politician who votes on Everglades issues should read, as it encompasses a slice of southeastern Florida ecohistory that is basic and profound. While it is delivered to us in Tom Shirley's wonderful storytelling voice, it is a history of the Everglades wetlands that has an effect on our lives every time we turn on a faucet.

Patsy West
Director, Seminole/Miccosukee Archive
Ft. Lauderdale

Preface and
Acknowledgments

If I could have a wish come true, I would take you on a trip throughout the Everglades and show you how unique and beautiful it was as I saw it in my early years in the 1930s. First we would travel across the Everglades at night on the only trans-Everglades roadway in those days, the Tamiami Trail, U.S. Highway 41. You could see the glow in the sky made by the millions and millions of fireflies. It was something gorgeous to see. In the headlights as we crossed the Everglades on the Trail, you could see tens of thousands of rabbits, raccoons, bobcats, otters, deer, gators, snakes, frogs by the ton. What an abundance of wildlife.

As morning came, I would put you in an airplane. We would head for the Ten Thousand Islands. I would show you the hundreds and hundreds of roseate spoonbills, their beautiful rose-colored wings looking transparent as they flew into the sun.

You would see the black-and-white wood storks, the great white and blue herons, the snow-white ibis, green-winged teals with their iridescent wings. We'd see a vast assortment of crocodiles and alligators basking in the sun.

Off the beaches there would be flocks of pelicans with bright yellow on their beaks. And along the mangrove coastline, dolphins would frolic in the water; manatees would float slowly by, next to sharks— many sharks of all sizes, as we flew over the Ten Thousand Islands.

And yes, there would be tens of thousands of islands—islands every which way. And waterways headed in every direction, just brimming with an abundance of wildlife.

Huge flocks of birds like this were once a common sight in the Everglades wetlands. The engineering plan of the U.S. Corps of Engineers and the drainage programs of Flood Control through the Corps' canals and levees created artificial floods and droughts that destroyed the habitat for the birds and other animals in the Everglades wetlands. (Photo by Tom Shirley.)

We would head on northeasterly across the Everglades wetlands, which would be covered with saw grass, brackish water, black mangroves, and red mangroves. There, the Everglades grasses would vary in color like an artist's palate from green to yellow to red.

Then we'd go farther north into the cypress swamp where the large cypress trees grew with the beautiful hanging grey moss. And again clouds and clouds of birds: ibis, spoonbills, white herons, blue herons, and ducks by the tens of thousands. As we flew, below us there would be so many clouds of birds that it would look like a grassfire in the Everglades that suddenly turned into a big, white, puffy cloud that just rose right off of the ground as they flew upward. What a breathtaking sight!

Back on the east coast in Miami, we'd fly across the Miami River, then on up the coast to a spot near the Broward County and Palm Beach County line. There you'd see really gigantic alligators! They would just die of old age there, as the food was plentiful, and they were at the top of the food chain. Of course, back then, the food chain ran from the smallest to the largest, but these alligators looked like they would be maybe 4 feet across the belly and were as black as a Goodyear tire—just hundreds and hundreds of them. No harm was being done to them at all. They lived in a free world back in those early times.

And, as we continued on up to just south of Loxahatchee, in what would become "Conservation Area 2," we would see ecologically perfect savannas and islands. And nothing but lots of game trails from one island to the other. You would look down on herds of deer, alligator holes (ponds) every which way, and again, an abundance of birdlife. What a gorgeous sight, a perfectly active wetlands ecosystem . . . that's why it's called one of the natural wonders of the world, the Everglades.

I want to give you the opportunity to envision what South Florida was like, what the Everglades wetlands was like before man altered it. And I want to share my experiences and observations while I was trying desperately to protect the Everglades for the future enjoyment of you and yours.

I hold a fawn during the Game Commission's deer rescue operation in 1966. (Photo by Toby Massey.)

I have fought for fifty-four years to assure that the Everglades won't be just a chapter in a history book. Nature created this most perfect ecosystem that produced life from the smallest insect to the largest predator and hosted an unimaginable variety of plant life.

In reading *Everglades Patrol*, I hope that you will begin to visualize the beauty of the Everglades as it was, through my eyes—a person who knew this land intimately—to understand the destructive directives that were carried out by Flood Control/Water Management, and realize that I did all that was in my power to save this priceless environment from extinction, for you to enjoy. I hope you will see the value to restoring the Everglades, not to a travesty of its former self, as politicians and grant writers envision, but a true restoration to the ecosystem that it once was.

*   *   *

I would not have written these reminiscences had it not been for my desire to relate all of the beauty, the great abundance of wildlife, and the perfect ecosystem that was the Florida Everglades wetlands. In this endeavor, I received the encouragement and support of family and friends.

I would like to formally dedicate this publication to four Gladesmen who have given freely of themselves to preserve the Everglades wetlands. They are Peter Gonzalez, Lee Chamberlain, Freddy Fisikelli, and Jack Moller.

Peter Gonzalez, a strong leader among the Everglades preservationists, hauled food out to stranded deer in times of high water and helped rescue and move the deer in emergency conditions. He has labored to plant native trees and eradicate the invasive exotic melaleuca trees. He has battled hazardous conditions to aid in putting out Everglades muck fires. A prominent designer and builder of Everglades vehicles, Pete and his sons were always available when called on to rush out to aid Everglades enthusiasts when they crashed or got bogged down or stranded.

Lee Chamberlain has been a very avid conservationist. In his work he was anxious to protect the rights of the Gladesmen and their culture to guarantee that we have access to public lands for traditional use and recreational activities. A past president of the Everglades

Pete Gonzalez is a great leader among men. He was an active conservationist in the 1960s, involved in such important projects as catching and removing deer, putting out Everglades fires, irradiating invasive melaleuca trees, and fighting for conservation and the rights of Gladesmen. (Shirley Collection.)

Coordinating Council, Lee has served as a policymaker. He is an Eagle Life Member and former member of the Board of Directors of the Florida Wildlife Federation. He worked with Florida senator Tim McPherson and the Division of Natural Resources to curtail the commercial sale of the melaleuca tree, which has been so detrimental to the Everglades environment.

Freddy Fisikelli, a true Gladesman, has been active in the Everglades since he was a child. He is a former president of the Half-Track Club of Dade County. In the 1966 flood created by Flood Control, it was he who led the fight to remove four hundred deer to higher ground. He has served on the Board of Directors of the Florida Wildlife Federation. He fought aggressively against the high-water conditions in the Everglades and the policies of Flood Control that created this situation. He was active in halting both the Cross-Florida Barge Canal and the Everglades Jet Port project.

Jack Moller was active with the Everglades Conservation Club and served on the Everglades Coordinating Council. He has been a shrewd negotiator in his efforts to protect the Everglades and has won many awards for his conservation efforts. He has also fought for the recognition of the Gladesmen's culture and heritage. He is our diplomat. (Photo by Rick Dilliston.)

Jack Moller, a former teacher, also grew up in the Everglades, becoming active in the Everglades Conservation Club on the Tamiami Trail. He served on the Everglades Coordinating Council, winning many awards for his conservation efforts. In the fight to protect the Everglades, Jack proved to be a shrewd negotiator with politicians and very agile at meeting new challenges. He, too, fought to protect the Gladesmen's culture and heritage, and he continues to be our diplomat and ambassador. For these Gladesmen, fighting for the true restoration of the Everglades wetlands to its natural state has been a lifelong dedication and passion, encompassing years of hard work. I would ask you readers to consider picking up this great challenge. We are running out of time. Please help keep the Everglades wetlands alive.

I would like to express my appreciation to Henry P. Cabbage, Public Information Director, Florida Fish and Wildlife Conservation Commission, for his patience and typing; and to my daughter, Melanie for typing, clerical assistance, and her many phone calls.

I am especially indebted to my editor and friend, Patsy West, Director of the Seminole/Miccosukee Archive, who worked closely with me from start to finish and helped me keep on target. She was wonderful.

My sincere gratitude and appreciation to my family, to Tommy, Troy, Barney, Melanie, and Ray for our memories and to the wonderful times we have cherished in the Everglades.

Needless to say, my closest supporter is Naomi, my wife of forty-three years, who experienced with me those extraordinary years of exploration and adventure, and all of the great times and hard times that went with them.

Introduction

The Everglades wetlands once flowed naturally south from Lake Okeechobee to Florida Bay. Everyone, from the earliest explorers forward, speculated on the possible drainage of the shallow flowing wetlands (a true "wetlands," which should not be classified as a "river") and its future uses. In the first decade of the twentieth century, drainage in southeastern Florida was initiated. In southeast Florida, canals were cut to Lake Okeechobee, and Okeechobee's water then drained into the Atlantic. As foretold, the drained lands became fields or homesites on the lower southeastern coast from Palm Beach to Miami. Even the former Everglades wetlands south of Lake Okeechobee became dry enough to be farmed.

But, during the Hurricane of 1928, wind and heavy rainfall swept over Lake Okeechobee, pushing floodwaters over the southern banks, drowning hundreds of farming families and their immigrant workers. It was Florida's first natural disaster.

President Herbert Hoover set about to see that this would never happen again. He supported the building of a massive dike four stories high around the lake. In this engineering feat, Lake Okeechobee's flow was further diverted through rivers to the east and west. So, instead of the lake's waters forming the Everglades, from that time on, most of the water flow to the Everglades wetlands was cut off.

Only after the Hoover Dike was built could the towns on the southern perimeter of the lake—towns that should never have been built in the Everglades floodplain in the first place—and the vast acres of agriculture that supported them be considered safe. But their safety came at the expense of the Everglades wetlands.

It wasn't long before the consequences of man messing with nature appeared: those very fields became a man-made desert because all of the water had been rerouted! While on the coasts, with the former hydraulic balance of the Everglades' water obliterated, there was salt-water intrusion from the Atlantic Ocean. And, in the drought-ridden Everglades wetlands that bordered the eastern cities, fires of putrid "muck" smoke smoldered away in the overlying peat bogs seasonally and intermittently for decades, wreaking havoc on the sinuses and allergies of all who lived in the vicinity.

The Everglades was still there, just in a *very* altered state.

Then came 1947, a year of heavy rainfall and two very "wet" fall hurricanes. This situation caused an overabundance of water to spill out from the parched Everglades basin and rush eastward through the rivers and creeks, filling the drainage ditches like it had never done before. Southeast Florida was by then bustling with cities, including some new western subdivisions on drained Everglades land. All were now underwater! This was no "killer" flood, but many areas looked a lot like New Orleans after Hurricane Katrina in 2005.

Of course, the hue and cry was loud! *Something* had to be done to assure that such a disaster could never happen again!

As a result of the 1947 flood, the United States Army Corps of Engineers was instructed to create a new protective antiflood system of levees (also called dikes) to protect the cities. The Corps eventually constructed some 2,000 miles of levees, canals, weirs, and their attendant pumps that were to be the "cure-all" for southeast Florida. The dikes would protect the cities from floodwaters and would retain water in times of drought for drinking and agricultural needs. The system was operated by the Central and Southern Florida Project for Flood Control.

Ironically, there was yet another issue to add to the future dilemma of drainage and water conservation in southeast Florida. Just weeks after the 1947 flood, U.S. president Harry S. Truman opened the nation's newest national park. The antithesis of artificial flood-control systems, the Everglades National Park was all about the *preservation* of a national wetlands preserve! Many years in the planning, the park would, over the decades, become a great diversity of Everglades ecosystems that would stretch across the tip of the Florida Everglades up into the Big Cypress, south to the Ten Thousand Islands, and east to the Florida Reef. The well-being of the internationally applauded Everglades National Park would provide yet another important issue in the future history of water-regulatory issues in the Everglades wetlands.

This book is a chronicle of the great Everglades: the abundance of wildlife that once was; its supporters, caretakers, custodians; also its detractors, poachers, fire bugs, Flood Control, agricultural pollution. The role of the game warden, the wildlife officers riding like the early TV hero Lincoln Vail across the Everglades on airboats; stories of stakeouts, airboat crack-ups, catching wildlife for research, saving wildlife from man-made floods, nights sleeping on the ground around a distant campfire, the interrelationships of poachers and the law. It will provide an overview of the Everglades as it was, one that readers will never see as the Everglades that I knew exists no more. It has been altered so as to be almost unrecognizable. Yet this story, too, begs to be told.

1

The 1930s

My Early Years in Miami

I was born in Kennedy, Texas, on November 6, 1930. Shortly thereafter, my father, Barney Vance Shirley, received a letter from his cousin who was married to Bill Sternkey, an internationally known tropical fish breeder. Sternkey went all over the world showing different specimens of fish that he had hybridized. He told my father in that letter, "Come to Florida! There's a mint to be made in tropical fish."

So in 1931, we packed up my mother, Estella Blanch Shirley; my sister, Doris Nell; and my brother, Barney Viron Shirley, and left for Miami on a boat named the *Mohawk*. Our family won a basket of fruit for being the "best-mannered family" on the boat from Texas to Miami, which was quite an honor for my mother.

This fish farm of Sternkey's was just east of Opa Locka Airport. It was within 100 yards of the old blimp hangar airport. I remember cutting my second birthday cake there.

Although I was very young, I can remember some of my thoughts and experiences and how it was in Miami in the 1930s. Starting at around age three, I had become interested in all sorts of animals—pelicans, sea gulls, butterflies, and reptiles. There was just an abundance of wildlife and insects to be seen everywhere you looked. Butterflies were flying all over the place. All the colors . . . and it was a popular thing to catch them. It was so popular that the stores sold special-made butterfly nets. And kits with framed pictures where you could put the various types of butterflies with their names.

I remember Biscayne Boulevard. The royal palm trees that today are so tall and line the boulevard were then only 3 feet tall!

There was a Seminole camp on the Miami River, just across from downtown Miami. I'd often see the Seminoles come into town. They were dressed so colorfully.

We went to Miami Beach over the Venetian Causeway. It was a wooden bridge, very long and made of heavy wooden planks. I remember going over it and listening to the *plankety, plankety, plank* of the boards. On the beach, the conch shells were strewn all over, so many of them that you had to be careful not to stub your toes.

And there were pelicans by the thousands. Formation flights of fifteen or more were very common, and they flew so close to the ocean that I thought their wings would strike the water. I didn't understand how they could coast so long without flapping their wings. I had no idea that they were gliding on the winds that came off the water. Then, from high in the sky, a flock would peel off into a dive like Stuka dive bombers going in for a kill. But just before they hit the water, they would fold their wings and crash into the water after a school of fish.

On the boat docks, pelicans were always there, sitting on pilings, waiting for handouts from fishermen cleaning their catch. Since I was just a child, I would be looking at the pelicans head-on. To me, with their piercing eyes and long beaks, they looked like the old grey-bearded wise man of the sea.

We had friends who lived east of Biscayne Boulevard at approximately Seventeenth Street. I was about four years old, maybe even younger. I would get up in the morning and venture out. We lived approximately 50 yards from the bay. I would go down to the bay in the morning and look into the water. I would see all sorts of sea life: octopi, crabs, all types of needlefish—all in abundance. There was a different type of fish I don't see anymore. We called them ink fish back then, maybe it was a type of "Black Sea pigeon." We drove a Packard. It didn't belong to us but to a friend of ours—and I remember going down what was then Twenty-Seventh Avenue, which was just a rocky road back then. We had another friend who lived right on Little River at West Twenty-Seventh Avenue. A neighbor of this individual had a pen of alligators. I remember experiencing that first smell of alligators. It was a great experience for me.

We lived with one of my parents' friends for quite a while, as times were poor.

We had a German shepherd dog named Charlie Boy, and it seemed like every Sunday, when we went out onto the back door step, there would be a chicken that he had caught. Of course, it was dead. Well, we had chicken for Sunday dinner, which came in handy. We didn't bother to scold Charlie Boy too much because he had done us a good deed.

One of the most exciting entertainments we had was to go down to Pier 5 on Sunday and watch all the boats come in that had been out sportfishing. There was an abundance of sailfish, king mackerel, and all types of fish, and we'd marvel at all the beautiful boats with shiny mahogany decks and transoms. All of them had fancy names, and all of those beautiful boats were owned by the wealthy, something that we could only dream of. Yes, Sunday at Pier 5 was a great gathering that we always looked forward to.

Around 1935, we lived two or three blocks from Edison School. I remember at night, I would be lying in bed trying to go to sleep, but the light from the Edison football field would shine in my eyes.

Then a bad hurricane came in. It was the granddaddy of all hurricanes, the famous Labor Day Storm of September 2, 1935.

I remember well that my mother made a little sign on the back of a piece of cloth giving my name and address.

I said, "What are you going to do with that, Mother?"

"I'm gonna sew it on to the back of your shirt," she said.

I asked, "Why you gonna do that?"

"Well, this is a bad hurricane," she replied. "You could be blown away, and I couldn't find you! This way, whoever finds you will know your address and your name."

That brought the first fear to me, of course.

We left our home and went to the Sears store at Thirteenth Street and Biscayne Boulevard. It was open for people who were searching for refuge. So we stayed in the Sears store during the hurricane.

I recall getting up the next morning and walking down the stairs. On the bottom floor of the Sears store was a foot of water. There was beach sand all over Biscayne Boulevard. It was a terrible storm. It was a frightening thing for me at the age of five.

Although small in diameter, the Labor Day Storm is still considered to have been the most powerful and destructive hurricane ever recorded in the Western Hemisphere. The wind velocity was estimated to have been between 200 and 250 miles per hour. The barometer dropped to 26.35—a record low. It caused a storm surge that swept westward across Cape Sable, destroying mangroves, whipping the tops out of royal palms, and laying waste to the coconut groves.

It drowned many World War I veterans who had been working on the Overseas Railroad in Islamorada. It derailed and overturned eleven railroad cars and tore up 41 miles of track. The hurricane killed more than 376 men, women, and children.

Another of our friends, Sam, lived just north of the Edison High School. He had a food store. My mother worked part-time at Sam's store. She would put me in a cardboard box under the counter at the register. I would doze off, but every time she rang up a purchase, the ding of the register would wake me up.

Sam had a hobby of collecting scorpions and black widows and watching them fight. I was fascinated. I figured that if Sam could do it, so could I! My mother gave me many scoldings, many times. I even remember getting out of the crib that they kept me in (for a long time apparently). I would get up very early in the morning before my mother and father got out of bed. I would go outside and turn over rocks and catch scorpions and black widows and put them in jars that I kept hidden under the house. That was my first hobby. I observed that the black widow could kill the scorpion, but after the black widow ate the scorpion, the black widow would die.

My father quite often had to go to the Everglades to collect various types of tropical fish. He made the first black molly by taking the speckled black mollies and breeding them until they came up with one that was completely black. I remember that this cross-breeding was recorded at the Smithsonian Institution around 1936 or 1937.

When he went to the Everglades, the mosquitoes were horrible, but fortunately, he came across this German doctor who'd traveled to South America fighting malaria. The doctor advised, "Barney, I'll tell you what you can do to keep the mosquitoes off of you. Get you a friend you depend on and a bar of Octagon Soap. Go out into an area of the Everglades where the mosquitoes are most abundant. Take off all of your clothes and let as many as mosquitoes as you can coat your body black. Just let 'em eat on you for about fifteen minutes. Be sure you take this friend with you because you'll probably pass out. Give yourself about a fifteen-minute period of getting bit by the mosquitoes. Then, wipe your body down with Octagon soap, and you can go back home. Make sure to take someone with you because you're going to pass out!"

Father followed the doctor's instructions, and when he went through that ordeal, he did pass out! But after that, when he went back to the Everglades to where all of the mosquitoes were, the mosquitoes would come within about a foot of him, but then they'd turn around and haul butt! So, that worked out pretty well for him.

Years later, we moved in to the Allapatta area. Allapatta means "alligator" in the Creek Seminole, Muscogean language. On Seventeenth Avenue and Thirty-Sixth Street was the Regent Theater. It was a wonderful place for us kids. Kids today don't know what they're missing. We had Saturday movies that had these serials. The serials were a little segment of a movie with little strips of mysteries such as Flash Gordon, Buffalo Bill, Tim McCoy, and many others. The movie only cost ten cents, but sometimes the line might be 80 yards long! Kids would stand in line for maybe an hour to get a good seat. Ten cents bought you a big box of popcorn, a Babe Ruth almost a foot long, and a ticket to see the movie. All the kids stayed to see the feature attraction at least twice. Other theaters had matinees especially for the kids.

Then there was the Talent Scout. Kids would volunteer to get up and do their thing—tap dance, sing, do acrobatics—all sorts of things. One kid did a dance with a belt. All the kids in the audience were whooping and hollering, and the one who received the loudest applause and the most hollers and whistles was the winner. It was a great time!

I recall that the Seminole Indians would come into the Regent Theater on a Friday or Saturday evening. The women had a special hairdo made by wearing a hair board. You don't see this hairstyle nowadays. The women were beautiful. They would come in, always barefooted, and do the shopping. I would follow them around at times to see what all they would buy. On occasion, they would bring their kids with them. They would tag along behind, but they always had a smile.

I recall watching the Indian men go to Allapatta Hardware Store, buying hammers, nails, saws, axes, ropes. Then they'd go into the

Allapatta five-and-ten stores. They'd buy candy to take into the Regent Theater. They seemed to like the gumdrops best. The Indians would always sit in the very back row, at the wall, in the seats farthest from the screen. They seemed to enjoy the cowboys as much as we did. I'm not sure how well they accepted the cowboy and the Indian movies.

Their camp was the neighborhood of Twenty-Seventh Avenue and Eleventh Street. It sat about 200 yards east of Twenty-Seventh Avenue. It was very picturesque. There was a slough there that fed into the river. The grass was very green on this prairie. The Seminoles had built a dock where they tied their dugout canoes, and nearby they had constructed their chickees. It was a beautiful setting against the blue skies, and I always looked forward to going by there and marveling at the Indians.

There were other Indian villages that were for tourists. One was on Thirty-Sixth Street and the Miami River, called "Osceola's Indian Village." The other one was in Hialeah at Fifty-Fourth Street and the Miami River near the "Seminole Bar."

Other Seminole camps were farther out on Highway 27, where at one time, they worked for the Ernest R. Graham family cutting sugarcane in the Pensuco Sugar Company's fields. The Grahams were sugar men way on back. Both Ernest and his son Bob Graham, who was to become a governor of Florida, became U.S. senators. They always did cater to the sugarcane industry.

At this date, Twenty-Seventh Avenue did not have asphalt on it. The town hadn't really progressed that far westward yet. Fifty-Fourth Street was considered "way out in the country" and was just a rocky road. That part of Miami was still pretty wild back then and unsettled.

In the early days in town, you'd see a boy peddling his bicycle delivering the *Saturday Evening Post*, or he had a paper route. In those days that was a sign of an energetic young man in the making, on his way to becoming a good businessman, who cared for his future. Others were delivery boys. Their bikes had a big wooden basket that fit on the front, or the bike had double saddlebags that fit over the back fenders to carry the magazines or newspapers or grocery goods. All the bikes had fenders to keep mud from getting on you and the supplies you were delivering.

Because this was the time of the Great Depression, during these hard times my parents made twenty-five cents an hour if they were lucky. I remember my father would get on my mother if she spent more than four dollars a week for groceries. For that four dollars, she got four great big bags of groceries, and that had to last us for a solid week. Back in these times, you didn't see many obese people. They all were slender, well-built, wiry people. They didn't even have any extras like paper napkins and paper towels; they used cloth napkins and cloth towels that could be washed and reused. Yet everybody seemed to be happy, joyful, and without worries.

2

The 1940s

Into the Everglades

My father was called off on a business trip to Tampa, and I got to go with him! We were warned ahead of time that you had to be sure to plan your trip ahead, that you didn't dare get caught crossing the 270 miles of the Tamiami Trail at night. Also, we were told to be sure to carry an extra can of gas and an extra can of water. So that's what we did to make our 270-mile trip to Tampa.

As we crossed the Trail, there were small Australian pine trees that had just been planted all along the Tamiami Canal on our right. It was a long journey, and I remember looking to the south at the grass plains, nothing but a vast open area of saw grass. We didn't see any hammocks to speak of—just open saw grass.

When Father's business concluded in Tampa, we started home. Sure enough, because it was such a long trip, night fell upon us. But in the dark, the sky lit up with fireflies—I mean just millions of them! Every place you looked, the sky just flickered like it was on fire . . . so many fireflies. And the windshield was spattered with so many bugs that we had to pull over and use the water to clean the windshield many, many times.

The highway itself was covered with frogs, snakes, turtles, raccoons, and possums—dead animals hit by other cars. It was an awesome experience for me that I will never forget.

I sure loved the Everglades. I begged and pleaded with my mother, trying to convince her to let me pedal my bicycle 25 miles out into the Everglades. It took a couple of months of my hounding her to death for her to finally give me her approval. I was around eleven or twelve years old!

The bicycle trip was quite a test of endurance, of course, but I took all the camping gear, and I got three buddies to go with me out Highway 27. There was Donald Henshaw, Dicky Clark, and Kenneth Russell. We got on our bicycles about two or three o'clock in the morning and started pedaling out to where Mack's Fishing Camp is located today on Highway 27 along the Miami Drainage Canal. Back then there was no fishing camp, just wild, wild Everglades. So we got out there before sunup and spent the day out there. It was an environment filled with snakes, turtles, otters, raccoons, opossums, bobcats, you name it, there it was . . . and thousands and thousands of fish.

When the Glades were draining, from November roughly to April, the fish would come out the Miami Canal into the marshland at the Dade and Broward County levee like you just can't imagine. As a result, two fish camps were built there in later years: Tom's, the oldest and largest, and Mack's. Both did a brisk business.

Later on, during my high school days, I used to make extra money going out into the Everglades and catching cottonmouth moccasins and various types of water snakes with my bare hands. I'd pin their head down with a stick, then I'd slit their belly and pull the skin off. I sold the skins to Brad Bradford at the tannery. Once during a season when the water was going down, lots of snakes were coming into Mud Canal. Mud Canal was a shallow ditch, dug in the 1920s, that ran from where the Miami Canal met the Miami River, all the way to the north where it met the South New River Canal in Broward County. On one hunt at Mud Canal, I filled two washtubs full of snakes!

Sometimes, I would go snake hunting with my friend Dave Scarborough, who had a 12-foot, flat-bottomed pram-type boat with a Sears 3-horsepower Elgin engine. Dave didn't like snakes, but we were a good team. I would spot a snake, and he would run the boat onto the bank, then I would jump out and catch it. I would average about a dollar a snake. That was big money for me!

Green Congo water snakes would always bite, so I would grab the body and whirl the Congo in the air to catch its head (the "pop")! Often enough during this maneuver, the fish and whatever else that the

As a boy, I caught snakes in the Everglades and sold their hides. Sometimes my friend and I had whole washtubs full. Here is one of the largest rattlesnakes that I caught and skinned out. (Photo by David Scarborough.)

snake had eaten would fly out of its digestive tract and splatter my friend in the head! At the end of the day, Dave looked like he had been whitewashed!

Once on our way home down the canal, we ran out of gas. The boat was full of snakes, some still squirming, and Dave looked and smelled so horrible that the gas attendant was too afraid to get close to our boat. He just passed us a can of gas.

When we got to the landing where I left my car, I said, "David, you and I have been buddies for a long time, but I can't let you ride with me like that. Jump in the canal and freshen up!"

He jumped in the canal, clothes and all! Then he threw his stinking shirt away. We got in my old 1930 Model A Ford and, tired as we were, we went home and dressed out all those snakes to sell to Bradford. It was a good day's work!

One of the most prolific areas in the Everglades lay north of Highway 84 and west of Ft. Lauderdale, which is now called Conservation Area 2. I remember swimming across the canal and looking over the bank. It was early in the morning and the sun was just coming up, and in the sky was just a tremendous number of spoonbills, egrets, herons, ibis, ducks—just all sorts of birds. I mean, the sky was filled with millions of birds, but that was the norm for the Everglades in those days. This area is now devoid of wildlife.

When the water was at the end of its natural draining season around April, I recall many times in the Tamiami Canal there'd be so many fish in the center of the canal, in, say, a quarter mile, that the water would be black with so many catfish, bass, bluegills, bream, all sorts of fish, but mainly catfish. They would be so tightly packed against one another, just like sardines, that some of the catfish at the center would be pushing each other out of the water!

Now, I know that sounds like an old fish story, but that's the way it was, and it was an annual event March through April before the disastrous fluctuations in the water table imposed by Flood Control's pumps and the dikes that held the water in and then the infusion of insecticides and herbicides by agricultural pursuits.

But in these early days, it was always a joy to get up early in the morning and go ride the highways and look in the canals to watch the otters play, sliding on the bank, chasing one another, and frolicking in the Miami River.

There were always a lot of manatees, or what they call "sea cows." There were plenty of them in those days anywhere along the Miami River, especially in the wintertime. At that time, they would come in by the hundreds to get up the Miami River away from the cold ocean waters, but the Thirty-Sixth Street locks built by the U.S. Army Corps of Engineers stopped their seasonal migration.

Again, Mud Canal was one of my favorite places to go. At the north end, at the North New River Canal, the fish would just drain in there from the marsh. There would be thousands of them. I recall one time, standing there fishing and feeling myself slowly getting deeper into the water. I didn't understand what was happening until I looked down and saw hundreds of thousands of fish intermingled in the duck weed. I was actually standing on fish! That's how many fish there were in the early years. In that same area, I was out collecting snakes one time. I was working back up toward south of the New River Canal and the Miami Canal junction. In the process of herding snakes, I was inadvertently herding all these thousands of fish back into the blockage point. I didn't realize it at the time, but all of a sudden the fish turned around and started to come back toward ME, the water just foaming! I sure didn't want be captured in there!

There were so many fish that now the water was just roaring! Big mudfish about 2 ½ feet long and large catfish were hitting me in the ankles and the knees. Boy, when they hit you in the ankle, you knew it. If I had fallen down, I don't know if I ever would've been able to get back up . . . such tremendous numbers of fish were there!

Years later, when I was with the Game and Fresh Water Fish Commission, I recall many times going out south on the Miami River Canal and there would be these little breaks in the north bank, where the Everglades would drain. At a certain time of year, the bass, bluegill, and bream would come swarming in there by the tons.

One evening there were two kids way back in the saw grass. They were herding these fish back in through the cutaways. They were back in there whoopin' and hollering, having a good time. I heard one kid holler out to the other, "Here they come, get ready! Here they come!"

Then I heard this swarm of water. You see the water was whipping into foam, as thousands of bass rushed through that cutaway, just thousands of them, turning the water into foam.

This was almost an annual affair. There would be so many fishermen gathered around there in their boats, catching these bass! Usually, they'd get into fights, hitting one another's boats trying to get in there to get the best position to catch the most bass, but those were sure good fishing times!

And ducks were extremely plentiful every winter. They would come in by the thousands and thousands. Their flights would almost black out the sky. This was the way it was. Especially south of what is now Alligator Alley (I-595), you'd look up and you'd see all these birds, just thousands of them, clouds of them. Well, you didn't know if there were swallows migrating in, or if it was ducks. You had to watch for quite a while before you could make out the difference between ducks and swallows, but the duck hunting was just unbelievable. Now you can go out in the same area and not see a single duck.

As a teenager, just for the sport of it, I would go out to the Everglades in a buggy or an airboat, and I would sometimes come across a gator pond. I would often get out and catch whatever alligators I could get, up to 12 foot or better, whatever—it didn't really make a difference.

To hunt alligators, we would carry conduit steel piping with us. The alligator ponds would have caves that the alligators made under the bank, and they could vary in length. They might go 20, 25 feet back under the muck and make a cave. That's where they stayed during the dry period, during hard winters, or during periods of drought or fire.

We'd take these iron rods and pipes, poke through the muck, down into the cave, and locate the alligator. The procedure was that I'd have somebody there to agitate the alligator in his cave and make him come out into the pond, while I would stand in the water at the entrance of the cave. When the alligator came out of the underwater entrance to its cave, he would bump me in the belly with his snout. I would slowly reach under his jaw, very gently grab him by his lower jaw and drag him out very slowly, trying not to excite him. This worked pretty well, and I did it quite often. That was what we did to entertain ourselves!

One night, David Scarborough and I had been out coon hunting out northwest of Medley. On our way home, we noticed that the water was kind of high at that time in the Glades and it was flowing over the road in one low place. As we got closer, we noticed something that we'd never seen before. It was a giant migration of eels, trying to leave the marsh on their way back into the Miami River. Literally thousands of them were crossing the road. I tried to grab some of them, but they were so slippery, it was impossible. I tried and tried and could never catch a single one.

These eels had come upriver by the thousands to go into the marsh to spawn, migrating miles from the ocean to the Everglades in an annual event, but when the Corps of Engineers built the Thirty-Sixth Street locks, it shut them out permanently.

Another of my favorite places was west of what is now Mack's Fish Camp on the Miami Canal. There in the saw grass was a willow strand that must have been a quarter mile long. It was a rookery where, each year, the ibis would come in, along with egrets and herons, and build their nests. They'd take up all the limbs available in this long willow strand and would build so many nests that there was no more room left. Then the extra ibis would build their nests in the surrounding saw grass, by bending it over and making a very comfortable nest for their young. I had never seen anything like that before. From a distance, the long willow strand looked completely white with so many birds nesting.

When the ibis are young, they're not white like the adults, but black. Many of the babies would jump out of the nests and fall on the ground. The ground would literally be black with the young ibis—just thousands of them. When the adults would come in to feed their young, they would find many of them on the ground, so it became like a community feeding program.

It was very impressive to go there each year, and in doing so I realized that the birds' seasonal habits coincided with seasonal water levels. It took many tons of fish to feed all those young chicks.

I got a chance to go back out on the Tamiami Trail again shortly after World War II began, around 1942. Gasoline was rationed and harder to come by, but a friend of ours who was in the Service was stationed at the Opa Locka Airport. He was able to acquire a couple of 5-gallon cans of gasoline. He also had a Model A Ford, and he wanted to take a trip around the Loop Road, which is 40 miles west of Miami, making a loop south of the Tamiami Trail just west of Forty-Mile Bend.

In the 1930s, there used to be a settlement on Loop Road called Pinecrest. There was the notorious Pinecrest Bar that had been owned by the gangster Al Capone, who had moonshine, gambling, and a dance hall with lots of women. (In fact, we were told that there was still lots of moonshine produced in the area.) In Capone's day, there were no rules out there with the law so very far away in the cities. When Al Capone ruled Loop Road, he had runners to alert him if the law ever decided to raid so that he could clean up his operation before they arrived. It sounded very exciting to me!

It was the Hurricane of 1935 that destroyed the settlement. When it was rebuilt many years later, it was called Gator Hook and became a hangout for alligator poachers.

So we gathered up our gear and gas cans and left one morning for Loop Road, with me in the rumble seat. When we got to that isolated spot, much to our surprise, there must have been around three hundred people from one end of the Loop to the other! As hard up as everyone was for money, gasoline, and so forth in those days, they were out playing, picnicking, camping, and just having a plain old good time. And the fishing was terrific. Boy, I sure liked the Everglades!

Frogs and Airboats

The history of the once lucrative frog-leg economy and airboats went hand in hand. In 1930, Joxey Redding built the Blue Shanty Store and Bar about 30 miles west of Miami on the Tamiami Trail. The Reddings—Joxey and his brother, Bobo—caught live frogs by hand for the lucrative frog-leg business that supplied restaurants.

Their transportation down the canals and into the Everglades where the frogs were plentiful was on a homemade barge, a type of boat 5 feet wide and 16 feet long. They pushed the barge with poles in the shallow waters of the Everglades north of the Trail.

The Reddings dealt in volume so they did not gig the frogs, but caught them live by hand. They put them in a large potato sack about 4 feet wide and 10 feet long. Their frog-hunting trip would last about three days. Then they would head home, where it would take them days to dress out all of the frog legs.

In 1936, Joxey located an airplane propeller. He made one of the earliest airboats utilized in the Everglades region. Utilizing a Model A Ford engine, he took the flywheel off and installed an airplane propeller, which gave it a "pushing" motion. Interestingly, at this time, his airboat was only used to *push* the large barge, which was still used as the staging area to catch the frogs and for storage. Of course, today's airboats use a "pusher-type" propeller.

Joxey's airboat had a rudder on the bottom and a rudder above. But he soon found out that the bottom rudder would hang up on the grass, so it was not effective. His airboat was controlled with hands on the carburetor.

After World War II, the aircraft engine entered the availability market. The usual engine available from 1947 to 1950 was 65 horsepower. In time, horsepower and speed were demanded. So Joxey located a 90-horsepower Franklin AC engine and made himself a *real* airboat! (Today, the horsepower has reached 750 or better!)

By the mid-1940s, the development of airboats was major, and as a result, commercial frogging began to increase. The frogs could be gigged from the faster-moving airboats with a homemade gig made of four straightened-out fishhooks. Some of the early froggers were able to gig more than 125 pounds of frog legs per night.

In 1946, Franny (Francis S.) Taylor built his first airboat from aluminum sheeting and riveted angle runners. This airboat was only 3 feet wide and 12 feet long with a 165-horsepower Continental aircraft engine. Franny set up an airboat shop at SW 107th Avenue and SW Eighth Street (Tamiami Trail) in Miami. The airboat shop was not much to look at. In fact, it looked to be an old chicken coop! But this shop produced many of the first commercial airboats that were known as "Taylor-Built Airboats."

I built my first airboat in 1949. One of my very happiest days was when I was in Miami Springs, and I found a man who had a 65-horsepower Continental "up stack" exhaust pipe. I think I paid seventy-five dollars for it, and I was on my way to making my first airboat! My buddy Roddy Bryant and I began its construction, fabricating it of plywood. To make it watertight, we used gauze strips coated in a product called Permatex. We had the boat completed in several months. These were hard times, and no one had extra money for a trailer, so we would put a 55-gallon drum under the airboat and roll it onto a pickup truck in order to transport it. It took Roddy and I two or three trips to get out of the Miami Canal because of engine breakdown necessitating repairs, but we were on our way.

This boat was 4 feet wide and 12 feet long. That was the only size that they made back in those days. Anybody who made one other than that size was considered "out of his mind"! A usual seat was a 5-gallon can. The bottom of my boat was completely flat. It would catch and

stop when I wanted the boat to slide sideways. It was very hard to steer because we did not have the leading edge on the rudder yet. If I was cruising down the slough and turned sideways a little bit, or if I was making a turn, it threw me out immediately with no warning! It was real rough during the winter months—being thrown out in that ice-cold water and then having to run the rest of the day wet. We realized that there was a flaw in the design. The bottom should have been beveled at an angle on the edge of the boat, so it would not sit flat on the water.

Also, with no grass roll, we spent a lot of time pushing the boat through the heavy saw grass stands. But it was simply all in a day's work, knowing that we would have to push the boat a half mile every time we went out. And wading through the saw grass, it didn't take long to wear out a brand-new pair of dungarees, especially in the knees.

I used a 1-quart tomato can for a gas overflow system. The rudder design was poor; the rake was poor. There were no push-button starters. A hand prop was the only way to go—and you would build up a strong arm pretty quick!

Prop guards were not a consideration during this period, as they would have added too much weight. With no prop guard, the only thing we could do to stop the prop from getting torn up with the willow limbs or whatever was for one of us to jump on the limbs and hold them back before the prop got to them. This was a very dangerous thing, but that was just part of the Everglades trip. We had no "grass roads" (airboat trails) back in those days, which meant we had to push through saw grass strands time after time, back off, and give it another try until we broke through! And, after burning up the engine twice, I found out that you just have to give the engine a rest once in a while.

There was a really tough strand of saw grass that was called the "Iron Curtain." It went south from an island called El Rancho to way south of where Alligator Alley now cuts across the Everglades. Traveling northwest, we always had to go through that Iron Curtain. The saw grass there was thick, 11–12 feet high, full of big fern stumps, and laced with thick vines. The iron vines were sometimes called "wait-a-minute vines." Those black vines were extremely strong, with sharp

The first airboat that I designed in 1949 was made out of plywood with oak runners. It was covered with gauze and sealed watertight with Permatex. I sat on a 5-gallon can with a quart tomato can used for the gravity flow. There was no starter and no prop guard. The airboat was flat-bottomed, and there was no leading edge on the rudder, so when I made a turn, I was usually thrown out into the water. (Shirley Collection.)

thorns, and it took a very sharp machete to cut through them. Then, during the struggle to clear the path, we had to be wary of poisonous snakes below and spiders above. It was horrible going!

In the 1960s, during the Vietnam era when I was with the Commission, the Pentagon called my office in Ft. Lauderdale and wanted to meet with me. They wanted my assistance in designing airboats for the military. They made arrangements for me to get any type of metal, props, or paints that I wanted. "Money is not a concern," I was informed.

I promptly made arrangements to meet with Franny Taylor of Taylor-Built. The Pentagon would have set him up with a new factory for assembly-line production for hundreds of airboats. But I knew that business with Taylor would be difficult, as he had a reputation for never giving a customer a delivery date or a price. The Pentagon wanted a complete airboat delivered to Washington in six weeks.

I first visited the shambles that was called "Lost City" located in the middle of the Everglades in 1949. Lost City had been the clandestine site of a very large moonshine business during the Prohibition days of the 1920s. In 1956, when I was with the Game Commission, I found the remains of this old Seminole canoe. (Photo by Toby Massey.)

Taylor, stubborn as usual, would not give me or the Pentagon any answers. Well, the deal fell through! Franny missed out on becoming a millionaire!

Later, Diamond Back produced other aluminum airboats. Then came a new type of airboat hull made of fiberglass. Larry Williams designed his new fiberglass airboat with a "step-hull" bottom. This new design added much speed, which is very popular now. The step hull was designed after the Hydro Speed boat with two different levels in the boat's bottom. The step-hull design gave the hull two surfaces to plane on. Gore Airboats was another famous fiberglass airboat production company. They received the contract from the Pentagon to build the airboats for the military. Unfortunately, these boats were poorly designed and were twice the weight of the aluminum boats.

But it was Gary Thurman who was the most popular designer/builder in South Florida. And Thurman's mechanic, Benny Webb, has built more airboats than anyone in the business, under the name Spider Airboats.

The airboat opened up the Everglades wetlands and its islands to exploration. I went to Lost City first in the 1940s, and then again when I was with the Commission. It was a remote island in Collier County that had been the site of a major moonshine operation in the 1920s.

3

Everglades Patrol

Getting My Feet Wet

My First Assignment—1955

One day in the early 1950s, as I was traveling the Glades in my airboat, I pulled in to an island where a game warden, Sigsbee "Sig" Walker, was entertaining a federal agent, Jake Wolfley. The agent had his .44 Smith and Wesson, and he said, "I'm gonna go out and get breakfast."

I heard him shoot about ten times within about fifteen minutes. Then he came back with a whole bag full of cottonmouth moccasins with their heads shot off!

He said, "Man, we're gonna have breakfast."

Sure enough, he skinned out all of those moccasins, cut them up in about 8-inch pieces, and fried them up for breakfast. Then, after breakfast, I saw him up against a rubber tree, snapping his finger on the rubber tree root and sticking his tongue out, dabbing it back and forth.

I said, "Jake, what in the world *are* you doing?"

"I'm still eating breakfast," he said. He stuck out his tongue, and he had a whole ball of ants rolled up on his tongue. He said, "Ants taste good."

At this time, Sig Walker was employed by the State of Florida's Game and Fresh Water Fish Commission as a game warden who patrolled the Everglades: *my* Everglades! That fascinated me. What a job! Sig was a very friendly, country fellow. I guess some would call him a redneck, but he had a very cultured way of speaking. He appeared to be a very pleasant gentleman. Everybody liked him.

By 1950, I had been in the Naval Reserve for five years, and I had worked for Southern Bell Telephone Company for the same amount of time. But when Southern Bell went out on strike, I put in my application for a commercial diving company, Bird Brothers, that had contracts with projects at Cape Canaveral's Space Center. I had been diving since the 1940s with treasure diver Tim Watkins, working shipwrecks off the coast of Florida. I knew that you could make good money as a diver, but I also knew that the pressure of the depths could be really rough on a man's life.

By this time, Sig had resigned from the Game Commission, and we had really become friends. He recommended me when I put in my application at the Game Commission. Sig joked, "Tom, the only thing I want out of you is that you keep me posted where the wild hogs are!"

An applicant to the Florida Game and Fresh Water Fish Commission had to be between twenty-five and thirty-five years old, a resident of Florida, and a high-school graduate with a valid driver's license. He had to be of good character and in good standing in his community. If he met those qualifications, he could take a comprehensive exam, pass, and go before an oral review board. If he passed review, he was then eligible to be employed. I knew that there was a probationary first year in which I would be expected to receive special training.

Special qualifications that also were considered necessary for this line of work called for the applicant "to be of a self-sufficient nature, so that he is competent to work alone in the wilderness areas without immediate supervision or assistance. He must be intelligent enough to operate mechanical equipment and vehicles. He must, in other words, be a rugged all-around man" (Dahne 19).

The other news in my life was that I had just gotten married! So I decided I would take the first job that accepted my application.

I was hired by the Game Commission on June 6, 1955. I went to Lake Okeechobee to meet Mr. Fred Stanberry in the office of the Everglades Region to be sworn in.

Mr. Stanberry himself did the honors: "Tom Shirley, repeat after me, I will solemnly swear to enforce the Florida Game and Fresh Water Fish laws. I will solemnly swear to uphold and protect all the wildlife and freshwater fish within the State of Florida, so help me God."

With my hand raised, I said, "I will."

I joined the Law Enforcement Division of the Florida Game and Fresh Water Fish Commission in 1955. The Commission was funded by the sale of hunting and fishing licenses and the payment of fines for breaking the Florida game laws. Here I am in 1961 in the only airboat that the Game Commission had for our Everglades patrol when I joined in 1955. We used Motorola radios that were so valuable for communication in our jobs in the isolated Everglades wetlands. (Florida Game and Fresh Water Fish Commission photo, Shirley Collection.)

I was then told that I would have to purchase my own gun. Law Enforcement back then, even in other agencies, was sort of like the Old West. To my great joy, I had been assigned to the Everglades! Now, the Everglades scares most of the individuals trying to join the Commission as a wildlife officer. In fact, in Tallahassee, when they are initiating a new wildlife officer, they ask, "Will you be willing to work anyplace in the state of Florida?" Of course, the answer is supposed to be "Yes!" but when you do say "Yes!" they'll have a big map of Florida, and real seriously, you'll be asked, "OK, will you be willing to work down south in the Everglades?" and point down at the end of Florida.

Well, that's supposed to be the secret way to get on the Commission. If you're willing to work within the Everglades District, then you're a courageous man. For me, it was like Brer Rabbit being thrown

in the briar patch! And that moment was the beginning of a long journey working to protect the wildlife and the fish of the state of Florida
and struggling to promote conservation efforts in the Everglades
wetlands.

I left Okeechobee and made the long ride back to Miami. Early the
next morning, I got up. I went out and picked up my Commission-
assigned airboat, gassed it up, and went to the Tamiami Trail. There
I launched my boat and headed north to my own new frontier, the
Everglades, that I knew so well.

I brushed through the grass, the saw grass plains stretching from
the east to the west, crossing sloughs that run for miles north and
south. I cruised across the Everglades wetlands, the breeze whish-
ing by my face and my ears. It was a great feeling of freedom that
I'd never had before. But fears came with it also, knowing that I was
now responsible for upholding all of the game and fish laws and for
the protection of the Everglades forever. What a great responsibility! As I shot northward, a great cloud of egrets, wood storks, herons,
and curlews rose into the air. It was a sight to see. There were ducks
by the thousands, snakes and turtles in the water scooting out from
underneath the airboat, and the airboat rushing by the coots and the
gallinules as they ran across the lily pads to get out of the way.

My Everglades beat covered the Game Commission's Everglades
Wildlife Management Area: Dade, Broward, parts of Collier, Monroe,
Palm Beach, and even parts of Hendry Counties. It was a vast area
encompassing Conservation Areas 2 and 3. The marsh area of the Ev-
erglades is about 50 miles wide and 100 miles long. It goes on up past
Palm Beach County, all the way south to the cape end of Florida to
Cape Sable, including the Ten Thousand Islands and the Florida Keys.
It was an area, in fact, larger than the state of Rhode Island, and I was
responsible for protecting all of the wildlife in it!

After patrolling in the airboat and checking all the camps in the
area, I decided to go ahead and make camp at the Grapefruit Head.
The Grapefruit Head is an intersection of Mud Canal and North Airboat Trail, about 65 or 70 miles northwest of Miami. It's a small island where rough-skinned lemons, wild oranges, and grapefruit grew.
It was a good place for an airboat to cross over before the day was
through.

I traveled the Everglades that evening under beautiful stars, puffy cumulus clouds, and a bright, bright moon that came up orange before setting in the west.

When night fell, I gathered up some logs and made a fire. I always take three logs and face them toward one another, like fires made by Amazonian Indians. That way, the fire would burn all night without going out and keep the varmints more of a distance away. And when the chill of the night falls, that fire sure feels good.

I threw out my tarp, bed roll, sleeping bag, puffed up my pillow, and tried to fall asleep watching the fire, watching the coals. Before I knew it, I was relaxed and feeling good. In the open air, the smell of the Everglades is excellent, and all the different birds were calling: the night herons, limpkins, whippoorwills . . . the sounds of the Everglades. I fell asleep dreaming about what the following day would bring.

Morning comes pretty quick. You hear all the birds coming in to feed. They would be squawking, hollering and screaming, singing, carrying on—it sounded like an orchestra. All ganged up by the hundreds, feeding within 200 feet of me. I loved watching the bright pink spoonbills feed in the water, running their spoon-shaped bills back and forth to catch the shrimp, the minnows, the crawdads. There's always one curlew. He's tipped up high on the highest branch around. He stands guard for all the other birds. When he squawks and takes off, that means all of them have got to go! It's a very entertaining and beautiful sight to see all the birds feeding in one wad. So wonderful that there was so much life in the Everglades!

I returned to civilization early that morning. The Commission office where I was stationed was located at the Ft. Lauderdale International Airport, where we had our own hangar for our fixed-wing plane and our helicopter. I cleaned my assigned equipment and made sure that it was ready and in good working order. I knew I had a great job ahead of me.

When I first signed on with the Game and Fresh Water Fish Commission, the programs we operated were what I would call "wholesome"! "Environmentally balanced" might be a more professional description. All of the Commission's efforts were geared to habitat in the Everglades wetlands and to the replenishment and upgrade of the wildlife in those habitats. Ultimately our responsibility to care for, protect, and even to replenish the wildlife meant we were to nurture the game animals, fowl and fish, in the Everglades District. This was to benefit not only the Everglades wetlands as an environment but also the conservationists, anglers, and sportsmen who utilized those areas for recreational purposes.

These men and women were our actual employers, you could say, as the Commission was state-funded only through the sale of hunting and freshwater fishing permits and the fines for violations of the game laws. The laws were ones that those same conservationists, sports-men, and anglers had voted to place on the books as state laws. They governed the types and numbers of animals, fowl, or fish that could or could not be taken in particular seasons and by which methods. We in Law Enforcement at the Game and Fresh Water Fish Commission then enforced those state laws. Because of the pivotal role that our constituents played in the livelihood of the Commission, our director, A. D. Aldrich, issued annual reports to the wildlife stockholders.

All of us officers were expected to work together in Game Man-agement, Fish Management, and Law Enforcement. For Law Enforce-ment positions it was mandatory, as we were expected to have full knowledge of all departments. We were known as wildlife officers, the "Men in Green."

My first job assignment was to meet a Game Management biologist in southern Homestead. A farmer had loaned the Game Commission a high Oliver-type tractor to mow down the short grass in the marsh to plant seeds of millet to attract ducks for the sportsmen's hunting season. At this time, the planting of wildlife food crops was a very im-portant activity conducted by the Wildlife Commission in their Wild-life Management Areas.

The Game Commission was also closely tied to the various anglers' clubs. The Commission had purchased a weed-cutting machine that needed constant repair. It was used to cut a path through the saw grass to make ponds accessible to fishermen. With better access to the water, they would buy more licenses and catch more fish. The anglers were a strong, organized body of fishermen. If our grass-cutting op-eration was not satisfactory, they would want to know why. So we had a lot of maintenance duties in our job just to keep our constituents happy and satisfied since they paid our salaries. In fact, in those days we at the Florida Game and Fresh Water Fish Commission were proud that we could operate on the proceeds of wildlife permits, licenses, fines, etc. and not be a pawn of state politics!

And according to an article in the Commission's magazine, *Florida Wildlife*, the year I joined, the presence of the Game and Fresh Water Fish Commission in our Everglades District promised a bright future for the Everglades wetlands. The article discussed how the rampant inroads of agriculture and urban and industrial growth had threatened the land and water resources in southeast Florida, but the Commission had "as its ultimate goal, the preservation and management of as much of the state's wildlife habitat as possible. In addition to providing for the present, to assure the future, a good game supply on readily available hunting lands" (Van Dresser 18).

So our governmental agencies had acquired large properties that they would administer for the hunters' and anglers' benefit. Environmental writer Cleveland Van Dresser wrote:

To the everlasting credit of the Florida Game and Fresh Water Fish Commission and the U.S. Fish and Wildlife Service, this had been done in South Florida. Had the land acquisition project not gone into effect, fishing and hunting over a wide section of the state would soon be nothing but a memory. Deep felt thanks must also be given to the Florida engineers who are directing a multi-million dollar water control project aimed at rehabilitating immense areas of land in 11 counties in the southeastern part of the state.

As far as wildlife is concerned, nearly one million acres of land and water has been set aside as a "conservation area." This virtual wildlife empire extends roughly from the northern part of Palm Beach County to the Tamiami Trail in Dade County, and westward on a line with Lake Okeechobee. The state part of the project—nearly 800,000 acres—is as yet unnamed. It is simply referred to as the "conservation area." The Federal part—140,000 acres—is known as the Loxahatchee National Wildlife Refuge . . . I have observed, first hand, many wildlife restoration projects of various kinds. In my considered opinion, none of them surpass the combined Federal-state project now coming into being in southeastern Florida. (Van Dresser 18)

Boy, did this sound like a wonderful future for our wildlife! But somewhere along the way, the concept of the management of *only* water overtook the Central and South Florida Project for Flood Control District's mandate to protect the wildlife, while the Florida Game and Fresh Water Fish Commission seemed to have no strength to stem the tide.

What Is a Wildlife Officer?

I really took to heart my job at the Commission and tried to emulate the directives set forth during my thirty-year career. I suppose I succeeded, as one of my colleagues, Vic Heller, who went on to become the assistant executive director of the Wildlife Commission (he retired in 2008), dubbed me "a game warden's game warden."

The Education Division of the Game and Fresh Water Fish Commission defined our duties in an article entitled "What's a Wildlife Officer?" in our magazine *Florida Wildlife* in 1961.

The wildlife officer "patrols the woods and waters in all 67 counties of the state. He does this on foot, by boat, in automobiles, in airplanes, by swamp buggies, and many other types of wilderness equipment. He is always on the outlook for violations of the law" (16), which are found in the Wildlife Code of the State of Florida.

The officer must know the hunters and fishermen in his area well. Most of them are armed with hand guns, rifle, or a knife. The officer must be cautious: "Florida Wildlife Officers, acting in the line of duty, have been assaulted, cursed, shot, cut, and on one occasion, murdered. . . . Attacks upon the Officer are, in effect, attacks against the state, and are prohibited by law, as in the provisions concerning resisting arrest or impeding an officer in the performance of his sworn duties. The officer cannot bear grudges against the violators. He must be fair, courteous and considerate in approaching all persons" (17).

He makes arrests on violations, files paperwork, writes reports, issues citations, may serve warrants or subpoenas, appears in court, seizes illegal devices: weapons, nets, seines, other implements utilized in the violations; confiscates fish and game found in possession of the violator.

The wildlife officer is to be at all times courteous and considerate, using his weapon only in self-defense. The job requires hard physical exertion, so the officer is a specialist in wilderness survival and self-defense, often working under severe weather conditions.

The wildlife officer is also responsible for conservation work, aiding researchers in both game and fish management. The officer assists in wildlife inventories, blood sampling, tagging, relocation; captures nuisance animals, makes public appearances, takes part in radio and television shows; is responsible for the maintenance, repair, and operation of a variety of specialized mechanical equipment.

The wildlife officer is further a public servant, who will aid in search and rescue and hunts for drowning victims and downed aircraft. Officers may be asked to aid in locating escaped convicts and is expected to assist in Civil Defense work and public emergencies.

The wildlife officer "is considered to be on duty twenty-four hours per day. He works as many nights as he does days, depending upon the pattern of violations and complaints in his particular area. He is always on call for emergency duty. . . . The good enforcement officer never follows the same schedule or appears in the same places at the same time. He continually varies his patrols and activities so that his routine is 'lack of routine.' He does this to confound the hardened and confirmed law violators" (16).

Early on, only men were eligible for the job: "Any male resident of Florida may apply for the position of Wildlife Officer" (18). As I have previously mentioned, written and oral examinations before a review board were required, and if accepted, the new officer enrolled in a special training school operated by the Commission. He received his uniform, insignia, belt, and gun holster. He had to furnish his own revolver. A pay increase of fifteen dollars per month was given to those who achieved a promotion to wildlife officer first class. Following one year's probation, the officer received a pay increase of three hundred dollars. There was a merit system in place that protected the officers "against false charges or dismissal without cause" (Dahne 18–19).

When I joined the Commission in 1955, they had only one Commission airboat for the entire Everglades District. In 1961, there were, on average, only 165 Florida wildlife officers in all of Florida. This amounted to roughly two men per county, but more officers were deployed in counties with greater needs. The officers were "required to enforce and uphold the law fairly, equally and impartially throughout the State of Florida. There is no other single law-enforcement agency in Florida faced with so large and complicated a task" (Dahne 19).

Dove Season—1955

Right after I was hired by the Commission in 1955 came the first weekend in October, my first "dove season." I learned to make a habit of getting my old mop stick when I was checking the dove fields, to make it appear that I was a hunter, too. Carrying the mop handle high above my head like a shotgun barrel worked pretty well. I found that I could walk right up on the hunters before they knew it.

So I was out patrolling on my way to a dove field in the woods around where the Doral Country Club is now, west of the Miami International Airport. All of that property was vacant for a long time. Because it was in the path of the air traffic, no developers were interested.

I noticed, oh, about seven or eight people way on off, so I raised my old mop stick, and off I went. Now, I was rambling around. I didn't walk straight at them. I walked from side to side and so forth, not taking a direct route. But, as I got closer, I saw somebody run and hide behind some bushes.

I thought, "Uh-oh, what have we got here?"

As I walked on up there, I saw about five or six cameramen. They're all acting kind of nervous. There's a big beautiful blanket and pillows lying on the ground. All of these cameramen? Something's going on!

One of them I recognized. He worked for one of the big newspapers in Miami. So I began to look around the bushes. It was near a canal bank.

I saw ripples in the water. I'm looking a little bit closer, kind of through the bushes at the edge of the canal, and I see a nice-looking foot there with red toenail polish.

I figured, "Uh-oh, something's *really* going on here."

All I could see was this foot.

I was going to act casual like—you know, keep things calm. So in a musical voice, I said, "Come out, come out, whoever you are! Come out, come out, wherever you are! C'mon out!"

So here she came . . . a beautiful blonde with long hair, big full lips painted all red and everything, and—holy moly! It was Jayne Mansfield in living color, all right! Naked as the day!

So I helped her off the canal bank and out through the bushes. She gave me a big smile . . . and I gave *her* a big smile!

The photographers were out there doing a photo shoot! I had read that Miss Mansfield was trying to promote herself to overtake Marilyn Monroe in the popularity contest. Well, she was far more beautiful than Marilyn Monroe in my eyes.

It was time for me to take a break anyway. I told the photographers, "You all go ahead. You're not breaking any Game and Fresh Water Fish Commission regulations as far as I'm concerned, so go right ahead."

I sat there and watched them do their thing for a while, then I got up, gave them a wave good-bye, and went on about my patrol.

I thought, "Well, this job isn't so rough, after all. You've got to take the good with the bad!"

A Fishy Business

There was an unbelievably high concentration of butter catfish in the Tamiami Canal. It was just black with catfish from Krome Avenue westward to Ochopee. We wildlife officers also had the duty to check fishing licenses. On weekends especially, we had a great problem just dealing with thousands of fishermen and the ensuing traffic problems that would exist along the Tamiami Canal. The fishermen along the Trail were so concentrated on both sides of the highway that the cars were parked bumper to bumper, sometimes extending a mile or more without a parking space. It was hard for us officers to find a place to park! Then, after departing our patrol vehicle, we would have to walk a half mile or more just to begin to do our job. In the fiscal year 1957–58, fishermen spent $979,127.25 to purchase 480,201 freshwater fishing licenses!

I spent a great deal of time at Mack's Fishing Camp located on Highway 27. It was a very popular fishing and recreational destination. That's Junior Jones on the roof around 1960. Mack's was where I usually launched my airboat to go out on day or nighttime Everglades patrol north of Highway 27. Mack's is still open today, located around 4 miles south of Pines Boulevard. (Photo by Tom Shirley.)

On the Miami Canal just off Highway 27, "Tom's" and "Mack's" fish camps did a big business. At this time, Tom's had seventy-five to eighty rental fishing boats. Mack's had fifty-four. A third camp on Highway 27 on the South New River Canal near Andytown was owned by Vern King, who had approximately sixty rental boats. His other facility on the Tamiami Trail at Cooperstown had twenty boats. The fishing activity was so great that it was necessary to call in to make a reservation for a boat. And most of the boats were rented for a half day only.

As can be imagined with the high volume of anglers, the bait supply usually fell way short of its demand, even though there were more than a dozen suppliers in Dade County alone to fill the demand for worms, minnows, crickets, and chubs. And the market for fishing lures was so great that the salesmen had to make two, possibly three, deliveries to the fish camps each week!

The fishing activity around Loop Road was so heavy that many times two of us officers would get together just to handle the checking of licenses. But in a full day's work there was not enough time to check them all. That's how bountiful the Everglades wetlands was in those days!

But in 1959, there was a drought, the worst in six years. The water table dropped drastically. In the Everglades, nearly dead bass and bream lay gasping in ponds and puddles, and the stench of dead game fish wafted up the levees. There was no relief in sight from the weather or the Flood Control District. Vern King explained to a reporter from the *Miami Herald* that "if they would open the gates just a trickle and let some of that water down here to make a current a lot of these dying fish could swim to the canals" (Moeser 6).

Water was being held to the north in the conservation areas, but not where it could be released by the South Florida Flood Control District to aid the areas near the fishing camps. The Game Commission reported that it was also not "biologically feasible" for us to move the dying fish to deeper water. Meanwhile, we officers had to stand back and forget the bag limit as hoards of people with jack handles set upon the dying fish, clubbing them and piling them in wheelbarrows to take home. At least they would be cooked up and eaten.

Filming Wildlife from the Air

I have a friend, Malcolm Roberts, who was the owner of Florida Fish Farms in Stuart, Florida. I went to school with him in Miami, and I made several trips to South America with him to purchase tropical fish. He asked me to shoot a movie of him for his concession at the New York World's Fair. At the concession where the film was shown in 1964, Malcolm had an albino woolly monkey and a display of tropical fish.

Malcolm had purchased a Piper Cub to make trips up to Stuart to check on his fish farm. Quite often, we'd go flying over the Everglades. I would film all the spoonbills, the egrets, the ibis. There were beautiful sights over the Everglades early in the morning, when the clouds of birds would fly and the alligators would be sunning.

So I was going out on patrol one weekend, and Malcolm said, "Tom, how about, I'll take my plane out there, and you can meet me? I'd like to patrol with you."

"That sounds like a good idea," I said, "but you'll have to land only where I tell you."

The particular place where we always landed the Commission's plane we called Sands Point, because the sand in that particular area is white, but it's very hard, very flat—a perfect place to land light aircraft. So I told him exactly where it was, and he was sure he could find it.

I said, "OK, I'll meet you out there at 4:30."

So at 4:30, I was on my way out there in my airboat, but way before I got to the spot, I saw an airplane there. Well, lo and behold, it was Malcolm Roberts. But he didn't go to the place I told him to land. He landed almost 2 miles back southeast from where he was supposed to be.

At least he hadn't crashed!

He came on with me back to camp, and we made the rounds and spent the night.

The next morning we went back to where he had landed, and he said, "C'mon Tom, get in—we can take a flight."

I said, "No, not me. I'm not going to fly with you. You're not even going to be able to get off yourself, much less with me in there."

"Nah, I can make it," he said. "I can make it. Get in."

"No, I'm not going to do it," I replied. "Let me go ahead since you've made up your mind that you're going to try to fly it out of here. Let me go ahead and search out the terrain and pick the best path for you to take."

So I got into my airboat and buzzed round. All the areas had too much water. There was one dry strip that looked reasonably safe, but to the south end of it, there was a gator hole.

So I came back and told him, "Now back down there, where the willows are, there's a gator hole. If you're going to go, you're going to have to lift off way before you get there, or you're going to crash the plane."

He said, "Don't worry about it, Tom. I'll be off way before I get there."

"OK," I said. "But, hold on a minute. I want to get a movie of this. I don't think you're going to make it. You're going to crash in that gator hole sure as the world."

"No, not me. I can make it," he said.

I said, "OK. Let me get my camera."

So I wound up my camera and got in a good position down by the gator hole, where I could get a good angle on all the action that I was anticipating.

Well, Malcolm took the plane way back north, trying to find the farthest run between him and the gator hole.

Well, here he came; here he came; here he came.

He made it through the willows . . . and that's as far as he got when . . . Bam! The plane went up on its nose! Mud, water, weeds, saw grass, and everything went every which way! But, as luck would have it, the plane didn't catch fire or anything.

So I rushed over to him in my airboat, and we looked over the engine. It had mud and grass all in the carburetor. But we took it and cleaned it up and cranked it up. The prop was bent just a little bit, not too bad. He was lucky.

He said, "Well, I'll taxi it back over there to Sands Point."

So I followed him all the way, about a mile through the marsh and the water with the plane.

The next morning, we were going to take off. I got in the plane with him, and off we went.

Well, we got up in the air all right, and we flew over the Everglades. I was taking great scenery shots. Everything was going well.

Then, all of a sudden, all hell broke loose.

Bam! Bam! Bam!

Boy, it sounded like the engine was coming apart. Well, we didn't know what it was. We thought maybe we had thrown a rod, so we were getting ready to crash. We were looking for a place to set down, but in the meantime, we headed on back toward Sands Point with the engine just clanking away.

We looked at the oil pressure gauge. We had oil pressure, all right, but we were getting ready for the engine to cut completely out any second. To our surprise, we set the plane down safely!

Well, what had happened was that the cowling had slid forward into the prop bolt, and all the clanging was the prop bolts eating up the cowling. So we pushed the cowling back in and fastened it where it would hold.

The next morning we took off again. Malcolm had a battery that he wanted to take back with him. So, with the extra weight, he had a lot of trouble taking off. He couldn't get up enough airspeed, so he ran north and south, north and south, turning around each time, trying to build up enough airspeed. Finally, after about four attempts of running back and forth, gaining airspeed on the ground, we lifted off and had an uneventful trip back home. That is what I sweated through flying with him!

Now, showing the 16-millimeter film, he jokes. He tells everybody that I sucked him into that alligator hole, that it was all my fault! But what hurt him the most was that in the film, you can see the camera jiggling. That's where I was laughing! I couldn't help it.

Wranglin' with Monkey Fishermen—1956

It was March 1956, and I hadn't been with the Game Commission long, when the director told me to get my airboat and head on upstate to Palatka.

"We've got a big problem with the monkey fishermen," he said.

Well, at that time, I didn't even know what a monkey fisherman was, but this was supposed to be a very secret operation. I was given orders to get to Palatka just before midnight because they didn't want the monkey fishermen to know an operation was being set up. It seemed there was a big feud going on between these monkey fishermen and the sport camp operators. So a little bit before sundown, I hooked up my airboat and headed toward Palatka.

I pulled into this fishing camp. It was all dark, oak trees around. I wasn't used to so many oak trees and moss. That part of the St. Johns River has a certain smell about it, a foggy, heavy, musky smell, real different from the smell of the Everglades. It seemed a lonely, spooky-looking place to me because I'd spent all my life in the Everglades.

There was a light on the side of the fish house, bugs flying all around, toads on the ground catching the bugs, and the crickets were really carrying on. I didn't see any of the officers around. But way off to the side in the back, I saw a building with a light on. I ventured over there, and there was a gang of about twenty wildlife officers. They were waiting for me! They commenced to tell me just what a monkey fisherman is.

There is a machine that is a glorified version of an old crank telephone generator. The Florida model is an $8 \times 13 \times 6"$ box that contains a simple but ingenious electrical generator with a storage battery, homemade electrodes, usually with bent copper tubing. When a fisherman drops it into the water, the electric current shocks the catfish. They go into a state of helplessness and float to the surface, where fishermen pick them up with a long-handled dip net. This "monkey machine" device was outlawed for use in fishing in all southern states.

But catfish were going for 12 ½ cents a pound! So the monkey fisherman could earn from four to five hundred dollars a week! And all they had to do was drop the end of these wires off either end of the boat, and the catfish just came spiraling up to the top of the water.

The local controversy had developed into a many-sided affair. Sport camp operators, sportsmen, wholesale fish dealers, and commercial fishermen who operated legally all took sides. And, although many cases against monkey fisherman were brought to trial in Putnam County, where most of them lived and operated, they always got off.

Recently, the State Attorney General's Office had investigated the problem and tried to work out some solution concerning the illegal fishing. The sportsfishing camps were very upset because the monkey fishermen came close to their camps with their high-powered boats, creating wakes. The other fishermen were very angry as all this illegal activity had been taking place in their fishing grounds. And the aggressiveness of the monkey fishermen made many people fearful for their lives. All around, it was a bad situation.

The violations continued despite law-enforcement operations. The Game and Fresh Water Fish Commission decided it was going to put its best officers and finest equipment to work toward bringing this business to a halt.

And, I could see that these wildlife officers were actually scared to go out there and apprehend these guys! That's when I learned that the monkey fishermen were getting very aggressive—ramming the officers with their boats, trying to run over them. They were just having a field day. And the courts were not backing the officers when they made arrests!

I figured, "Man, I'd better be set for anything that's going to happen out there!"

The officers had never seen an airboat before, and they went out and looked at mine, marveled at it. I could see that it kind of intimidated them.

I said, "Well, I'm going to go and see what I can do with these monkey fishermen, but with all of the rock pilings, concrete posts, and debris in the water that you've been telling me about, I'm going to have to have somebody go with me who knows the river. Who's going to go with me?"

I had no volunteers out of all those guys! They all said, "Not, me. I'm not getting' into that thing!" gesturing at my airboat.

But there was an old man there, an old wildlife officer named Wayne Watkins.

"I'll go with ya, Tom," he said. "Cuz you're gonna have to have somebody to direct you. Them guys are gonna try to lead you into troubled waters."

We waited a little longer, because they told me that the fishermen's best activity falls around midnight. The other officers scattered around various sportsfishing places with their boats, because when things got going, "There's going to be some boats scattering all over the place, while we are trying to make an arrest."

We cranked up. Oh, I guess it was about 10:30 p.m., and we looked out there and saw three or four lights working.

Monkey fishermen were really difficult to apprehend. The main reason was that their equipment was so inexpensive. Their electrical units cost less than nine dollars each. So when an officer got too close, the violator simply dropped the machine overboard. The only sure cases were those with full material evidence, so most cases were lost right there.

I checked my airboat to be sure everything was operational and in order—the red light and a full tank of gas. I also had what they called a dairy pistol that shot a good-sized flare. It was a pistol that the Air Force uses for planes, to signal one another and so forth, like to signal for taking off and coordination. The pistol shot out two balls of bright-red flame. So I loaded it up where it'd be handy in case I needed it. And off we went!

I was trying to psyche myself up to be prepared for anything. Those lights were still working out there, back and forth. It sure looked like they might be monkey fishing.

As we got close I could see that these fellows had the best boating equipment money could buy—the biggest-horsepower boats with two motors on the transom. So they could move out pretty well. Money was evidently no problem since they were making a great income off the catfish.

Luck was on our side. As we were approaching the three boats, there was a train coming on tracks not too far from us, making a lot of noise. So I figured it was a good opportunity to get pretty close up on these boats. But then they saw me, so I turned my red light on. The three boats split up. Old Wayne was sitting behind me. He beat on my back, yelled, and pointed:

"Go after this one. He's a ringleader. Get him, Tom!"

So, boy, I poured the coal on, and off we went. I came up beside him pretty close, but he kept going. He made a move at me with the boat, trying to throw the wake at me and swamp me.

So I chased him, but he kept on going, didn't pay me any mind. I was looking ahead to be sure he wasn't trying to run me into any of those concrete pilings. It was a wild chase.

He wouldn't stop, so I thought, "Well, it's a good time for me to use that flare gun," and I pulled it out. We were moving on about 60 miles an hour, kicking on down the river. I shot out a flare.

There was a guy on the bow of the boat, and it was pretty close to that fellow, about 4 inches above his collar. Man, that was really close! That flare just lit up the world, but the boat kept going.

Well, I put another shell in the flare gun, and I fired another one at him, and, boy, it was going right at him. I could see his eyes now, big as saucers, and he ducked. I thought that flare was going to go right down the back of his collar. They still kept going.

I didn't have any more flares, and they were still going strong. So I pulled out my revolver and started shooting, splashing water about 20 feet in front of the boat, where they could see it. They saw the splash in the water, but he kept going, and I kept shooting.

I shot a couple of more times, but they kept going. Then I shot so close that they could barely see the splash in the water, but water splashed in the driver's face. Suddenly, they got the picture. So they stopped, and we got into the boat. They had about 200 pounds of fish. Of course they had thrown the monkey fishing equipment overboard. I said to the driver: "Man, you stopped just in time. My next shot was for your engine!" We put them under arrest, took them down, and put them in jail.

They said, "We'll get our attorneys on you. You won't have a chance getting a conviction." Unfortunately, that was the truth. I told him to do what he had to do, but all they said was, "I'll see you in court!"

There hadn't been a conviction there in many, many years. The monkey fishermen were paying two attorneys two cents a pound on all their catches! If the fishermen got into any trouble, the attorneys would represent them. So there was no fear of getting caught. The next morning, boy, the town was in an uproar!

Headlines of the *Daytona Beach News-Journal* read: "Shots Fired at Fishermen: Two Facing Charge at Palatka." One of those two was *me*!

Well, we wildlife officers had now publicly declared war on the monkey fisherman, so it was really going to be a hot and heavy affair. The Game Commission would of course see all the headlines. I was sure that they wouldn't know what to make of all this. So I wasn't sure what they were going to do to ME, even though I was working under orders.

The judge called me in one morning for a session. So I sat in the judge's chambers, and I could tell, boy, he wanted to get on me big time. I was in trouble, and I knew it.

He said, "On what grounds do you think you can shoot at somebody?"

I said, "Judge, I can use any manner of means to apprehend an individual without bodily harm. I didn't hurt anyone . . . not any of those men."

So, well, the judge looked at me with a questioning expression but made no reply. I didn't know whether I was out of hot water or not. I got up and left.

But as I left, there right in the courthouse were all those monkey fishermen who had gathered for a big meeting, and boy, were they hot! They were shouting about what all they were going to do. They were going to get their guns, and they were going back on the river. They were going to be on the river that night! They were really agitated.

They saw me and yelled, "OK, Mr. Tom Shirley, we'll be out there tonight. We'll be waitin' on ya. Come on out. We'll be out there. And we'll see who's who!"

I still didn't know what backing I was going to get from the Game Commission. The commissioner for that district had come in and met with me, but of course *they* didn't know what to do. That's why I, as an experienced outsider, had been sent up there. The locals were on the fence . . . They didn't know what side to get on, and I didn't know which side was going to back me!

Earl Frye was our assistant director. The director, A. D. Aldrich, had recently come from Oklahoma, but Earl Frye really ran the whole show at the Game Commission. So finally, Earl Frye reported to the press, "We asked Tom Shirley to come up here to stop monkey fishing. He did it. He did a good job. We're going to back him."

Man, that was good news to me. Earl Frye was the guts of the Commission. If he would stand up for me, I felt I was on good ground from that point. So our next move was to get ready to go on the St. Johns River that night. It was going to be a big show. We got word that there was going to be a lot of boats out there tonight. And they were going to have the news media—they were going to have TV. They just knew that we were going to go up there and shoot up everything. It was going to be a big show, bright red flares and all!

So we prepared for it.

We cranked up our boats about 11:00 p.m. and saw several lights out there working. Then I saw one boat that cranked up and, bam, he took off in another direction. I figured, well, what he was doing was gathering up all the monkey-fishing equipment. They put it in his boat, and he snuck off down a creek off the St. Johns. (I understood later that he stayed out there all night in another other creek way back in the woods!)

So we got up running toward the boats. And then we saw that they were coming toward us!! One of them charged at me, trying to throw water in my boat. I took out after him, and my airboat took in a lot of water.

Well, taking in that water . . . the prop blast would pick it up and send out a big sheet of water like a big fog. So I chased him. I spun the back end of the boat around to give it full power, and I just drenched him with a big blast of water, really let him have it! He lost his headlight hat, seat cushions, raincoats . . . Man, this was great sport!

If I wanted to, I could have blown the caps off the equipment and out of the boat, but my blast of water didn't bother them a bit. Those guys still wanted to mix it up.

The big fight was on as other boats joined. So we were running around the St. Johns River—wakes and backwashes galore! It was like the Pacific Ocean. So we ran around in a big fracas while all the people on the shore were watching the lights, the action, the roaring of the speedboats and the airboat, right before their eyes! One reporter wrote, "The river became a maelstrom of flashing lights and roaring motors" (Scaggs).

I was having a ball!

I would chase them, I'd come up beside them, turn the back end of the airboat around and blast them, just drenching them, almost blowing them out of the boat, but these guys were so redneck, they didn't care about getting wet. They were having fun, too!

So finally it simmered back down. Gradually they all went back to a dock with a beach. I figured, "Well, I'll go on back there and beach with them. And let's see what's going to happen then?"

So I went up there. All their boats were beached, and they were grouping up and talking. So I parked my airboat right beside them. They all gathered round to marvel at it since they'd never seen an airboat before!

After that, I was known as the "Everglades Man with the Devil Machine."

They all marveled at the airboat, and we stood around and shot the breeze for a little while, and everything was great. They asked me what kind of engine I had? Where could they buy one? What's the cost? How fast *is* your Devil Machine?

I told them it was "fast enough to catch anything you've got!"

After all of that fierce action, nobody got in trouble. There wasn't any shooting or anything so it worked out well. Before leaving, I stood up in my boat and hollered to the eighty or so men in around twenty boats, "The next time a wildlife officer turns on his red light, it means to STOP! It's my recommendation that you *do stop*! We are here to enforce the law!"

Then, while patrolling on the banks of the St. Johns River, we came upon the boat of a suspected monkey fisherman. Apparently he'd heard us coming and had run off to hide. In the boat was an electrical generator, a long-handled dip net, and a head lamp. I took down the trailer tag number on the truck and ran a 10–28 check. The tag was registered to the infamous editor of the local newspaper. No wonder that the Commission didn't receive the cooperation we deserved from the media!

Before I left, I made the rounds to the sportsmen and asked that if they saw any monkey fishing activity to call our office in Ft. Lauderdale and let us know. I told them we would respond immediately.

I didn't hear anything but found out later what happened after I left. The violators, the monkey fishermen, made up a list of the camp operators they didn't like and posted it at the post office. They were going to get them one at a time, and sure enough, they went by the list.

They beat up the camp operators something horrible. They beat up this one guy, bloodied his nose and injured one eye really bad. The camp operators were really scared.

Word got to Governor LeRoy Collins. The governor called Game Commission Director A. D. Aldrich and said, "Now you have to bring an end to this fracas between the monkey fishermen and the sportsmen. You have got to get to them and clean this problem up. If you can't do it, as director, I'm going to replace you and put in another director there. So you better secure this problem" (*Florida Times-Union*).

So the judge found the two individuals I'd caught and got a "guilty" verdict for them. That was the first guilty plea that they'd had in, I think, twenty years, and the judge himself was almost released from his duty. The governor told him, "And you'd better straighten this thing up, or I'm going to replace YOU!"

In fact, I heard later on that he did replace the judge. I don't know if that was a fact or not, but that's what I was told.

Since then, I've heard nothing about monkey fishermen. I asked people, "How's the monkey fishing doing on the St. Johns?" and they don't even know what "monkey fishing" is anymore. So it looks like that problem was solved.

But, to tell the truth, this had to be one of the most enjoyable episodes that I ever had with the Game and Fish Commission!

Cop versus Cop—1956

Well, early one morning, I was going out on patrol, departing from Mack's Fish Camp. On the weekends, it was always bustling with people going fishing, hunting, renting boats, just having a good time.

So this particular morning, I launched my airboat and I was headed down by the river. I was going to be checking fishing licenses.

I came upon this fellow. He was a large man, a large black man, around 400 pounds. I noticed that he had a .38 strapped to his side.

Well, I made mention . . . I said, "It's against the law to bring firearms into the game management area."

So he said, "Well, I'm a police officer out of Dania, and I have to carry this firearm with me, cuz I always have people gunnin' for me."

"I understand your problem," I said. "I'll go ahead and work along with you, but you're going to have to take and keep the firearm where people can't see it."

So he agreed he'd keep it in his fishing tackle box. So that was all right, and I went about my business.

Several weeks later, a couple of men came in and said, "Hey Tom, there's a big colored fella down there who said you weren't man enough to take his firearm from him."

Well, I said, "I'll look into that. I'll take care of it."

So I turned around and sped back home to get my airboat and check it out.

I got back, put my airboat in, and went on down Miami Canal looking for the guy. His name was Jerry Harris, but I couldn't find him.

So I came on back and thought I'd catch him later.

But in checking things out, I had seen these individuals in their swamp buggies hitting all the gator holes. Well, it was the dry period, and a lot of people were out there, and I knew what they were doing!

So I immediately went back to Opa Locka Airport and made contact with one of the Naval Reserve helicopter pilots. They would always help out because of my Reserve connection.

So we took off. We went out and flew over an area where, sure enough, there had been alligator hunting going on. We sat the 'copter down in some mud spots, and I got out and walked around looking for evidence. Lo and behold, I found one of the poacher's wallets! I opened it up, and it belonged to a fellow named Benz, out of Clewiston, but there was nothing else to be found.

So we got back in the helicopter, but while we were trying to take off, one of the pontoons broke free and the other stuck in the muck. That threw the chopper to its side, and the blade began to chop at saw grass roots, muck, and everything. We came real close to turning the whole helicopter over and crashing in a ball of fire, but it broke loose just in time!

OK, so it seemed this was going to be an exciting day. I could tell already.

On the way back, we flew over Miami Canal, and I saw Jerry down there fishing. I looked, and sure enough, he had that pistol on his side.

We went on back to the airport and landed. Then I went and got my airboat and went rushing back to the Miami Canal, where I knew I was bound to come up on Jerry. I knew he was going to give me problems. I planned to be real nice to him, asking him how fishing was and so forth, but there he was with his gun in plain view.

I said, "What kind of pistol you got there, Jerry?"

"That's my .38," he said.

"Well, you're going to have to give it to me," I said, "because you're under arrest for bringing it into the management area. I was giving you a chance, and now look what you've gone and done."

So, he said, "Tom Shirley, I'm not gonna give you my pistol, and I'm gonna go ahead and keep fishin', and I'm not gonna pay you any mind." He was from Chicago and had a real attitude!

"Well," I said, "One way or another, you're going in, Jerry. You take your choice."

"I'm gonna keep right on fishin'," he said, and he commenced fishing.

Well, there were two other fishermen there, close by in their boat.

They saw a ruckus in the making. They cranked up their boat, and boy, they got out of there fast!

I was still trying to get this resolved.

"Come on, let's go," I said. "Let's not have any problems. Give me your gun and let's go."

And I saw him look down at his paddle, and I knew what he was thinking. He was going to assault me with that paddle.

I had hold of the front of his boat. I figured, well, if he stands up to hit me with that paddle, I'll pull the boat forward, and he'll fall off the back end. That'd take care of him.

So anyway, he still wasn't planning to go in with me. He stood up, and I saw him looking down at his pistol at his side.

I said, "OK, Jerry, from this point forward, I don't want you to touch that pistol, you understand? Do not touch that pistol."

All of a sudden . . . boom . . . he went for his pistol!

Luckily, I outdrew him.

He stood up and froze. My hammer was back, and boy, I had it aimed right between his eyes.

The first thing he said was, "You drew on a fellow officer! You got your hammer back!"

And by that time, boy, his face grew wide—big, big, big. And it blew out in a bunch of tears . . . an unbelievable amount of tears! His face was just completely wet with tears!

Well, in retrospect, that was a lesson for me. I should have gone ahead and shot him because his gun barrel was only about two feet from me.

I reached over and took his pistol. I told him to crank up, go on back to Mack's Fishing Camp. "Because *now* we're going to have to go in to the Sheriff's Office." So he cranked up and off we went.

We got to the fishing camp. I got in my vehicle and said, "OK, follow me."

He said, "No, you can follow me," and he dug out.

Well, I took a shortcut to the highway, and I blocked it off, blue light flashing, and went through all the motions, knowing he would go around.

He went around all right!

My truck was clocked at 110 miles an hour. But he had a new white and orange Crown Victoria floored, and, man, was he gone! He left me like I was tied.

So I radioed ahead to the Sheriff's Department, "I've got a vehicle headed east on State Road 84. Hold him for me."

So I'm racing. When I caught up to the police, there were three of them on motorcycles, and they had Jerry pulled over out in a field.

So I pulled up, and they said, "What's the matter?"

I said, "Well, Jerry's given me some trouble, so I'm taking him into the Sheriff's Department."

This time Jerry raised up, and here came the tears again. He was ranting and raving, just going berserk. His neck and face had swelled up way out of the ordinary, and here came those drenching tears again.

So, I said, "Jerry, are you going to go in with me?"

The three police officers stepped back, very nervous of the situation, and one said, "Tom, this guy's pretty irate. He seems like a dangerous character. We'd better call the wagon on in."

I said, "Well, hold on a minute."

"Jerry," I said, "are you going go in with me, or am I going to have to call the wagon on you?"

He said, "OK, Tom, I'll go in with you."

So we loaded up and off we went.

We got to the Sheriff's Department. I went in there and started to book him, and he starts welling up, crying again—tears just running down his face by the tub full.

The people in the Sheriff's Department saw all this. And, man, they vacated the place.

Jerry began to cuss me. He walked over and said, "Tom, if you come through Hollywood, I'm gonna book you at 120 miles per hour."

Then he walked over to a steel grate door—quarter-inch steel—and he started boxing it like a boxing bag. He tore his knuckles to the bone, blood flying all over the cell. Meanwhile, he was saying: "You'll be sorry that you ever apprehended me. I'm sure gonna press charges!"

"Well, fine, Jerry," I said. "If you want to do that, we're going up to the Solicitor's Office right now," which we did.

We walked into the Solicitor's Office and told him that I wanted to press charges, and Jerry wanted to press charges also.

Well, with all this excitement, and Jerry acting so irate, the solicitors, boy, they cleared out of there. They were just plain scared. So I figured that I was going to have to come in next week to file charges, which I did. And I should have filed felony charges on him, but I didn't. I wanted to give him a break.

A week or so later, the case came up at the Broward County Court House. They found Jerry guilty as charged for resisting arrest, excessive use of violence, and bringing a concealed weapon into a courtroom. The *Miami Daily News* reported on the verdict on May 14, 1956.

So time passed. I was back at Mack's Fishing Camp again. Two men came up and said, "Tom, you got problems."

I said, "What's that?"

One of them said, "There's two black men down there with guns saying they're going to do away with you."

I said, "Oh, well. OK, well, I'll have to look into that."

So I left.

I went back to the airport and got my airboat and came all the way back to Mack's Fishing Camp and launched, and I was off, going to find the two black men who were looking for me. I searched everywhere, all the way over Miami Canal, south of the river, I couldn't find them. Apparently, they had picked up and left before I got there. Well, perhaps that was the best thing.

A week or so passed, and I saw Jerry's boat out there again, with a 3-foot billy club across the deck.

So I launched my boat. I was going to go down and check out Jerry's attitude.

Well, I went down, and sure enough, he was fishing as usual. I came up against the boat and said, "Mind if I check your fishing license?"

So he gave me his fishing license, and I handed it back.

I said, "You mind if I go through your boat and look for a gun?"

"Nah, go ahead, help yourself," he said. So I helped myself.

I spilled out the tools, a little bit rough-like, and put them all back nice. I handled his fishing tackle box, kind of rough . . . no pistol.

So I said to Jerry, "Are you going to give me anymore problems?"

He said, "No, Mr. Shirley, I ain't gonna fight you no more."

So I replaced the tool box and the fishing tackle box where I had found them.

I stepped into my airboat. I told Jerry, "You have a nice day," and I left him.

A couple of weeks after that, I was driving down in Ft. Lauderdale and I heard someone hollering at me from a seven-story building. Somebody was yelling so loud, "Hey Tom! Hey, Tom!"

So I looked out the vehicle window and up there, about four stories up, I saw Jerry. He was up there plastering. He was working as a plastering contractor.

I waved to him and hollered back. So it looked like we had patched up our problems.

Jerry eventually bought a big airboat and a half-track. I'm pretty sure that he was the first black man to use such equipment in the Everglades.

Flairs and Hot-Air Balloons

Each year, two individuals would come down from Tallahassee to make a survey of all our equipment and keep everything working and in proper order. At that time, we would request new equipment that we'd like to have, making capital purchases and so forth. These individuals were very good to us. We would design different boats and buggies, and they would put those items in the budget to fund, allowing us to complete projects and supply ourselves with equipment that made our Everglades patrol and law-enforcement jobs easier. We had great cooperation at that time. Those old one-on-one procedures were very effective and appreciated, and the Commission made great advances during those years.

There was an economic upswing in South Florida that filtered into the Commission's coffers. Gasoline for airboats, new full-tracks or half-tracks, all sorts of vehicles, camping supplies, food, a wide variety of rental equipment, and Motorola radios. Gradually, I had the necessary equipment and supplies to really meet the challenge to enforce the law.

My response area had two full-tracks, two half-tracks, one swamp buggy, three outboard motorboats, one ATC (all-terrain cycle), and light airboats. I had access to a helicopter, a fixed-wing aircraft, and a twin-engine aircraft. We really had it covered.

Back in the early 1960s, when Homestead Air Force Base was very active during the Cuban Missile Crisis, we had a game officer, Steve Carter, who was assigned to the Homestead area. He became great friends with high-ranking officials in the Air Force. He could get all kinds of sleeping bags and other equipment donated to the Game Commission.

So I began thinking of what we could use or adapt to our needs in Law Enforcement. For instance, I had acquired some very large, several-million-candlepower flares, the type you drop from airplanes with timing devices and so forth.

Well, we had great problems with the group called the Homestead Outlaws who hunted south of the Loop Road and engaged in all manner of illegal activities. This included "jack-lighting," or "fire hunting," at night by shining light in the deer's eyes, which was an illegal practice at any time. This group frequented the Tentacle Rock area—which was very hard country to travel unless you knew it well, especially in the dark!

I figured that with these flares, I could get our Piper Cub to patrol at night. We could have our officers surround the area with the airboats, weasels, half-tracks, and full-tracks. Then, we could drop the flares from the airplane, and, boy, we could really put on a raid and catch some of these longtime poachers, who were long overdue to be apprehended.

But just before making final arrangements, Steve told me, "Lieutenant, before you do this, we're going to have to get permission from the Air Force to set off these flares."

Well, in reality that was going to take too much time and red tape, and as a result my plans would doubtless be leaked. So I decided that I'd better drop it, but it had been a great thought, and I sure bet it would have worked really well!

Steve also had access to helium and these weather balloons, so I thought about that, and I got creative: "Well, if we could get enough helium balloons, we could fasten them to a chair, and we'd have our own helium balloon setup where we can go across the Everglades!"

Well, halfway joking, I talked to Wendell Clemmons. He's an officer who worked South Dade quite a bit as well as the saw grass area. I said, "Clem, I think what I'm going to do is assign you to this program.

We're going to get about a dozen of these big weather balloons. We're going to fasten them to a lawn chair. We're going to turn you loose in this rig. We'll have a long rope and we'll tie it to a half-track or full-track, and we'll patrol the Everglades with you in this chair!"

"Now, I have a .22 pistol. If anything happens, if the balloon rig breaks loose and you go sailing up to 100,000 feet or so, well, you take this .22 pistol, and you pop those balloons to come down at whatever rate you want to."

Well, he didn't think too much of this idea. He didn't know whether he was up to that sort of dangerous thing or not, but I kept him sweating for quite a while.

Joking or not, we carried on that conversation with the other officers for several months. I still felt that in theory this would be novel, pulling a man in a balloon behind a full-track, especially over the grassy areas, to check vehicles. And, if the hunters threw any evidence out, we'd be able to see them do it! I was that desperate to curtail the efforts of the Homestead Outlaws!

Moonshiners—1956

I was on routine patrol in my vehicle just north of Hialeah, around where 183rd Street is now. Back then, in 1956, it was wild country. There was an old coral rock house that belonged to the Graham family. About a quarter mile, maybe half a mile east of there, I smelled something that needed investigating. So I followed that awful, nasty smell of rotten corn.

I followed a track to a moonshine still that was going big time! Boy, there were barrels of corn and a big vat that still was producing 'shine in a big way.

I figured, well, this is a major, organized setup for sure.

The police normally patrol that kind of activity, so I couldn't understand why this illegal operation was going on—when it appeared to be so wide open!

I had worked with the Alcohol and Tobacco people before, and they had raved about this one agent. He was in West Palm Beach, and he had a reputation for catching his man every time! So I figured he was the guy to handle this.

I called my officer, a lieutenant up there in West Palm. I said, "You contact this fellow from the Alcohol and Tobacco Department and tell him I'm sending him information on where he can make a bust!"

So I sat back and waited.

About a half week later, I received a report that he "didn't catch anybody," but that he'd destroyed the still.

That was the last time I put my trust in the Alcohol and Tobacco guys. It seemed obvious that the local police department was part of this operation.

Late one night, I was patrolling by myself in my airboat south of Highway 41. I was going down some of the canals, running north and south, and I came upon a still.

Well, I looked at some of the equipment, and I recognized this burner. A burner is a 3-inch-diameter metal pipe with a hole drilled in it. Butane gas is hooked up to it, and when it's fired up it produces a really hot fire. This kind of device was used to warm up the corn and water to start the fermentation process in making moonshine.

One of the officers that worked for the Game Commission had a burner like that . . .

I didn't say anything, I didn't disturb anything. I just looked at the still.

Later I saw Sig Walker with a load of 5-gallon cans in his trunk. So I put two and two together. The rumors were right. This was my old buddy Sig Walker's still! The former game warden had become a moonshiner.

Since I had lost faith in the Alcohol and Tobacco people, I figured I would just go ahead and destroy this one myself. So I stepped back a bit, pulled out my .44 Magnum. I shot six times, making a big letter "T" in the big vat, destroying this operation and letting Sig know that Tom Shirley had been here!

Swamped

In the latter part of the 1950s, my boss, Officer J. O. Brown, loved to design and make airboats, which he thought were just great. He wanted to make a little 10-foot airboat with one of these hopped-up,

90-horsepower Continental engines. So we went to Jimmy Jordan's. That was our shop.

We built three of these little boats according to his design. All of our boats then had galvanized bottoms, which were very good for running over dry ground. The first one we made, J. O. took out on the Perry Airport runway to test and see if it would run dry.

Oh, he thought it was just wonderful! He ran it up and down the airstrip. Sparks were flying, and he was having a ball. Well, he ended up burning the whole bottom out of boat on the first run, so we had to take that sheet of galvanized metal off and put on another one. But he was so tickled that the airboat had proved itself. He figured that he had designed the greatest airboat ever!

Well, I didn't like the design of his boats. In fact, I thought they were terrible. They were small, and they weren't fast. They'd get out of the hole fast, and they'd run dry pretty well, but as far as their life as patrol boats was concerned, they were almost useless. You couldn't even get out to the back to change a spark plug in deep water. If you did, the boat would tip down with your weight, and water would come in over the side. It was just a horrible boat! But it was the boat that I now had to use on patrol!

I went down south of the Loop Road in the mangroves in one of those boats. That particular time, I went to Jack Hawkins's camp where there was a radio tower. I crawled up the tower to look over the area where I was going to try to catch these fellows coming in through the mangroves from Chokoloskee. I chose the route I would take, and I went back up into the mangroves in the airboat, looking—picking out a place where I could jump these fellows when they came back from their poaching. Whether they came back late at night or early in the morning, I could jump them in an area of the mangroves where they couldn't turn around and run from me.

So in searching for this particular place, which I thought I had found, and, in the attempt to turn around, the grass roll hit some mangroves, which don't give—they don't give at all. They're real hard and sturdy and strong! Well, my wake came over the back end, and just like that, my airboat sank! So there I sat in the mangroves.

I got out, and the ground was just like soft butter from sediment. There was no chance of lifting that boat up to get it above the water line where I could bail it out. Believe me, I tried and tried, but there was no way.

Well, I had a problem! Night would fall, and I'd be eaten alive by the mosquitoes. Back then, we didn't carry mosquito dope. We just sweated it out. But down in the mangroves in that particular place, they'd pick you up and carry you off—huge, black, mangrove mosquitoes! So I looked way off in the distance. I could just barely make out a place that the poachers call Gator Hook Strand. I figured, well, if I get out and walk as fast as I can, maybe I can find the camp that's on the other side of Gator Hook Strand.

Ironically, that camp was the one that belonged to Sig Walker, former game warden, now adversary poacher and moonshiner!

But right now, if I could get to Sig's camp, it would be my only salvation to get away from these mosquitoes!

So I got out of the sunken airboat. I had a little three-cell flashlight with me, but I found that the batteries were dead. I hoped that I'd be able to find Sig's camp in the cypress before dark, but everything seemed against me right then.

I took out walking westward. I walked and walked and walked. I walked sideways, forward, and backward, every way to get out of that spidery-legged mangrove forest and still head in the right direction. I was tired, really fatigued. And even at this snail's pace, I had to admit to myself that I was going as fast as I could. There was no place to lie down except in the water, but I knew that if I did that, my muscles would stiffen up, and I wouldn't be able to go any farther. So I just kept walking.

Finally, I got to Gator Hook Strand. There I found an airboat trail that went back southward. Now, somewhere off of that trail was Sig Walker's camp.

But by now it was dark. So, in the dark, I was walking, looking for another airboat trail that would bear off to the right, which would lead to Sig's camp. I walked as fast as I could, but I was dragging, really giving out, and now desperately looking for that trail that by now I felt I had missed!

I walked on about 100, 200 yards to the south of the island, and sure enough, I noticed a particular tree. That's when I realized that I *had* already passed the airboat trail. But even that was a good sign! So

I managed to walk back the way I had come, and I picked up the trail. Boy, was that a beautiful sight!

I went in to Sig's shack, slammed that screen door, and I got in out of the mosquitoes. Sig's camp had old rusted screen wire on it. You could punch a hole in that old screen, but so long as it kept the mosquitoes away that night . . . I was finally safe! I could hear those mosquitoes just a-honing and a-buzzing on the other side of that screen. But, boy, I felt like a king, just sitting there in Sig's bed without being eaten alive!

Early the next morning, as luck would have it, I heard a Super Cub. It had a particular noise to it, a cracking noise in the engine. I knew that noise and knew that it was *our* airplane! So quickly I went out and built a little fire, throwing some green leaves on it to bring up some smoke.

Well, sure enough, our pilot saw it and came buzzing down at me. I pointed in the direction where the airboat lay sunk. He searched, spotted the airboat, and realized what had happened.

Soon he flew back over me and dropped a note: "What the hell are you doing out here? Stay put. We'll get you out. I'll send Dave Baldman after you."

About five o'clock that afternoon, Dave Baldman came in his airboat. When he picked me up, he had another couple of guys with him. The four of us were able to lift that rinky-dink airboat up enough to bail it out. And I took off for home, sure glad to get out of that mangrove before another night came on!

Since that disaster with J. O. Brown's airboat design, I used my own personal airboat. It didn't always run better than the one the Commission had furnished me, but otherwise I sure could count on it! On the job I had plenty of gas and oil, and the Commission serviced my boat for me, so it was an even trade as far as I was concerned.

I decided that I wanted to build a new airboat of my own design. I made it with a top deck in the shape of the wing of an aircraft in an attempt to create a "lift." The bottom rake was kind of short to give it a compression effect—to give it a lift on the bottom—but this airboat gave me lift on the top *and* the bottom, so it worked out beautifully. The transom was extra low. I think it was 6, maybe 6 ½ inches, which was extremely low. The hull was made of 80,000-gauge aluminum sheeting. The bottom was 6 feet wide and 12 feet long. The grass roll was a very new design that I fabricated with ½-inch conduit covered with expanded metal, which was absolutely "out of sight" at this time! Everyone made fun of it and called it the "Cowcatcher." The rudders were tapered in at the top, which helped put the boat into a bank in the direction that you wanted to turn. It was powered by a 165-horsepower Franklin, which really didn't have a good reputation back in those days, but it sure worked great for me!

My new design looked like something from outer space, and it caught everybody's eye! It was *way* ahead of its time!

But all the sportsmen and hunters gathered up and said, "Tom, that ain't gonna work. That boat's gonna sink." Nonetheless, they all hung around admiring and studying it.

Being so skeptical, they were anxious to find out if it was even going to float! So, south of the Dade County Airboat Association on the Tamiami Trail, about 20 miles from Miami, we had a course that was a measured mile. This was before radar guns. We ran by the stopwatch. My airboat was clocked at 96 mph with the RPM (prop revolution per minute) at 150 on that measured mile course! That was the average speed, but at times it exceeded 100 mph. For fear that the airboat would indeed go airborne, I didn't have the gas all the way open.

It was a beautiful airboat. And if I was running the grass, it would run the highest grass. It would leave the water completely, swoop up, and ride high in the grass, just like riding waves in the ocean. It really was like that, like I was a surfer! When it was filmed, it looked so smooth. That boat came out completely satisfactory, as far as I was concerned.

It was extremely effective when I was patrolling boats in the nighttime without a light. I'd ride toward them, not on the water, but over the saw grass and, "Plop!," I'd land right beside them in the water before they knew what was going on.

With this boat, I didn't have to worry about anything except the Lord's Hammocks. If I wanted to check a boat, I could go across the sloughs and the high saw grass where the others couldn't go. It would go anyplace.

One particular night, I was patrolling, and I didn't know if I'd come across a gator hunter or a frogger or both. It was generally impossible

I designed this aerodynamic airboat in 1961, shortly after I was made lieutenant. Light as a feather, it would swoop up and ride the highest grass like riding waves in the ocean! Photographer Toby Massey took this photo while on assignment with *National Geographic* in 1967 to illustrate the article "Dragons in Distress" by Archie Carr.

to tell. That was the trouble, because an innocent frogger many times would be put in the fortuitous position to poach an alligator and skin it, and believe me, many of them did!

I had seen his light working. So I was sneaking up on this individual, and he was just at the edge, behind Sawgrass Strand. I was coming across the high saw grass, and just as I left the saw grass and hit the Lily Slough, he turned around, and his light illuminated me. All he saw was something coming out of the sky, pouncing down beside him!

Well, to say the least, it scared the fool out of him, and before he knew it, I was on his boat. I asked him if I could conduct a search of his boat, and he was shaking and trembling, and he said, "Yes sir!" So I went ahead and checked the boat. Well, I had him checked and frisked and everything before he even knew who I was or what happened.

But after he settled down, boy, he began to cuss and rave at me: "You just . . . scared the mortal hell out of me! Never do that again!"

So I laughed, and he looked at the boat a bit and marveled at it and so forth. But he was still very mad at the whole situation. So, having checked him out, I said, "Have a nice evening; I hope you catch a lot of frogs." And I rode off into the dark of the night with my lights out, just floating across the big saw grass strands with little effort. It was sure a great joy, driving that boat.

Well, that night's work didn't go over too well. The guy I apprehended wrote Tallahassee a very uncomplimentary letter stating, "Something should be done . . ." Because I scared him, he "almost had a heart attack," etc. "So stop Tom Shirley from using Gestapo tactics."

But that soon was old news, and it was business as usual. On another night not too long after that episode, I checked him out again, and all was just fine.

In 1961, the Game Commission asked me to build three airboats of my design, then hired out three more to be built for use by my twenty-eight officers. Here I am commanding my Everglades District airboat squadron in an international advertisement for Motorola Radios. This was during the heyday of the Florida Game and Fresh Water Fish Commission in the 1970s, when the state's sportsmen and conservation organizations worked actively and enthusiastically with the Game Commission. As a result of the revenues from this relationship, the Commission had top priority on vehicles, equipment, and supplies for our Law Enforcement unit in the Everglades. (Photo by Jim Brantley.)

I had made lieutenant in 1960 and had the responsibility of over-seeing the duties of eight officers covering the Everglades District. And my airboat was deemed such a success, so perfect for patrolling the Everglades wetlands, that I was asked to make boats for the Commission. My men and I built three of them, and we hired out the labor on the others. I have a wonderful memory of them.

4

Everglades Patrol

All in a Day's Work

Deer Studies and Nicotine Darts—1960

Along with my initial duties in Law Enforcement for the Commission, I spent a great deal of time and energy assisting our biologists. Frank Ligas was working primarily on a study of Everglades frogs for a future publication, and Charles Loveless was working on a very important publication on the Everglades deer herd. I assisted both of them in catching and tagging deer for various studies.

Around 1956, I had become involved in a capture-and-treat program for our deer herd. One of the parasites that we tried to control on the deer was screwworm, the larval stage of a type of fly. There had been really bad epidemics in the later 1930s across the southern United States. Here in Florida, it was thought initially that the deer was the carrier of this great threat to the state's valuable cattle industry. Huge deer hunts were carried out. Florida next planned to kill all the deer on the Big Cypress Seminole Reservation in 1939. This effort was thwarted by the Seminole leaders who protested to Washington, setting the state up against the federal government. As a result, an emergency study was made. The findings showed that screwworms were carried by many animals besides deer, including raccoons.

Any cut or abrasion can result in a screwworm infestation. Also, when the buck deer grows new horns, the flesh around the horn can get irritated at the base. I would locate a deer feeding in a prairie or slough and check to see if it had a wound. If it did, I'd chase it in the airboat, pull alongside of it and leap out onto it. Then I'd wrestle it to

There is water, water everywhere.

As I was so successful in capturing and handling animals, I was often called on to work in the Game Management Division. *Life* magazine published a series of photos in 1957 by photographer Stan Wayman that showed me capturing deer for treatment of screwworm, the parasitic larvae of a fly. I would run up close to the deer in my airboat and then leap out to subdue it. (Photos by Stan Wayman.)

...'t get started

A FIGHT

Once the deer was caught, we officers would treat any open wounds for screwworm infestation. This was one of a series of photos that led to a spot for me on the TV show *You Asked for It! Left to right:* Tom Shirley, unidentified, Crist Nolan. (Photo by Stan Wayman.)

where I could treat it with a medication that we purchased in a grain store—a foul, creosote-smelling liquid. I'd rub that stuff on them really well, and it was very effective.

When I worked with Charles Loveless from 1955 to 1957, the wildlife and the Everglades ecosystem remained top priority. Charles extolled the Everglades deer herd in an article in the Commission's *Florida Wildlife* magazine: "The Game Management biologists have learned that the 'Glades can and does support one of the best deer herds in the State. The annual hunting take from the 'Glades now ranks right along with the Ocala and Elgin Field deer kills" (Loftin 41).

In that same article, "Classroom in the Everglades," Charles reportedly noted that "60 percent of [the Everglades deer's] food is made up of white water lily and swamp lily." And importantly for what would come to pass in the future, Charles noted from his study of water levels that "when the water gets too high, they all have to take to the tree islands. Occasionally when the water stays too long, they may strip these islands bare, peeling the bark off the trees. And if the water does not recede in time, many of them simply starve to death" (Loftin 41).

His study discussed the water levels that would be optimum for the survival of deer and other animals and stressed the levels and conditions that would prove fatal to wildlife. The information documented in this study was critical to the health of the animals and the historic tree islands in the Everglades wetlands.

We spent a lot of time nurturing this really excellent Everglades wetlands deer herd. An article in the Commission's *Florida Wildlife* magazine in 1955, the year I joined, discussed how the Commission had initiated a major research project in February 1953 to protect the wildlife. It was called the Everglades Impoundment Investigation, and it was a continuing project to "inventory the wildlife resources, correlate water levels with plant succession in an effort to predict future trends, to recommend to the Corps of Engineers optimum stages for pool operations" (FGFFC 29).

This sure sounded like the Commission was planning to stay on top of the plans of the Corps of Engineers and the Flood Control District. And an article in the July issue by Cleveland Van Dresser stated that the engineers, including Lamar Johnson, former chief engineer with the Flood Control District, "were fully aware of the high value of wildlife that could be affected by the project. Since construction started six years ago, hardly a levee is built, a waterway dug or a pump installed that does not take wildlife values into consideration" (19).

So initially, according to the Corps, according to Flood Control, the ecosystem of the Everglades wetlands and its wildlife was top priority. If water levels were dangerous to wildlife, they were to be adjusted. If any agency exceeded their limit and endangered the habitat, it was clearly unlawful. I questioned everyone on this, and they verified that there would be laws on the books concerning the protection of the wildlife.

Toward the end of 1960, I took a six-month leave of absence from the Game Commission in order to take over management of a tropical fish farm, Carol City Fisheries. I learned a lot, the work was very interesting, and it also made me very prosperous. During this period, however, I continued to work on Commission assignments on the weekends, and I donated my time and equipment to them.

For my new employment, it was necessary to locate new suppliers of exotic tropical fish that were available in South America, as the business was competing with other importers. I would be breeding fish by the millions, traveling, importing from tropical countries. This was far more exciting than my Commission job at that time, and the pay was certainly better.

I needed to find someone to move my cargo, and I came across a fellow, Hank Goodman, who had a B-25 bomber. He had rerigged the plane to carry cargo, so I contracted him to fly my fish out of Iquitos, Peru, approximately 3,000 miles from the mouth of the Amazon right in the heart of the Amazon basin.

This was one of the happiest times of my life, because I've always wanted to go on an adventure to South America and see the really wild country.

It was nighttime by the time we were packed up and ready to leave for South America. I was to fly co-pilot. We took off at midnight. Hank Goodman radioed Key West Air Station and asked them to contact Cuba to see if we could get permission to fly over the island.

Well, this was right when Castro first took over. In fact, this is the time period when he had purchased his first Russian MiG fighters. I had read in the newspaper that five of them had just come in. I was sure that they were anxious to try them out!

Key West radioed the Cuban officials to see if we could get permission to fly over their island. And, of course, they radioed back, "No chance."

Hank was heading toward the island to go around it, but, all of a sudden, he turned out the light and pushed the throttle wide open. And over the island we went!

We had the radio turned to the Cuban frequency. They were raising hell! So I was sitting in the cockpit with the earphones, listening to all of this. And I was looking around for the MiGs with their automatic sights that fire the guns and all. They were really the most advanced fighters at the time. Anyway, we made it over the island! No problem—just a little bit of excitement.

We continued on to Iquitos, flying over the Andes. We had to gain altitude just to fly through the valley, but to make a long story short, I made contact with the fish dealers that I needed for business and made arrangements for Hank Goodman to fly my fish to the United States.

And when we flew back home, of course, we went right over Cuba just like we did before! And we made it back, no problem.

It wasn't long before my six-month leave was about over and I received a call from the Commission's director, Earl Frye, who said, "Hey, we want you to come back full-time!" Well, I had hoped to buy into Carol City Fisheries by that time, but the owner wasn't interested, so I went back to the Commission.

While I was in Iquitos, I became fascinated with the local Indians and their blowguns. When I returned to the Commission, I made one of my own design. I used aluminum tubing and golf tee darts! I then contacted a veterinarian friend of mine for nicotine.

I shot darts that would inject the nicotine. It was very, very effective, depending on the dosage, as effective as a 30.06 bullet, and it took effect in seconds. Data show nicotine to be one of the most violent of all poisons. Humans just don't realize how it poisons and stimulates the body.

If an alligator is shot with nicotine, he freezes like a two-by-four. You can pick up a 10-foot alligator by the tail and pull him out of the water like he's a frozen board. That's the effect that nicotine has on the gator's nervous system.

But it was for deer studies that this technique proved the most valuable. With the blowgun, I would shoot the deer with a very light dose, just four drops, and it would usually bring the deer right down. Then the biologist could tag and release within minutes, with little or no fear and trauma inflicted on the animal. This technique proved so effective to the Biology Department that they made arrangements for me to work with Charles.

Nicotine sometimes had a funny effect on the deer. Say that I would shoot a deer from the airboat as it was feeding in the slough. It would then run into a nearby hammock island. I would wait about five minutes and then go in and track him down. I'd catch him, and we'd conduct our study, tag, and release.

When the nicotine began to take effect, you could see that the deer knew that something was wrong. They couldn't run away, but some of them sure could stand there and fight. The drug turns some of them aggressive. There was one in particular like this. He was about a 10-point, a beautiful deer. I walked onto the island, and, boy, he was

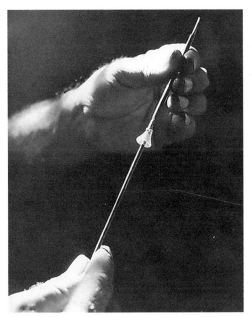

In 1960, I took a short leave of absence from the Game Commission and went to Iquitos, Peru, to conduct some private business. There I saw the natives using their blowguns. When I came back to the Commission, I brought the idea of using the blowgun to fire nicotine darts made of golf tees to tranquilize the Everglades deer for treatment. This method proved to be far less stressful for them. (Photo by Red Cilamatt.)

waiting for me! He had his ears down, and as I walked forward, here he came, wide open, coming at me. I mean, hard, hard, hard, like an old rushing bull!

Meanwhile, it had been rough going for me to get to him. I was all tied up in some vines. That was lucky for me because he ran toward me full force, ready to hit me right in the chest with his antlers. The only thing that saved me was that he got hung up in the vines, too! I was able to back up in the vines about 10 feet, but he got loose and came at me again.

Every time I backed up, he'd come at me. Finally, I had to ward him off with my hand. By then, he had managed to push me back about 50 feet, all the way back to the airboat! Every time I backed up, he would charge me. That was one strange effect from nicotine!

On another day, I was working with Frank tagging deer and moving them from one area to the other. I had knocked one deer down with the blowgun dart, but somehow I had overdosed him and he wouldn't come around. So both of us got down on the ground and began to give him artificial respiration. Frank was blowing in through the nose, filling up the lungs with air, and I'm pushing on the deer's rib cage to push the air out. We had a pretty good rhythm going, with Frank blowing in the nose and me pushing on the chest, but I guess I got mixed up, and once when Ligas blew, I pushed at the same time.

Now, it's pretty common for a deer to have a leach in its nose. In this case, when I pushed, several leaches blew right out of the deer's nose into Frank's mouth!

He kind of gagged and spit them out! He said, "Tom, you dirty, dirty dog!"

I said innocently, "I didn't mean to do it!"

We worked on the deer for about fifteen minutes. Slowly it came around, got up, and hesitatingly walked off. We continued to catch and release about eight more.

During that day when we were catching deer, I was crashing through islands in the airboat. Back then, it wasn't against the law for airboaters to do that. I would crash through the islands and chase out the deer to be able to shoot them with dart gun. But it was the season for spiders, and those hammocks were just packed with great big spiders—about 3 inches across with big webs, maybe 4 foot across, maybe larger. We'd be doing this all day long, and I'd come out looking like a cocoon with so many spiders and webs on me.

These spiders—golden web or banana spiders—are not usually poisonous, but after a full day's work, so many spiders had bitten me that I broke out with a fever. I wound up in the hospital for a couple of days. So from then on, we quit crashing through the hammocks with such abandon. But the deer project, aided by the use of the nicotine darts, was considered a great success.

At the time, I was implementing my own deer impact study program as well. I would use the blowgun with nicotine to knock the deer out so I could pick him up and safely move him. From where I captured him east of the Miami Canal, I would tag him and move him 10 miles or so west to see if he went back to the original location.

This was a worthy program, and when Game Management found out about it, they were impressed. They wanted to work with me on this study, so I joined up with biologist Frank Ligas, and we went out tagging deer. At times we found that they did migrate back to where they had originally come from.

One day, Earl Frye, the director of the Game Commission gave me a call. He told me that he had met the manufacturer of a drug called "Capture." They were interested in hiring me as their representative. But I declined since by then I had become totally dedicated to my job at the Wildlife Commission and to the Everglades wetlands.

A Dead Poacher and a Firearms Bust—1960

There was a deer poacher from Hollywood, Florida. He wasn't on my "most wanted" list, but he was consistent enough that I wanted to catch him. I even knew his routine. He'd have his wife drive him out to the Snake Creek Canal in the early morning, and in the late afternoon, she'd come back to pick him up with his deer.

So one morning I get this call. It's his wife, absolutely distraught! She had gone to pick her husband up the previous evening. She'd waited and waited. Finally, she took the chance of being found out and called and whistled. But he never came. She just knew that something terrible had happened.

"He's never done this before . . . Please, Lt. Shirley, will you find my husband?"

So I got our pilot, and we flew out over the area where I knew he hunted. And sure enough, there he was! He lay dead and bloated by the bodies of two huge bucks that he had killed in a good day's hunt that could have been better for him. He'd suffered a massive heart attack. We turned this case over to the Dade County Sheriffs' Department.

Another morning, I was patrolling north of the Tamiami Trail. This was way before Alligator Alley was put in. I went on up north in my airboat, about 20 miles.

There was a string of island hammocks that had a good population of deer and some hogs. I had heard that some individuals were going out to do some illegal hunting.

So, after running up there, I drove into an area that was a good place to hunt. I always made it a point to pull into the shady side of a willow strand. That way, when the sun came up, I'd be hidden in the shadows, and it gave me a great advantage in watching the activity taking place in the area.

Well, I pulled up to that shady place and sat there. It was April or May, the time of year when the Everglades was drying up. I sat there for an hour or so. The birds started flocking in—curlews, ibis, spoonbills. The big beautiful white-and-black wood ibis were just gorgeous. The birds gathered up and settled in and didn't even notice me sitting in the shadows of the willows. Hundreds of them came in. What a sight it was!

As the water level dropped in the Everglades, pools with an abundance of food would be left in low areas. There were shrimp, fish, minnows, eels—all types of foods that these birds dearly loved were right there. Pink spoonbills were there by the flocks. To see all of these beautiful birds feeding right up close, maybe 100 feet from me, still gave me a thrill.

I was being highly entertained while I waited there for the deer poachers. All of these beautiful birds with a blue sky behind them. The wood ibis would feed, then take off in groups. I'd watch them go up in the sky and circle, getting higher and higher and higher. They'd get so high, you could barely see them, until they'd go out of sight riding the jet streams back to their nests to feed their young, maybe 100 miles away!

Then I heard airboats off in the distance. I thought, "Sure enough, they're going to come in here; they're going to be hunting these deer, right out a quarter mile in front of me."

They were getting closer and closer. The birds began to get nervous.

Finally, the airboats got close enough that all the birds—the spoonbills, the ibis, the wood storks, and all the herons—took off. They just lit up the sky with all of their colors, flew off, and set down about a half mile from me.

Meanwhile, two individuals pulled up to a head nearby, parked their boat, and went onto the island to see if they could get hogs or some deer.

Feral hogs in the Everglades wetlands had just become a new legal game animal in 1955 in several of the Wildlife Management Areas. The Everglades Area was one of them. Hog hunting had immediately become so popular that Jim Powell, the biologist with Game Management, had been put in charge of a restocking program before the 1956 hunting season.

Truckloads of trussed-up Florida wild hogs were delivered to the Everglades area weighing between 200 and 300 pounds. They were fast and have a really nasty disposition, and those captured hogs were extra mean. Officer Louis Freeman and I had the job of cutting their binds. Boy, we found out right away that instead of fleeing from us, they wanted to turn and charge us with their tusks!

There was a photo by *Miami Daily News* photographer Toby Massey in the June 1956 *Florida Wildlife* that shows Louis and me preparing to release two hogs and another photo of a hog chasing me as I (in a blurred action shot!) bolted for the safety of the truck! That was some fun!

So I waited for these guys for about an hour.

Then I heard them and cranked up my airboat. As they came out of the woods empty-handed, they were sure surprised to see me! I arrested them for bringing firearms onto a Wildlife Management Area, but released them on their own recognizance. On court day, they paid a fine of about three hundred dollars each.

I was always excited about aircraft. That's why, in 1951, I joined the Naval Reserve Fighter Squadron based at Homestead Air Force Base. I gave the Reserve nine years, and even when I joined the Commission, the Reserve got top priority.

I mentioned before that I had designed my airboat like a plane, and it really did have quite a lift. I just never pushed it. But I was as curious as I could be to see how much of a lift it really had! That airboat was *so* ahead of its time!

In fact, I built that boat years before the U.S. government came out with its Blackbird airplane design that created the fastest plane built to date. During the government's research flight, they found that they could not control it! So they redesigned the tail using a tapered design, the same design I had previously adopted for my own airboat!

When my airboat reached about 65 mph, it would break friction from the water and really take off. It went so fast that you couldn't even hear the engine noise, only the roaring of the wind passing by. So, in an attempt to keep it from going airborne, I always kept an 8-inch concrete block in the nose.

The extra power, the weight, and air friction on this boat were very exceptional. I figured that my body and the total airboat had less air friction than the Stinson aircraft, which flew at 125 mph. The Stinson, like my airboat, also had a Franklin engine. It was such a great boat that once I made lieutenant in 1961, I made three of these airboats for the Commission and had three more fabricated.

Well, I was ready to see just how high it really would fly! So I decided to set up a trial. I was going to try to run the measured mile in thirty seconds, which would be 120 mph. There I was on patrol in the Lone Palm Slough, clipping along pretty fast. The water on the course was about an inch deep. All went well until the nose came up!

I knew that one day the boat would go airborne! But I thought that I could get it down by giving it full power, counting on the engine pushing the nose back down. But it didn't. The boat just kept gaining altitude! My airboat travelled 200 feet before crashing down.

I was thrown out and kept rolling ahead of the boat with my arms at my side. The boat traveled along close behind me as it cracked up. My brand-new boat was broken in half, the prop was destroyed, and all of the spark plugs were broken off the top of the engine. A crescent

In this series of photos from 1961, I was seeing just how fast my newly designed airboat could go in a mile run on Lone Palm Slough. I had given my boat's aluminum hull an aerodynamic uplift, and sure enough, when I removed the weight used to hold the nose down and gave it full power, it took off and went airborne! I was thrown out and rolled through the shallow water just ahead of the boat, which was cracking up behind me. Nothing was broken but the boat; nothing was hurt but my feelings. (Photos by Red Cilamatt.)

wrench that had been lying inside the deck crashed through the crown nose making a really big hole. What a force! There was also a knapsack attached to the back of the front seat. This knapsack had a 9-inch monkey wrench inside. If I had been sitting in my seat when the airboat dove down into the ground, the knapsack and wrench would have smashed me in the back of the head!

After going airborne, I decided that if I wanted to fly, I would get in a plane!

I made it back to town.

Then Sig Walker—after I'd shot up his still, and after all the years I had tried to catch him poaching—came back into the picture. On the morning after my accident, I heard that Sig had gathered up a bunch of men and gone way out into the Everglades and brought my airboat wreckage back to his airboat shop in Hialeah! And he and his crew were already rebuilding my airboat for me! That's the kind of relationship that he and I had in those days, even though by then we were at opposite ends of the Game Commission's laws!

I was always a bit experimental. On several occasions over the years, my truck would break down while I was headed to or from assignments with my airboat in tow. So I would get out of the truck, tie the airboat on the trailer, and put the emergency brake on the truck. Then I would jump in the airboat, start the engine, shock the gas throttle one-quarter open, jump out of the airboat, get back in the truck, shift into neutral, release the emergency break—and off I'd go at about 45 mph!

I recall once, years earlier in 1949, going through Hialeah at about 3:00 a.m. with my airboat revving up and sounding like a B-29 bomber. You should have seen all the lights come on behind me down the streets. And when I pulled into my yard, a neighbor came running out to investigate. I had to do that on several occasions!

The last time this happened, I stayed in the driver's seat of the airboat, and my friend Stan Kern drove the truck. We "pushed" the truck all the way across Alligator Alley and Highway 27, some 50 to 60 miles back to my home. I figured that if I was ever pulled over by the Highway Patrol, I'd just say that I was keeping my airboat engine cool, while breaking it in after a new overhaul. I was also pretty sure that a patrolman wouldn't have realized that the trailer hitch was capable of pushing the truck. I just took my chances on this novel way to get back home!

The Homestead Outlaws—1961

Even before I was employed by the Game Commission, I had read in the news about the bad reputation of game violators from Homestead, Florida. Homestead is a major farming district, where country farmers were joined in their illegal exploits by some of the "dust pilots" who sprayed their crops. As a result, they had the best thing going— excellent pilots and superb Curtis-Pitts planes.

These fellows were using their airplanes in deer hunting, either shooting them from the air or, most often, tracking the deer for hunters who would ride in for the kill on ATVs.

So, in mid-April 1961, I scheduled a flight in one of the Commission's planes south of the Loop Road to try to catch these poachers. The Game Commission had a new pilot who had been transferred from Ocala, so he was new to our area. I met him about five o'clock that morning to explain what we called the "kamikaze flight." I asked him if he knew the Japanese attack procedures.

He said, "Yep, the Japs always use the sun in their attack mode."

"Well, that's the same thing we're going to do today," I said.

So we took off. We headed toward the Loop Road off the Tamiami Trail. This is an area where the Homestead boys had their own grassy airstrip. There were quite a few deer to be had in that location, which was protected at the western edge of the Everglades National Park, but for these guys, there were no boundaries.

So we took off, flying at about 3,000 feet. The sun was just coming up, and it was going to be a beautiful day. We flew over the area and saw two Piper Cubs on their airstrip. It looked like they were up for a busy day of hunting.

It was about 7:00 a.m. as we circled high in the sky, with the sun behind us. One of the outlaw gang walked out and got into his Piper Cub.

I said, "Well, the hunt is going to be on soon, so keep that sun to our backs."

The Piper took off. I had my 16mm Bell and Howell movie camera.

That was going to be my ace in the hole to make a good case on these guys. Let the judge see for himself how these poachers used the airplane for hunting deer. So we're looking at the Cub, watching it down below us. I reminded the pilot not to cast a shadow on them while we were keeping the sun at our back.

Two full-tracks took off from one camp. The full-tracks were very effective in this rocky terrain south of Loop Road and in the Everglades mud and marrow. I got my camera all ready. We were going to catch these guys today. Everything was in our favor.

As we looked down following the full-tracks, we saw that there were four men in each vehicle. Time passed, but probably not more than fifteen minutes. We were still circling and watching that plane because he was going to signal to the full-tracks by diving down toward the deer, then pulling up real quick and kind of pointing the tail of the plane at the deer. When that happens, the full pack moves in and does the rest.

So keep in mind that we're still keeping that sun to our rear. My camera was ready. We were looking for some good shots of the action at just the precise moment.

Sure enough, the Piper dove down, dabbed his tail, and here came the two full-tracks from different angles. We could see the deer run into a little myrtle bush, a bushy area for cover. The tracks moved in, the hunters all ready, while their plane circled high to watch the action. So the hunt was on for the weasels.

The deer took off with the full-tracks after him. The guns were just a-blaring, smoke coming out. I had my camera hanging out the side of our Super Cub and was shooting away myself! When apprehending poachers, we always make it a point to note what everyone wears; usually they wear a ball cap, different colors. We always look for the smoke coming from the barrel of the guns—and the corresponding hat—so we know who's doing the shooting.

On one weasel, the hunter was a fellow with a red cap on. Boy, he's blaring away, with smoke just pouring out of his barrel. The shooter in the other weasel track had on a white cap. Boy, he was blazing away, too. Always remember now, we got to remember that track, the color of that track, and the color of the cap of each guy who shot at the deer.

That was a red cap and a white cap. I'm still shooting away. What great footage I'm getting!

We had to continue to keep that sun to our backs. We dove down. We were going to get closer so I could attempt to film the individuals' faces and the whole scenario. We flew down into a steep dive.

All of a sudden, I looked off in the distance and saw a jet turning our way.

I said, "What's that jet doing there?"

He was barreling down, coming right at us! I couldn't understand what was happening. He was coming closer and closer and closer and WHAM! He comes right beside us. That almost blew us out of the sky.

I looked at the jet, and it sure looked to me like an F-104 Needle Nose, one of the super fast jobs that goes more than two or three times the speed of sound. It had little old short wings, maybe 10 feet long. It's built for speed. The leading edge is as sharp as a knife's blade, and they have to put a cover over it because if somebody walks into it, he can seriously cut himself. That's what it looked like, and it was right there in our faces! The pilots call it "the flying casket." Then it was gone!

Well, we were in the middle of our own action! We went back to the scenario below and didn't think anything about it.

I was really engrossed, finally getting to film all of the outlaws' violations as they were taking place. We were just in the initial stage, but I was sure that we could make the identifications when we apprehended them at the end of their hunting day.

All of a sudden, ZING! Here came that jet again, and WHOOSH! it passed us, almost flipping us out of the sky! And he waved his wing! Again I didn't know what to think about it.

But I said, "Something's wrong here, something serious!"

And only at that moment did I think about the escalating crisis in the news. They were calling it the Cuban Missile Crisis! Were there "no-fly" zones? Where were they, and how were they enforced?

I said to my pilot, "Did you file a flight plan?"

He said, "Yeah."

"Where at?" I asked.

He said, "Well, just west of Coral Gables."

"Well, Dagonne! That wasn't good enough! We're *way* southwest of Coral Gables and in deep trouble. We must be in a no-fly zone!!!"

Here came the jet again. ZING!

It passed us about as slow as it could go and still keep in the air, but he waved his wing and then he turned back eastward.

Well, now we got the message all right.

"We've got to get out of here! Turn this Cub around and give it full power. Go as fast as you can!"

So we headed on back east, but I sure hated to. All of that work, watching all of that illegal action, and here we are interrupted, with no chance of having a successful day in court with the footage we took!

As we headed eastward, we flew over the turnpike. Man, what a sight that was! It was a scary sight to see just how far this Cuban Missile Crisis had escalated between us and the Russians. There below us were convoys of military vehicles, lots of them, hundreds of them, almost as far as you could see, coming south on the Florida Turnpike.

The pilot said, "Man, would you look at that. It looks like an invasion in the making!"

Obviously the United States was really taking this threat seriously.

I went on patrol later that night. Stopping at a hamburger joint, I happened to run into one of my old chiefs from the Naval Reserve.

"Chief, what's going on?" I asked. "I've got helicopters flying over my house day and night. What's happening?"

He said, "Tom, we've got twenty-seven Russian subs sitting off the coast of Florida. More of them are coming. Those helicopters have sonar gear, and we're trying to keep tabs on all of the subs and their locations."

Chief was so angry because Cuba had just shot down one of his squadron's aircraft. But there was a double standard. There would be *no* retaliation from the United States.

He said it was a beautiful night tonight and that if I looked up at 2400 hours, I would see the vapor trail of a Russian bomber going over Florida to Texas and returning on the same route to Cuba.

Boy, that day in April 1961 is one I'll not soon forget!

Well, what we didn't know was that these subs were equipped with atomic warhead missiles capable of demolishing cities. And they were all set to go! As Secretary of Defense Robert McNamara later told us on television, "In the olden days, we killed troops, but today it's not like that anymore. Now, we wipe out nations!"

In 1960, I had divorced from a very bad marriage. I never intended divorcing; even at the time, I couldn't comprehend the idea. But, seeing my misery, a friend advised me, "Sometimes a divorce is better than trying to stay together." It became a foregone conclusion. Back in those days children were expected to stay with their mother, and my erratic work schedule at the Commission would not allow me to have them. Tommy was five and Troy three. Losing my sons was just a terrible tragedy for me and very emotionally rough on the boys as well. I sure wished that I could have been with them that night.

Flying with McLoud and Cone—1961

Flying with John McLoud was always an experience. Just before a deer-hunting season opened in November 1961, the Game Commission had hired him on, a new helicopter pilot fresh out of Vietnam. He was a dandy! Oh, he was full of vinegar, let me tell you. He could really handle a helicopter and was gung ho! Man, I could see some exciting times ahead for us in the upcoming hunting season!

Since I was the officer who did inspections, we were a great team. It was a fine job for him and a daring job for us, because he loved to buzz people very low and very fast.

On the second day of his employment, I met him at the Ft. Lauderdale hanger. We were all set up to patrol the Everglades to Big Cypress and the area south of Loop Road. We had fueling stations set up at Forty-Mile Bend on the Tamiami Trail and Levee 28, north of present day Alligator Alley (I-595).

There were many full-tracks, half-tracks, and airboats in the saw grass, and when I spotted someone I wanted to check, I pointed them out, and John would jockey the helicopter around, usually where he could come up from behind . . . sort of sneak up on them and check them before they had a chance to throw out any illegal deer or whatever.

In so doing, a lot of times we'd come extremely close to these sportsmen. Most were good jokers. They'd get a big kick out of being scared and being buzzed so low and all that. Most didn't seem to

These hunters are riding on an early version of a half-track in 1965. By the 1950s, we could go where only the Seminoles' dugout canoes and the native Gladesmen's skiffs had gone before. Airboats, full-tracks, and half-tracks allowed hunters, conservationists, scientists, recreationists, fishermen, and poachers full access to the Everglades wetlands. *Left to right:* Ronnie Anderson, Lonnie Corbett, and Jimmy Saucey. (Shirley Collection.)

mind, but we got on the wrong side of some after a while, because McLoud was coming in so close that he was blowing their hats off! They would (doubtless) cuss, have to stop their full-track, and cuss again when they had to jump off into the water and muck to retrieve their hats.

But that really got old after a while, and it didn't give them cozy feelings toward the Wildlife Commission! I had to try to tone McLoud down.

Then, late one afternoon, we were on our way back to one of the fueling stations. We flew over the Rotenberg Landing at the northern end of Conservation Area 3 on the Broward and Palm Beach County line. And as we flew over the area, I saw a group of fellows there. One of them picked up a 30.06 rifle with a scope and zeroed in on me.

Well, man, that looked bad. I don't like looking down the barrel of a 30.06 with a scope. I have to tell you, it scared me! So I grabbed my pistol, and, boy, I came out with it fast. I was going to have to bust that fellow. Well, just before I pulled the trigger, I happened to recognize him. It was Al Henschel!

Well, we were good enough friends that I knew Al wasn't going to shoot me, so I trusted that he knew I wasn't going to shoot him! But there were a couple of seconds there that it looked like there was going to be a killing, one way or the other.

On that first day of hunting season in the Sawgrass Area, the permitted hunters had killed around 250 deer from a total season kill of usually around 800 plus. So it was a very good season beginning for them. We continued patrolling until sundown, checked all the hunters, made several cases. It was a very active day. Man, what excitement! And I was getting paid for this!

But I just couldn't get those Homestead Outlaws out of my mind . . .

Again, we were without a pilot. But there was Wayne Cone, who worked in Game Management. He loved Law Enforcement work, and he'd recently obtained his pilot's license. I asked him if he'd be willing to fly for me.

Well, he was thrilled to have the opportunity! And we began making plans.

We were going to work for two solid weeks if necessary. We would get up really early and be at high altitude right at sunrise, south of Loop Road where the Outlaws did their illegal hunting.

It was still dark when we left the Commission's office at the Ft. Lauderdale Airport.

We flew south all the way down into Monroe County. We remained at a very high altitude between the sun and the hunters on the ground. We saw their airplanes take off and the hunt begin.

Everything was going well from our end. Then all of a sudden the engine cut off—no power at all. Boy, the old prop just stopped, and man, our hearts stopped, too!

And worse yet, we were over the Tentacle Rocks! These rocks were peculiar to this area on the rim of the Everglades. They were razor-sharp outcroppings of coral, oolitic limestone, that stuck up a foot or more out of the ground like fingers. If we tried to set down here, we would be chewed to bits! No way were we going to come out of this alive!

Well, we were gliding down. We were getting lower and lower in altitude. We were going to crash . . . But just then, Wayne Cone realized what might have happened. He had switched the gas tanks and turned the wrong switch off!

Quick thinking, he switched the other gas tank to "On" and hit the starter button. The engine coughed a couple of times, and just before we cracked up in those rocks, the engine started!

Boy, what a beautiful sound! So we regained altitude. Fortunately we had not revealed our position, and we forged on ahead.

And those guys were still intensely focused on their hunting. Finally, I was able to take my pictures of the whole thing, with them shooting from the weasel—and all of it on film!

We were in court. One of my fellow officers had charged them with a separate offense. That trial went on for about six hours. The Homestead Outlaws were found "not guilty" due to "insufficient evidence."

Well, then it was *my* turn. They knew I had the film that showed their violations, and they pled "guilty" to all of my charges!

That was the first time in many, many years that the Commission had made a case against them that stuck. Wayne Cone was really pleased, because *he* had been the pilot that had made a case against the Homestead Outlaws!

The Masked Rider

In my younger days, before I joined the Game and Fresh Water Fish Commission, my friend John Turgeson from New York had just built himself a new airboat. His brother and a friend came down to visit John, and he wanted to take them out into the Everglades to impress them. We launched our boats at Mack's Fish Camp and went to the Grapefruit Head.

We got there and were stretching and relaxing, and we usually wound up shooting a pistol a little bit, setting the sights or whatever. So I took my German Luger out and was looking at it. John said to his brother and his friend, "Here, watch this!"

So he took a penny out of his pocket and stuck it on a tree.

He said, "Tom, see if you can shoot it out!"

So I aimed the Luger and fired, and BOOM! I shot the penny! I pushed it right into the bark of a grapefruit tree. (It's still there today, though the bark has grown over it!)

John was still trying to impress his guests.

He said, "Well, that's nothing! Watch this!"

So he pulled out a dime and put *it* on the tree.

"Ok, Tom, see if you can his that!"

So I pulled out my pistol. BAM! I hit the dime, and it went sailing off.

So we all turned away walking, still talking, but then, John said, "Well, that's nothing. Watch this!"

John walked about 25 feet away and stuck a cigarette in his mouth. He said, "Go ahead Tom, take it out!"

Well, I've done that before, with other people, my brother and so forth, but I had never done it with John. So I took out the Luger and took careful aim. BAM! I blew it right out of his mouth, and he acted like we did that every day! Of course the guys were really impressed. I was, too. I'd lucked out!

So we walked off to settle down and eat our sandwiches. John got me off to the side: "God damn you, Tom, I didn't want you to do it! I just wanted you to shoot and I was gonna spit it out. You could have blown my nose off!"

"Heck, I didn't know," I said. "I thought you really wanted me to do it!"

So he shot me a bird.

I looked at him, laughed, and said, "Well, let's not play *that* game again!"

In retrospect, this incident proved to be a very unsettling experience for me. I never even told my sons, as I would never recommend such dangerous bravado as that for anyone!

But I have proved myself shooting.

People have asked me how I got to be such a good shot. Well, when I was around four years old, I had to strain to cock a BB gun. But every spare moment I had, I was shooting. First a BB gun, then a .22 caliber pellet gun, then a .22 caliber rifle.

From 1943 on, I would get on my bicycle with my .22 rifle or a shotgun to go hunting. We also went target shooting in the Everglades wetlands where the Doral Country Club is now. My favorite pastime was throwing up objects and shooting them out of the air.

I recall that a drugstore cleaned out a stockroom of hundreds of small jars and bottles and dumped them. My friend Roddy Bryant and I found them in the woods and put them to good use. We would throw them up, then spin around and shoot the bottles out of the sky before they hit the ground.

I shot so often that I could tell you which manufacturer made the bullet! They say that all of the same caliber bullets have the same speed. That's not so. SUPER X and Western are the fastest. I knew them so well that I could tell without looking what brand of bullet I was shooting!

When I joined the Game Commission, I was already a very confident marksman. I knew that I could hit my target, whatever it was, and right away I became the top shooter and captain of the Commission's Everglades Region Pistol Team.

One cool winter day, south of Loop Road, I made myself a little camp on Cabbage Island that was only about 20 feet in diameter, but it was a good location, close to a main airboat trail. I figured it would be a good checkpoint to see whoever might come by.

Early morning came, and I cooked my breakfast—eggs, ham, grits, and so forth. It always tastes good out there in the woods! I even threw in a couple of frog legs.

Later, some boats came along. It was extremely cold, so I had one of those black wool Navy masks that goes over your face. It's very effective in extremely cold weather, especially when you're driving an airboat 40, 50, 60 miles an hour and that cold just cuts right through you big time.

So anyway, because it was so cold, damp, and wet that morning, I figured I would wear the mask. Several boats came by, and I pulled up beside them. I usually got right up beside them, off to the right, so I could look over into the boat and see whether they had taken any game. I could search them pretty well without them even knowing I was there.

I stopped one boater and asked if I could search his boat, and he said, "Yes sir!"

So I went through his boat and found no illegal deer or anything. I got back into my boat and went on. Meantime, a fellow I had visually checked out before, named Crazy Red, came up beside me while I was checking out another boat. Crazy Red had a very bad reputation. It was said that he had killed two men in Miami.

When I finished and got back into my boat, Crazy Red yelled, "Damn you Tom Shirley! Don't you *ever* pull up beside of my boat again! You scared the mortal hell out of me with that mask on. I oughta shoot the hell out of you."

He was really, really irate and perturbed. He kept saying, "I ought to shoot your ass!"

There was another individual in the backseat of his boat. I could see that *he* was really getting very uneasy about the situation. I said to Crazy Red, "Well, if you want to shoot my ass, just go ahead and shoot my ass right here."

So he's looking at me, and I saw that he had a 30/30 and some other rifle in the scabbard. I figured, well, if he goes for that gun, I can out-draw him. Meanwhile, the guy in the backseat, boy, he's really getting nervous. So Crazy Red and I are sitting there eye to eye, and I'm waiting for him to make a move. He had his hand in the pocket of his leather jacket. I figured we were going to have some good action in a little bit. But Red cranked up and took on off. So I went on ahead and checked out several other boats.

A couple hours later, I went back to the landing. There was Red, angry and talking to another individual I knew, a gator poacher by the name of Bob Ford. Crazy Red and Bob Ford had gotten into an argument. I heard Bob Ford say, "Well, I'll fix you!" and saw him pull a big old switchblade on Red.

Red said, "Nah, you better not do that," and he pulled a .38 out of his pocket!

Wow, that got my notice, because he had his hand on that .38 the whole time he and I were having that argument!! He'd have gotten the jump on me for sure!

So they continued talking and raising hell with one another, but that all panned over, and fortunately nobody was hurt. But it sure taught me a lesson about being more careful!

Those Everglades City Boys

I was working with Officer Dave Bowman. He was assigned to the area south of the Loop Road. So we decided, well, we're going to go catch the poachers Joe Brown and Virgil Lopez. You name it, and these fellows were in the middle of it. They were especially notorious for bagging gators and jack-lighting deer. So we set out in airboats south of the Loop Road. We worked our way all the way around toward Everglades City and the mangroves.

We got out and parked our airboats back away from Gator Hook Strand. There was a series of lakes back in there that was real good for the poachers.

We took a mosquito bar with us, canvas, some sardines, Spam, a few snacks, peanut butter, crackers, and so forth—not too much, just enough to keep us alive for a while.

And it was going to be real tough going, through some real rough terrain, and in heavily mosquito-infested areas. But that was where they chose to hunt, and that was where we had to go if we wanted to catch them.

It was good walk from the airboats into the swamp and cypress heads where these guys were going to camp, but we had to halt and strike out on foot so they couldn't hear our airboats.

We set off and walked through swamp, getting eaten by mosquitoes. They would coat us totally black! They'd get into our eyes. They were in our noses, so it was hard to breathe because we couldn't open our mouths; they'd get in our throats. It was truly horrible! And the person who got the worst of the mosquitoes was the guy who was following behind, so Dave and I alternated. Boy, the back of his shirt would just be coal-black with mosquitoes. He always wore long-sleeved shirts, but I didn't wear long-sleeved shirts, so the mosquitoes really tore me up.

Finally we made camp on Cabbage Island, the tiny 20-feet-square island with a couple of cabbage palms on it that I've mentioned before. It was at the east end of the lakes where these guys gator-hunted.

We were sitting there. We heard where they were hunting. We heard them talking. They'd already shot a couple of times. They were probably skinning out an alligator right then. It was late in the evening, so we eased up there, trying to sneak up on them.

We came up on another little cabbage island where they had their camp. Well, they had been camped there for maybe four or five days right among these mosquitoes. Some of their hooks and lines were lying about the camp. What they would go through just to get a few alligator skins is unbelievable, but they're rough and tough, and that's their lifestyle. They love every minute of it.

We waited there for them to come back to the camp, where they had left their extra gear. But we had to endure another night of camping there ourselves, knowing that they'd come back. Sure enough, the next morning real early, here they came; we heard them paddling the boat.

They got about 50 yards from us, and I heard Joe Brown say to Virgil, "Hell, I'm goin' back. I've had enough gator hunting. Let's get out of here."

Well, they were about 50 yards from us when they turned the boat around and began heading back through the series of lakes. We had to break camp really fast and head back to Cabbage Island, where our airboats were. But when we finally got back to the airboats, Dave Bowman said, "Tom, I'm goin' home—I've had enough."

I said, "Well, I'm going to go ahead and see what good I can do."

So I got in my airboat and ran around and tried to come up on Joe Brown and Virgil Lopez.

Well, they had evidently hidden their little Everglades skiff back in the mangroves. There they sat in an airboat. I could see that they were real edgy. I know Virgil Lopez well, and his hands were shaking. I always watch a man's hands when I'm talking to him. There are different things I look for—like if he's jumpy and nervous, or if he's licking his lips—to see if he's lying or scared.

Well, they looked scared.

I noticed an airboat trail. I thought I'd just see what they'd been up to.

So I followed the track of the airboat trail way on back in and around a pine island, cabbage palm heads, cypress stands, in and out all over the place, really some big stumpy areas.

Well, they sure had something they needed to hide.

I went on back and finally came up on a trail. There was a little old cabbage palm island that was barely 30 feet across, and a woman sitting there. I got out and introduced myself, and I asked her name. At this point, I can't recall if it was Joe Brown's wife or Virgil Lopez's wife, but I talked to her. Her name was Sara. She said she had come out there with her husband. They had come out there for their honeymoon.

"Honeymoon? Way out here in the wild with all these mosquitoes?" I asked.

"Yes, sir, Mr. Shirley," she said.

"Well, what do you have in the cooler there?" I asked.

They had a kerosene-type refrigerator that they had brought out there, so I opened up the refrigerator, and there was some freshly cut deer, so I said, "Well, what are you doing with that deer?"

"We gotta eat something out here," she said.

Well, they didn't think anything about killing a deer and eating it anytime they wanted to.

I said, "Well, that's against the law, and Sara, since you're the only one here, I'm going to have to place you under arrest just like I would one of the men. I can't turn my back on a situation like this. Your husband's been playing games like this with me for years, so I'm going to have to write you up on this," which I did.

In court, she pled guilty and received a $250 fine, which was a lot of money in those days.

Virgil Lopez and Joe Brown used to go into Coconut Palm Camp. They'd spend the night up there. I used to get a lot of complaints on those guys from Ed Mitchell and other hunters who had camps near these individuals. These two poachers would come in and help themselves to the hunters' food and supplies.

It was indeed a real challenge for me to try to keep up with the poachers coming out of Chokoloskee and Everglade City, as I have mentioned. Most of them were commercial fisherman, really tough individuals from families that had been fighting the mosquitoes and living with them for generations. I give them all the credit in the world for that!

In more recent years, many of them have turned to drug smuggling. The terrain where they live and the mosquitoes make it an ideal place for such activities. I guarantee that the drug officials who come down from New York or New Jersey wouldn't last five minutes in the dark in those mangroves fighting off mosquitoes!

For that reason, Everglades City and Chokoloskee became a dream land for smugglers. There was a boat that came in there called the *Midnight Express*. It came all the way from Columbia for a drop off. People from Chokoloskee and Everglades City were there to take its drugs and put them in the hands of the distributors. Finally, the feds came in and arrested more than two hundred individuals involved in the drug trade. Drug busts in Chokoloskee continue to make news on a more or less annual basis.

A Dusting in Homestead

One morning I had scheduled to fly on a helicopter patrol across the Everglades, the Big Cypress, and down toward the Ten Thousand Islands. It is beautiful country that runs from freshwater southward, to brackish water marsh and mangroves, then empties out into the ocean.

In this particular area were those airstrips, just west of the Everglades National Park, that we had to keep an eye on, the ones used by the Homestead Outlaws and their pilots. There were also several well-known people who had private strips there, like Curtis Pitts, the inventor who designed and built the Curtis Pitts special bi-wing airplane known for its aerobatic performance. Pitts's planes put the United States at the top of the world of competition aerobatics for the first time! Anyway, Curtis had a landing strip down there, along with the Homestead mayor, Fred Rhodes. We would be checking all the strips in the area on our routine patrol.

It was a beautiful day as we flew southward. I looked way ahead and saw a Piper Cub on an airstrip. There were two men around it, so I told the chopper pilot, "Let's check him out."

So we were flying toward this airstrip. The two individuals appeared to be Beau Jeffries and his cousin Jimmy Roberts—some of the guys I'd had trouble with in the past. Well, they started running toward the Cub to make their getaway.

I told the helicopter pilot, "Let's set the helicopter down in front of them so they can't take off!"

By then, these two guys were in the Cub, and it was heading east, down the runway to take off. It was a race for us to get in front of them before they took off, but the Cub didn't slow down!

They had called our bluff! We came close to having an air crash, but the helicopter pilot pulled away just in time! But the Piper Cub got away.

We followed, of course, but the Cub had better speed than we did. So they left us . . . and we had to pull off the chase. There was nothing we could do at that point. I would just have to conceive another plan.

This area was always a major patrol problem for us, but it sure was a field day for those poachers. So during most of my career I was focused on apprehending these guys.

I had an idea where they kept the plane. So real early the next morning, I got up and drove all the way down to Homestead and into a particular agricultural area. There were still plenty of acres of native palmetto and pine trees, but also a lot of orchards planted in mango and avocados. It was in this vicinity where I felt they landed the airplanes and took off the cargo, whatever it might be. There was a dwelling there with a fence around it.

I got up pretty close to the fence and climbed up in an avocado tree where I could observe the area. I could see any airplane landing or leaving. I felt that this was a real good observation point. After I was there for a while, the sun came up, but I was comfortably settled in. Then, all of a sudden, a pit bull and a hound dog came out of the house. They started sniffing the air and began to bark.

I thought, "Oh, boy, I'm given away now!"

I sure didn't want the occupants to catch me sneaking around spying on them! It would have been highly embarrassing. Of course, that's what my job calls for if I need to enforce the law—and that's what I was trying to do.

But the dogs wouldn't go away and I realized, "I've got to get out of here now!"

About that time, an individual walked out the back door. He spotted me even though I had my camouflage netting on. Luckily, he wasn't dressed. So he ran back into the house.

I was trying to get away, attempting to make ground between me and the dogs, but I had to cross this huge tomato field where the tomato bushes were about 2 feet tall. So I made my way through this tomato field, as there was no other place for me to go. Two men came running out of the house and saw me. They ran back in and got their guns.

At this point, they didn't know who I was. For all they knew, I was some prowler. Now there were four of them. They got into a car and they began to circle the tomato field. I was standing almost in the middle of it, so I was really in hot water.

I sure didn't want to reveal myself, so I lay down right in the middle of that tomato patch, glad that I had my camouflage on.

By now, as they were still circling in their cars, they didn't know exactly what part of the field I was in. Then they began to walk through the field, and I lay there, just as still as I could, cozying up tight under those tomato bushes so they wouldn't see me when they looked down those straight rows, glancing left and right. Now, one fellow was just about ten rows away. I thought sure I was caught.

And I thought, "Boy, this is going to be very, very, embarrassing for me: Tom Shirley caught in the middle of a tomato field!" So I was really sweating it out.

They stayed looking around there for about an hour. They were cussing and yelling, calling out threats, and so forth. I realized that my only chance was to be patient, be patient. Just wait them out . . . wait them out while bugs and ants bit and crawled all over me.

And that's what I did. I lay there until about 8:30 that night when it was good and dark. Stiff as anything, I snuck out of there! That was one of my close calls that I'd sure not want to go through again— the most embarrassing day of my life! I just wrote that day off as a misadventure. My ace in the hole was that Beau and Jimmy didn't *know* that it was *me* in that camo! I needed to keep it that way, as sometime I would surely catch those poaching Homestead Outlaws. But I sure didn't want them to be able to gloat over how they humiliated me!

Alligator Victim?

One day while on patrol with my news AM radio on, it was reported that a child was taken by an alligator in Opa Locka. When I investigated, a woman told me that she had seen a small boy's head, a splash, and the head going under and never coming up again!

A big crowd gathered, with all of the media reporting the event. I removed all of my hardware and entered the water. The canal led to a 6-foot culvert, part of the drainage system that drains all of Opa Locka. With my flashlight I entered the dark water and began searching for the small child's body.

Block by block I searched, always turning left and right in the culvert. The county engineer came out to assist me. I was truly hoping that I wouldn't get lost in the dark in the miles of pipe.

After cleaning up at home, I returned and searched all of the canals in the area but found no body or any alligators at all.

The next morning, I returned to the area where the child had disappeared. While watching the canal, I noticed a sea cow (manatee) nose the surface for air. With the bristly whiskers on its snout, I could see how the witness might have mistaken it for a child's head.

And the news wrapped up their latest report, noting that fortunately *no* child had been reported missing. What a relief!

The child described was about the same age as my sons. I sure missed them. Our divorce was especially rough on Tommy, my eldest. When I had meetings at home, I would ask him to call me back in, say, two hours, but he would say, "No Dad. I'll hold on until you finish your meeting," and no amount of persuasion would change his mind. He would patiently wait on the line all that time, until I had concluded my business. Even at the age of seven, he could track me down even when I was in meetings in Tallahassee, especially when he realized that I could be paged.

Once, however, I was in Tallahassee when a rumor spread that I had been *killed* out on Loop Road. Plausible enough, with the business I was in. But poor kid, he was so relieved when he heard my voice!

Gator Roberts—1964

The Roberts family was kin to the pioneer Gladesman Uncle Steve Roberts from Flamingo, Florida. Some of the Robertses had been notorious outlaws dating back to the days when they illegally hunted for plumes from the Everglades birds. By the 1920s they were fishing, making charcoal from the forests of buttonwood, growing cane, making moonshine, and running some rum from Cuba. You name it and they were into it. They were all Gladesmen who lived off the Everglades wetlands and sometimes found themselves on the wrong side of the federal or state laws.

Then, in 1947, the Everglades National Park was opened, and the Roberts family was run out of the Monroe County area around Flamingo. There were, of course, very hard feelings—maybe even some killings over it, because they figured they owned part of the Glades. Actually, even to this day, the Roberts family harbors some bad feelings against the park and the rangers. After all, the Park Service took their home and livelihood away from them. Most of the family moved to the Florida City/Homestead area.

During my patrol years, the Roberts boys had a hunting camp south of Loop Road that was still within Monroe County. Because so many violations occurred with their use of airplanes to hunt and kill deer out of season, not to mention killing does, the people south of the Loop—the camp owners and the sportsmen—started putting pressure on the family.

It was because of this that the Roberts clan moved their hunting camp south of the Tamiami Trail, sort of southeast of the Airboat Association property. That placed it in the strategic area of the Tentacle Rocks. The Robertses liked their privacy, were heavy drinkers, and they were used to doing things their own way, so Tentacle Rocks was a perfect place for their new camp.

One evening late, on a really dark night, I came patrolling down the Tamiami Trail in my car. One of my officers named Jones was ahead of me by about forty-five minutes. He radioed me that he had seen an airboat with two individuals come up to the edge of the highway. He had shone his light in there and seen a doe deer.

Well, the poachers saw Jones and took off!

I asked Jones, "Can you identify these individuals?"

He said, "Yes, one of them was Gator Roberts."

I raced down to the Airboat Association, where I had my airboat.

Well, I knew twenty-two-year-old Luther "Gator" Roberts pretty well. I'd had dealings with him before. He was already a legend, perhaps the most notorious gator poacher in the state of Florida and one of the Homestead Outlaws gang!

So off in the airboat we went. I had to work the airboat around the rocks and confront all the obstacles of that territory to get there. We got to the Robertses' camp, and it was all lit up.

When we pulled up, I said, "OK, you pick out the men that you saw, and then we'll put them under arrest and take them down and put them in jail."

We walked up to the camp in the dark. The Robertses were pretty well liquored up and feeling rough and tough. The odds were certainly in their favor with two of us and ten of them!

"OK, Officer Jones," I said, "pick out the two individuals you saw in the airboat with that doe deer. We take fire-hunting and doe killing very seriously."

So he picked out Gator Roberts and commenced to pick out one more.

They had a really bright gasoline lantern so it was hard to see beyond the light. I was standing at the doorway. By then, the Robertses had all come out and surrounded me.

Gator said, "Well, I'm not going!"

I said, "Yes, Gator. You're going to come with us one way or the other. Officer Jones saw you with the doe deer in the airboat. So you've got to go jail."

He said again, "I'm not going."

I was facing the lighted lantern so I couldn't see too well, but I saw old Mr. Roberts Senior grab hold of a 30–30 rifle. He came out the door, jacking one in. And I told Gator, "Gator, you'd better get the gun away from your father because I'm going to have to put him down. You'd better hurry up. You'd better hurry!"

So his dad lowered the gun. But about that time, I heard the cocking of other guns.

I couldn't see because of the bright light, but I heard them cocking. I drew my pistol, but I didn't know who was going to shoot or where they were.

About that time, two young men jumped off the roof! They had had a bead on me the whole time! It was Gator's eighteen-year-old brother Jimmy and their cousin Beau Jeffries who had dusted me that day! This was fast becoming a bad encounter.

Jimmy said, "Jones, now who do you think you saw?"

Well, I saw a questioning look on Jones's face.

Officer Jones couldn't truly identify who it was because Jimmy and Gator looked so very much alike!

Oh, well, the case was over. As much as I hated to, Officer Jones and I got in the airboat and drove off.

On the way back to the Trail, I noticed the oil pressure was going down. I looked down and saw that those Roberts boys had cut the oil line! But we were able to make it back to the Airboat Association.

OK, the next day I received word that the Roberts' Fish House at U.S. 1 in Homestead had a bunch of illegal game. So a couple of officers and I went over there and searched the business. Sure enough, there were eleven deer there, not legally tagged. So I had to confiscate all of the deer and write the Robertses up. Well, of course, that made them furiously mad.

We turned the dead deer over to the Boys Club. And word spread that the Robertses of Homestead were out to get Tom Shirley and his crew.

Later on that night I received a phone call from another Homestead boy, Fred Kannington. He said, "Tom, we're gonna be out there in force tomorrow. You'd better be ready; we're gonna have deer in our camp, and we just dare you to come into our camp and search it. We're all gonna be there. You can reckon on that."

OK, based on that information I called up some of my officers. I got hold of Gary Phelps, George Eddy, John Maples, and Jimmy Thompson, and we got our airboats and went to make camp south of Tamiami Trail. We waited and waited for a couple of days, but they never showed up!

But early one morning, we heard a boat running.

"Gary, you and George Eddy go out there and check that boat," I said. "See who it is. See if it's any of the Roberts guys."

Gary jumped in the boat and ran out there quite a ways, a couple of miles, and came up on Jimmy and Gator Roberts. Gary tried to stop and check them for their airboat registration, but they wouldn't stop! So Gary came racing back to the airboat landing at the camp where we were waiting.

He said, "Lieutenant! It's Gator Roberts and his brother, but they won't stop."

I said, "OK, we'll try to stop them."

So all of us got in our boats—Gary Phelps, George Eddy, John Maples, and me . . . Boom, off we go.

So we had a race. I was trying to cut the Roberts brothers off before they could get into the pile of rocks. I made a bypass at Gator Roberts and his brother, but they wouldn't stop. I got closer.

I banged the side of their airboat. They still wouldn't stop. Then they ran right across in front of me, and I almost turned them over.

Gator Roberts had a 30–30 in the scabbard of his airboat. He grabbed that 30–30.

I drew my .44, and I was going to bust him right off the seat. I wasn't going to put up with any more people drawing guns on me. But when I whipped my pistol around, he threw his rifle to the bottom of the boat. However, he still wouldn't stop, so we had a dog fight going on.

The airboats were bangin', bangin', bangin'. Finally, I ran across the deck of the Robertses' boat!

And, he stopped! Stopped so abruptly that Officer John Maples's airboat rammed him head-on! The collision was so hard that it knocked the pistol right out of Maples's holster, and it fell to the deck of the Robertses' boat.

Anyway, we stopped them, and then put them under arrest and took them downtown and booked them.

Well, that was OK for a while.

A couple of days passed, and then I got a call from the Sheriff's Department: "Hey, you'd better not come down here because the Roberts brothers brought charges against you. They filed charges against you in Homestead for assault with a deadly weapon, to wit, an airboat."

"The Highway Patrol knows there's a warrant for your arrest, so you'd better be careful."

Well, the warrant had been issued in Homestead, so that was the only district that legally had the power to arrest me. But at least when I went to the Justice Building in Miami, I was aware of what was going down.

I knew a fellow that worked for the State Attorney's Office, Jack Storm, a great individual with a deep, deep voice. I'll never forget him. I told him what happened.

"We'll go on down there," he said. "You'd better let me follow you, just in case something comes up," which I did.

I went down and filed on some cases. Everything went fine. But since the Roberts boys had filed charges against me, I was eventually going to end up in court, and I was going to need an attorney to represent me.

Being that the Robertses filed in State Court, the State Attorney General's Office could not legally represent me—State vs. State—so Jack said that he would represent me as a probate attorney. That's what he did.

But first, I went to Homestead before the judge, and boy, he threw the book at me! He was going to put me away because, he said, I was "a dangerous character"! Luckily, he only had the power to turn the case over to the Dade County Criminal Court. But nevertheless, I had to face court in Dade County.

During that time period, one of my officers, Gary Phelps, had a conversation with Gator Roberts. Gator told him that he could kill Tom Shirley, pay ten thousand dollars to his lawyer, and get away with it!

Well, that was a serious allegation. I told Gary, "You remember that statement!"

But I was in serious trouble myself. A reporter from the *Homestead Leader* had kind of taken a liking to me. She gave me the name of yet another attorney who could represent me, who had pull within the Dade County office. So I met with him, and we talked about his representation of me.

My new newspaper acquaintance also told me, "I have information and I know individuals, I'm not going to stand by and let them do any harm to you while you're enforcing the law. If necessary, I'll reveal the names of individuals working for the Solicitor's Office who are involved with organized crime! I will *not* see them abuse you wildlife officers!"

A week was set aside for both of these cases, the state's against the Robertses and the Robertses' against me. Beautiful Hellen Marvonious of the State Attorney's Office coached all of my officers on their testimonies. In those days, legal issues were left up to the lawyers who were hired, and their ethics were seldom questioned. Obviously the "good old boy" network was alive, but you just hoped that it was working to your advantage. There were no TV shows that discussed legal matters, and this was before the Internet, so all advice in the presentation of the case was welcomed. All we knew, as arresting officers of the law, was that these guys were guilty.

Well, the Gator Roberts case came up in Criminal Court. All of my officers went in and testified about what had taken place, about the dog fights in the airboats and all of the fracas and danger faced in the chase after the brothers' arrest. Then I took the stand and testified for about three hours. The charges we cited them with were "aggravated assault and reckless operation of an airboat."

The court recessed. When we came back, our next testimony was going to be the testimony that Gator Roberts had told Officer Gary Phelps that he could kill me and his attorney could get him off for ten thousand dollars.

Well, that was a deadly testimony. The Solicitor's Office advised Gator's attorney that it was coming up. Judge Jack Falk and the Robertses' attorney had discussed this testimony in confidence. It was serious and would look really bad for Gator when Officer Phelps testified.

Judge Falk slammed down the gavel, "Bam!" and called a recess. He wanted to block this testimony if possible.

So my attorney, Jack Storm, the Robertses' attorney, and I were out in the hall. We started discussing the case, which is illegal, really. Gator's attorney says, "Tom, you have four charges against Gator and Jimmy Roberts here. We've got to do something."

"Well, I'm not going to drop any of the charges," I said.

And he said, "Well, let's try real hard, because it's very important."

Gator Roberts of Homestead was a notorious poacher I chased around in the Tentacle Rocks and off Loop Road on the rim of the Everglades south of the Tamiami Trail. He once told one of my officers that he could kill me, pay ten thousand dollars to his lawyer, and get away with it! Nonetheless, we remained acquaintances. (Roberts Family photo, 1963, Shirley Collection.)

I said emphatically, "No! I'm not going to drop any charges. My *life* is important too!"

So we went back into the courtroom.

Judge Falk said, "Well, how are you doing? Did you work anything out?"

Gator's attorney said, "No, sir. Tom Shirley won't cooperate!"

So the judge hit the gavel again. Bam! Bam! Bam! And he called another recess.

We all went out into the hall again. Gator's attorney said, "Hey, Tom, you've got to do something. I'm representing these guys. I can't plead them guilty to *all* the charges. Drop a charge or two."

I said, "Nope, I'm not going to!"

So we went back and faced the judge.

"Well, what happened?"

"Nothing!"

Bam! Bam! Bam! Another recess was called.

Out into the hall again, my attorney and the Robertses' attorney began discussing dropping charges and so forth. So, after this third recess, back in the courtroom, Gator and Jimmy pled "guilty as charged" to assault and battery.

Judge Falk lectured them on having respect for the law and fined them each seventy-five dollars, which their father paid! The judge also placed the boys on a two-year probation.

"Bam! Bam! Bam!"

And, because of the serious allegations against Gator, his charges against me eventually vanished. That was good news!

Years later, this case against the Roberts boys that had involved the whole Roberts clan had a happy ending for me. The matriarch of the family, the boys' mother, was going to have her one-hundredth birthday party, and she wanted to invite ME! Well, I was in Peru at the time, but I heard about it and it was an honor, after all of the scraps the Robertses and I had been through!

TV Shows and Zoos—1967

When I first got on the Game Commission, the director called me. A new director, A. D. Aldrich, was coming in. Aldrich had been the manager of the Oklahoma Zoo, so as a favor to the zoo, the Commission wanted us to supply them with a collection of Everglades animals.

The director figured I would be the man to do it. He told me to work with the Oklahoma Zoo staff that was sent to Florida to aid us in capturing the alligators and other animals. So I made arrangements. I got the swamp buggies and everything, and we had about eight employees from the zoo ready to assist.

We located gator caves. I would show them the procedures on rodding out these big alligators from their caves. They would rod the alligator, agitate him to where he'd come out of the cave. I would be in the water at the cave entrance. The gator would swim out and bump into my belly. Then I would grab him by the underjaw and pull him out, just like I had done as a kid!

We got them up to 12 foot or better. It was working pretty well, and we had caught quite a few alligators.

But one guy decided, "Well, let me try that."

So I got out of the water and began to rod out the alligator while this guy got in the pond.

Then here came this alligator swimming fast out of his cave, and he bumps into the zoo fellow. Well, instead of gently reaching in there and grabbing him by the jaw, the guy just dove in and grabbed the alligator around the waist. Boy, the guy's coming out of the water . . . the alligator's poppin' his jaws. I thought he was going to take the guy's head off! The water was splashing, and all hell's breaking loose. The other zoo guy jumps in the water. He's going to help! Now they both came face to face with this alligator. Its jaws are still snapping back and forth! Somehow, I jumped in, and somehow, after the panic and mayhem from the two guys and the alligator, we managed to subdue it. It was just very lucky that the fellow didn't get his head chopped off by that big alligator!

So at the next alligator hole, I was back in the water as before. They rodded out one, and I could tell by the signs that it was another good 12-footer, so I was going to be extra careful. They rodded him out, and he popped me in the belly. As usual, I reached under there very carefully with my fingers for his jaw—and I was feeling with my fingers— and I feel this big tooth!

I move my hand slowly under the muddy water, there's another tooth. I change hands. I feel more teeth. There were teeth all over the place.

Then I realized, "He's just lying there with his mouth wide open!"

There's a first time for everything. But my thought at that moment was, "Why am I here doing this?"

So I cut my losses and just got out of the water. I had been doing this all my life, but I said, "To heck with it. I'm not going to catch any more alligators with this method!" For me, right then, I was finished. I guess that was a sign of growing up!

Next I worked with Marlin Perkins and Jim Fowler on three separate episodes of the Emmy Award–winning TV show Mutual of Omaha's *Wild Kingdom*. Now, these episodes were more or less scripted, but that didn't mean that spontaneous things didn't happen. They most always did! After all, wild animals by their very nature present the "unknown entity" that no action script can duplicate. And aside from the animals, almost every time *Wild Kingdom* came down to the Everglades, there was some major catastrophe involving equipment. Somebody was going to get hurt or some potentially dangerous situation would occur.

One time we were working with a panther and a bear out in the Everglades. I was on my airboat. Wildlife Officers Wendell Clemmons and George Eddy were working with me. In this particular episode, Marlin was out in the marsh. Jim Fowler, the new young host of the show, had hold of a big bear. He was really a bad, mean 600-pound Florida bear from Wilford and Lester Piper's "Everglades Wonder Garden" in Bonita Springs. His name was Tom, and I understood that he had starred as "Slewfoot" in the MGM movie *The Yearling.*

They had two ropes on him, but I could see a potential problem. Marlin was in the water, and that bear was really trying to get to him. From the way the guys had hold of the ropes, I could see that it wasn't going to work out as they planned.

So I cranked up my airboat, and I was just waiting for the inevitable to happen. Sure enough, that bear broke loose, and, boy, he went after Marlin Perkins!

Then Marlin was running . . . from fear! No acting then at all! I mean the real action, the real fear—it was there, I mean to tell you!

My airboat was running, ready to go. So off I went, but that bear was right on Marlin Perkins's tail. He was going to get him, chew him up, and spit him out! I ran my airboat right over the top of the bear and spun the boat around. At the same time I spun it around, it knocked Marlin into the airboat. Pretty slick!

The bear was still reaching for Marlin while it was underwater. They got all of this on film!

Boy, it looked great!

So the cameraman said, "Can you do that again?"

I chuckled.

Actually this footage is still around today on the Internet as Animal Planet clips of Mutual of Omaha's *Wild Kingdom,* the "Swampwater Safari" and "The Florida Everglades" episodes. When you see that film with Marlin running through the water, looking over his shoulder— and the fear—that's the real thing!

Anyway, that's the way movies go. It was a close call. And in the same episode, the company had rented a big, wide, powerful airboat to carry that same bear in a cage with the filming equipment. Wildlife Officers Wendell Clemmons and Jimmy Jordan and I loaded up the bear in this big boat. We were about 5 miles north of the Tamiami Trail.

Clem was driving the airboat. Jimmy Jordan, Clem, and the bear were there together. They cranked up and headed south toward Tamiami Trail, but the throttle on the airboat stuck wide open! It was wide open, doing 70, 80 miles an hour!

Clem couldn't stop it! He was scared—everybody was scared. It looked like we were going to have a big smashup with the bear and two wildlife officers. Something awful was going to happen if they didn't stop pretty soon.

Clem's hollering, to Jimmy: "Do somethin'! Do somethin'! I can't stop! It's runnin' wide open!"

So Jimmy Jordan starts grabbing spark plug wires. He starts splicing off plug wires. Well, that engine has two plug wires per cylinder, so Jimmy had a lot of wires to pull. But finally the engine died down and they reached in the cubby hole and repaired the throttle. But they were sure pleased when that boat came to a stop!

On another film shoot for *Wild Kingdom*'s series on the Everglades—and this was truly one of the most fearsome things that ever happened to me—we were again working in the Everglades, north of the Tamiami Trail. We had three cameramen bunched up all together. Then, we had a platform set up with a whole gang of officers on it. There must have been three or four, maybe even five wildlife officers.

The director wanted a shot of me and Marlin Perkins in the airboat. I was to come around and come pretty close to them on a curve, which I did.

"One more shot, one more shot, a little bit faster, a little bit faster," they said.

Well, this was a new airboat that I was operating. It was extra wide, an extra foot wide, so it leaped a little bit different on the water than my usual boat.

So they said, "Okay, Tom, one more drive. This'll be the last one [of course]."

So I came around, I was making this turn, driving toward them almost wide open. They wanted me to come close. Well, each time I came closer and closer—very, very dangerous, that plan. But okay, I figured this would really be the last time. So here I came around there, one more time than I had anticipated.

And I saw that I had cut too close, I was going to wipe out the whole crop, all the cameramen, the director, my officers—I was going to ride them wide open. There were going to be bodies splattered all over the place. I could just see it . . .

I could never, never again have pulled off this particular reverse motion again, but I put the boat into a reverse turn. It was just a reflex that came from somewhere in me that I didn't know existed. The boat spun around, showered them with water and wind. The rudders hit the cameras and knocked them down. The cameramen fell backward and everything got wet, but it could have been so much worse, even deadly, that it scares me to this day. I would never want to go through anything like that again. And all just to give them one more thrill shot!

But the excitement of the *Wild Kingdom* shoots continued. On another day, we were catching alligators with Marlin Perkins and Jim Fowler. We had just caught this big 12-foot gator. He was extra mean. He was one of those aggressive alligators that likes to get up on all fours and come and get you!

So we had him on the ground, shooting film. Marlin kept on walking next to the alligator, and I told him, "Marlin, don't do that. He'll whip around there, and if he doesn't bite you, that heavy beak of his can break your leg from right underneath you!"

Well, I told him several times, but he'd forget, and he'd go walking beside that alligator again.

Well, sure enough, that alligator turned around and cracked Marlin in the knee. Just knocked him down and flipped him through the air. Luckily, the alligator didn't bite him. But that's another close miss on that series of jinxed shoots.

Then, later that same day, we had that alligator in a big box sitting on top of a full-track. If you recall, a full-track is like a big swamp buggy on military tank treads. It goes through the Everglades easily. This great big box must've been 10 feet square or larger.

Well, sitting on the edge of this big box on top of the track, there's a famous cameraman. In 1959, he had shot the highly acclaimed nature documentary *Jungle Cat* in South America for Walt Disney.

Anyway, he was an excellent, professional photographer with top-notch equipment. He was perched up there on the edge of this box with his tripod and camera. Well, our pilot, Lewis Conrad, was in the driver's seat of the track. The track was idling in neutral.

Then, by accident, Lewis bumped the gear shift and knocked the full-track into gear. The buggy jumped forward. When that happened, the photographer and his equipment fell into the big box with this mean alligator!

What a horrible thing! He couldn't get out because the walls were too high. And he was in there with this monster alligator. I was standing outside, and I could hear the alligator whap him! Then the photographer and his camera came flying up in the air above the big box. Boom! He goes up. He comes down. The alligator hits him again!

Camera and photographer were up in the air again. Bam! He hit him again. This went on about three or four times. Finally, the alligator knocked him outside, where he fell to the ground and broke his ankle. So that stopped filming that day.

Like I've said, it just seemed like every time *Wild Kingdom* came down, we had some sort of catastrophe. That sure was a close call for that photographer, who was really lucky that he just got away with a broken ankle!

My next stint with the media was when *National Geographic* wanted Toby Massey, photographer for the *Miami Daily News* (he shot the cover photo for this book), to do a story on the Florida Everglades and alligators.

So Toby and I loaded up the airboat and took off to hunt a nice big one. Soon we found a 10-footer. I wrestled him for some time, and Toby shot lots of photos. It's always risky wrestling a gator. You can't always second-guess them, but, hey, it was only this one time. We finished and Toby promptly mailed off the film to *National Geographic*.

But the photos were returned! It seemed that they couldn't use them. The crotch of Tom Shirley's pants had split open, and his white underwear was showing!

So we had to return to the Everglades and do it all over again! This second set of photos was used in January 1967 for an article by noted

For a 1967 *National Geographic* article by noted herpetologist Archie Carr, Toby Massey shot photos while I loaded up an alligator. (Photo by Toby Massey.)

Florida herpetologist Archie Carr entitled "Alligators: Dragons in Distress."

A Family at Last—1967

It had been a rough seven years following my divorce. I really didn't socialize. I devoted all my time to my work. Nights out in the Everglades 80 miles away from everything, I would think of all the people cozy in their beds with all their creature comforts and their loving families all tucked in. I missed my boys so much. And here I was, slapping mosquitoes while protecting the state's wildlife . . . It was a lonely time.

The divorce was especially tough on Tommy, my eldest. I would visit, but when it was time for me to leave, he'd be hanging onto the car door, even when I was gingerly backing out of the driveway. He was just beside himself, and he'd run through the neighbors' backyards and again grab onto the door as I attempted to leave the neighborhood. That was a really, really rough time for us both.

In 1966, I met Naomi. My boys liked her. And one day I was very sad, and I told her that I really, really wanted to get my sons back.

She said, "Well, Tom, I'll help you get your boys!"

We married in 1967, and a few weeks later, we took my sons Tommy and Troy and Naomi's daughter, Melanie—our new family—with us on our honeymoon to Yellowstone Park and the Redwood Forest. We drove 9,355 miles in my 1965 Pontiac! That was the first of a great many wonderful family trips.

Then a few weeks after we returned, the boys' mother brought my sons to live with me. What a happy day! And the happiest of all moments was that first day that my boys were back with me. I was in the Commission vehicle leaving for my job. Naomi and all the kids came out, kissed me, and saw me off to work!

A Trip Up the Great Amazon—1969

Every time I went out in the Everglades I thought about how it used to be for the native inhabitants. I wondered what the earliest Indians had been like, the ones who lived on shell mounds and made their tools out of big conch shells. And what about the Seminoles and Miccosukees who had lived out in the Glades since the 1700s? What was it like for them to move there from way up in southern Alabama, coming south to live and farm on the Everglades wetlands islands, making their homes in palmetto-thatched chickees and navigating across the Everglades in cypress dugout canoes?

I had read about the Seminoles' Everglades hunting practices in the late 1890s in Harry Kersey's book, *Pelts, Plumes, and Hides*, about their trading days in the Big Cypress at Bill Brown's Boat Landing, which he established in 1901 on the shoreline between the Big Cypress and the Everglades. Bill loaded up alligator hides in his oxcart and took them to market in Ft. Myers. One time, he had 1,270 gator skins, and three weeks later, the Indians brought in 800 more from a one-week hunt! The largest alligator on record was 19 feet 2 inches.

By the 1950s, I had met a few Indians and I had visited some isolated camps on islands down in the wetlands north of the Tamiami Trail. But, for me, even those isolated camps didn't show me how

Again accompanied by Toby Massey, in 1956 we visited the Seminole Indian camp of Camilla Poole Tiger (Otter clan) just north of the Tamiami Trail at the edge of the Big Cypress. (Photo by Toby Massey.)

they had lived before modern times. I wanted to see really primitive Indians in their daily life.

I had continued to make trips to Peru and the Amazon since that first one I took to Iquitos, 2,800 miles from the mouth of the Amazon. I remained fascinated with the Indians there, their blowguns and their culture, but I wanted to see more. And, I wanted to see the Amazon jungle and wetlands "as it was"— before it stood a chance of being altered.

I really loved the Amazon! I wanted to go to the wildest part that I could . . . and still have a reasonable chance of coming back alive!

I had worked with a fish and wildlife dealer, Mike Tsalikis, since my first trip down. He was a Greek American who was the main business-man in the area. He had given me the phone number of a contact, a ham radio operator, who might be able to put me in touch with some-one in the remote regions of the Amazon River.

So one night in 1969, about 10:00 p.m., I called Mike's contact, who lived in Hialeah. I told him of my interest in going to South America and up the Amazon to see the head-hunter tribes of Jivaro Indians. He got right on his ham radio and contacted a missionary living far up the Amazon.

Right then and there, he put me on the phone with him!

So there I was, comfortably sitting in my living room, speaking to someone in one of the world's most remote jungles! And next thing you know, my wife, Naomi, and I were going on a trip to the Ecuadorian and Peruvian Amazon!

I contacted Copec S.A. Airlines. They had a Constellation that flew cargo into Iquitos. Our cargo consisted of fourteen metal telephone company boxes full of food, clothing, flashlights, batteries . . . everything you could imagine. We arrived in Iquitos, at the mouth of the Amazon, but our final destination was upriver some 2,800 miles away.

We were turned down by a number of men we asked to find us a guide, but finally we found a woman who had escaped from Poland during World War II and who had been a pilot in the Royal Air Force. With Mary Segon's help, we found a fisherman/guide/cook. We rented a boat with a 25-horsepower Evinrude motor and loaded up all of our supplies. We took on fifteen 55-gallon barrels of fuel and started out on our journey, traveling hard upriver before sunup until after sunset every day for eleven days. Day by day we'd go hundreds of miles farther up the Amazon. It was like stepping back into time.

Arriving at our destination among the headhunting Jivaros, our river guide, Guillermo Godoy, tried to reassure me: "Tom, you'll like the chief. He has five wives, and he's killed thirty-six men! You'll like him!"

Well, the natives had not often encountered white people. And Naomi had beautiful blond hair, which was a source of discussion, awe, and maybe even fear. In fact, these people had a reputation for being one of the most primitive of societies. And we were all on our own to make friends, as Guillermo was not an interpreter.

Well, I brought out my tape recorder and began to record their voices and play it back for them. They were so enthused that it could have gone on all night! Then I showed them what an insect looked like under a magnifying glass, while they brought me big grub worms the size of your thumb to eat. Those worms were one of the staples of their diet, and they ate them with as much enthusiasm as we would a box of popcorn! I declined the invitation.

I was warned never to shoot a deer, as it might be someone's grandmother or another ancestor. But the chief asked me on a jaguar hunt for a big old black jaguar that was giving them trouble. His five wives came along. To my embarrassment, a little child around nine years old was called to carry my 90-pound gear, which he did with no apparent effort. The endurance of these people on the up-and-down hill trek through jungle, under and over fallen trees, through creeks, while maintaining a very fast pace, was amazing!

I was further embarrassed at how, after not too long in this rain forest, my cotton clothing began to reek from sweat and the constant humidity. The Indians, however, wearing practically nothing, washed

In 1969, my wife, Naomi, and I headed on a great and potentially dangerous adventure up to the headwaters of the Amazon River to visit the headhunting Jivaro tribe. I wanted to see the Amazonian wetlands and its inhabitants in a natural state, before they were altered by modern civilization. We traveled 2,500 miles in a boat with a thatched roof. Carrying fifteen 55-gallon drums of fuel and supplies, we traveled sunup to sundown for eleven days to reach our destination. (Photo by Louis Moray.)

A member of the Amazonian head-hunting Jivaro tribe that we traveled so far to see. (Shirley Collection.)

off often in streams. I guess that's why they went naked. Clothing really has no place in such an environment.

It was night at our hunting camp. There was this really bad electrical storm, but I decided to go ahead and try to hunt the jaguar. He was out there all right, just raising Cain because of our presence. I had my red light, and because animals are color-blind, he couldn't see it. So I took off, barefoot and in my jockey shorts. It seemed odd to me that the Indians didn't hunt at night. Then I found out why.

I felt something crawling up my leg. I flicked it off and kept hunting. After a while I felt something again. I looked down and the ground was covered with "bullet" ants by the thousands! Nighttime must be when they come out! These bullet ants are very dangerous. Their bites inflict great pain, and then the area that's bitten swells and goes numb for twenty-four hours! But I managed to get back to camp without getting bit.

The bullet ant of the Amazon rain forest inflicts a terribly painful bite, one of the most painful of any insect known. The bitten area remains numb for twenty-four hours. This is one of the Amazonian insects that we definitely did not want here in Florida! (Shirley Collection.)

Unfortunately, we never did get the jaguar because the chief needed to lay in a supply of coco leaves. That's what gives them their strength for the day. But it was a real disappointment for me.

The Amazon region is indeed a harsh place to live. In the water were small canero catfish that swim up a bather's urethra to the bladder and can be deadly. Then there are the larger canero said to swim up larger bodily orifices by the hundreds! They are, in fact, more greatly feared by the natives than the piranhas, those man- and animal-eating schools of sharp-toothed Amazonian fish. There are also electric eels in the Amazon, and then there are just plain giant catfish, man-eating if the opportunity arises, that weigh in at close to 1,500 pounds, as long as 17 feet, and with a mouth span of maybe 3 feet!

In the rain forest are anacondas as big around as a 55-gallon drum that can be 60 feet long! Big enough to make a tribe abandon their village if one of these guys takes up residence nearby. What a place!

Looking back, this trip was indeed a bit risky. The prevailing cultural traditions of these tribes dictated, for instance, taking revenge on anyone the medicine man divined had caused an incident or death. Since we were strangers from the outside world, I sure hoped that nothing bad would happen while we were there and so isolated from civilization.

It was, then, a bit disconcerting when just before our departure date, a little girl from our Jivaro village drowned. It was sad, and I helped the men look for her. But then we thought that maybe we should take our leave. And we did so with no complications.

Then there was more excitement downriver. Just before we stopped at the village of Requena, Peru, they had been hit by a raid from a rival tribe who lived 250 miles away in the jungle. The raid was for young women and supplies, so everyone in the village was crying. It was sobering to think that the Requenans would never see those young women again, and Naomi was quite freaked out by it all.

Several days farther downriver, we were greeted with more tragedy. A young woman had just died from what was said to be a canero attack. She had been making love in the river. Even with all the tribal tragedies left in our wake as we kept moving downriver, we managed to make it back safely from that wild country.

Back home in Florida from that time on, I found myself frequently comparing the Amazonian wetlands with the Everglades wetlands. It made me consider that there were some practical applications that should have been made here. For instance, in other major tropical waterways in the world, such as the Amazon, there are what they call "traveling islands," big chunks of vegetation that have the potential to clog waterways but don't because the native manatees eat the vegetation and keep the waterways open.

At that time, we were having a terrible time and great expense going into eradication of the introduced water hyacinths that were taking over our waterways. Since the native Amazonian manatees have no trouble cleaning plants out of the river and keeping the waterways open, why couldn't our manatees do the same? It sure would have saved the state some money.

But we have interfered too much with nature. By controlling our rivers with barricades of dikes and locks, the manatees are kept out of their habitat. We lost a lot of manatees when they could not get up the rivers and canals to warmer water in order to survive the low temperatures in the prolonged cold fronts of 2010.

At the Port of Miami, another of my duties with the Commission—especially in the months following the end of the hunting season when my workload lessened—was to produce an annual report on the import/export of exotic species. I was routinely required to inspect importers/exporters doing business at the port and also to police local pet shops and tropical fish companies. I was to make sure that they were complying with regulations on the books and not carrying species banned from import. I also was called to make recommendations of what animals, mainly fish, should be banned as detrimental and/or dangerous to introduce to South Florida—such as bullet ants and caneros!

The trip up the Amazon and other trips I made to Iquitos and Pucallpa while engaged in my fish-importing business aided me to better serve the Commission, my personal enterprise, and my love of travel!

Fire, Smoke, and Tornados—1971

Usually, by the time the hunting season closed in January in the saw grass Everglades area, the winter conditions of frost and drought had made a lot of the plants brittle and brown and ready for a fire.

It often happened that on the last day of the hunting season, February 5 or so, some individuals made it an annual event to go ahead and start fires all over the Glades in the northern end. Actually, fires are good for the ecology of the area and for hunting, but starting fires was also against the law. So it was up to me to try to catch these individuals, even the conservationists such as Ray Rotenberger and Al Henschel. They were the most famous "fire bugs" who operated every year on the last day of the season.

One time, there was a fellow working out of the camp El Rancho, south of where Alligator Alley is now. That individual, Snow, was also a fire bug. I was trying really hard to catch him at work.

I'd seen him setting fires from way off, and I was easing up on him, getting closer and closer. I got close enough, but he was just on the other side of a big saw grass strand. I had to get through this strand in order to apprehend him. I worked around farther north behind him and attempted to jump the saw grass strand with my airboat.

Well, I got halfway across that strand of very, very thick and high saw grass and wax myrtle in my airboat. As I have mentioned, I had designed it to coast up and over the grass, but in this particular situation, this strand was so high that my boat got stuck on some wax myrtle trees! And just in front of me, the willow strand stopped abruptly, dropping off some 4–5 feet. I needed to slope the bushes down so I could get in the boat and take off.

So I got out of the airboat, which was stranded about 4 feet off the ground, and began to chop the myrtles with my machete. Of course, without my weight, the airboat rose up higher, and I wondered if I could climb back in. It was so high that I couldn't reach the gas pedals. I had had to work my way back to the stern so I could get in the airboat to find my machete. Then I chopped the wax myrtles out from underneath the boat, working frantically, as I was really running out of time to beat the fire. By then, it was about 80 feet from me, with flames about 35 feet high. I could feel the heat, and that fire was coming on pretty fast with the wind behind it!

Boy, was I in trouble!

I had to get out of there, or I and my airboat were going to be burned for sure. I chopped and chopped with the machete. Finally, I was able to climb up into my airboat from the back, move forward, and give it full throttle. What a relief when it dropped down smoothly off the myrtles just as I had hoped. Then I pulled away like nothing had happened!

But Snow had already gone.

As I mentioned, fires are very good when it's the right time of year. When the ground is still moist, it doesn't burn down too far into the muck, and the grass burns back just to the ground. It's also just before the spring season, when the fawns are born, so timewise, it is perfect to produce a good deer herd, as plenty of the rich, fresh grass that sprouts after a fire is great for the young deer that are coming along. However, starting fires is still illegal.

One evening I was patrolling in the Commission vehicle across the northern part of Conservation Area 3 on the levee west of the Miami River, called L-4 Levee. A lightning strike had caused a big fire there. I was going out to investigate, driving westward. The flames were pretty high—I'd say 40, 50 feet high. It was a big, heavy, heavy burn.

Well, I was driving on down the levee, and everything was fine. The fires were getting kind of close, but there was no turnaround place, so I had to go down several miles to turn my vehicle around.

But by the time I had turned around and was headed back the way I came, the wind had changed. Now, it was really blowing northward, which meant I had to go through some of the flames. I was driving my vehicle through smoke and small flames around the levee, but I couldn't turn around or safely back up, so the only thing to do was keep going forward!

The wind changed again, fanning the flames bigger and bigger.

I had to keep going. Then it got to where I figured it wouldn't take too long before I'd be right through it, but as I drove, the flames only got bigger and the smoke thicker!

Soon I couldn't see through the flames. I couldn't see the road on the levee. But I couldn't stop. Blindly, I had to drive faster, trying not run off the levee. Now it was getting hotter. I kept driving and driving, and the flames were so hot. The car was hot. The windows got scorching hot. But I kept going.

I'm glad nobody was with me, because they would have surely panicked. Hell, I probably panicked myself! I was doing all I could to control myself and take care of the situation.

The air in the vehicle got so hot that I feared I was going scorch my lungs, so I took my last breath and I held it and still drove as fast as I could through the flames and the smoke, trying to keep on top of the levee.

Finally, I broke through the flames! The car's skin was so hot . . . the windows . . . the metal on the windows . . . was so hot, it burned me! I had made it through the flames just in time.

I opened up the door and just rolled out and got a breath of fresh air!

That was a close call. It sure taught me not to mess around with a wildfire.

Many times prior to that, I had put out grass fires with my airboat, running trails and fanning the blades on a drive-through to blow out the flames. That worked pretty well.

Over the decades, I've seen rabbits running from the flames. They're pretty smart. I've seen young rabbits and old ones. They all seem to have a rare knowledge, an instinct. They would run to an airboat trail or buggy trail and stay there, knowing that the flames were coming. On that clear patch of ground, they would gamble on the flames not burning on the trail. So they hid right there until the flames went over them . . . hopefully. Sometimes it worked, sometimes it didn't, but the rabbits knew, by instinct, how to escape from fires.

One time, one of my officers, Jimmy Sistrunk, and I made a trip out to my camp in the saw grass to help me sink a well. The whole area we crossed had burned flat, right down to the black, black muck. You could see for miles—no grass. We got in my little jeep half-track, and Mich Rudy was in a regular jeep. The Everglades was so dry, you could travel anyplace over the burned saw grass area.

We continued on southwest of the camp to the Big Cypress, which was a long way from the burned area, but the effect of that smoke had been toxic. I noticed that there were holes in the ground where snakes had come out and died because of the fumes.

I saw buck deer dead. In the still of the night the smoke settles to the ground, and there's no escape. It settles to the ground, and it's toxic enough to kill a mature buck, not to mention the turtles and snakes underground.

In my early years with the Commission areas, like along what is now Hollywood Boulevard and Pembroke Pines Boulevard, was Everglades. It was all wild. Then the Corps of Engineers got busy digging the canals and so forth in there to dry the area up. Because of that unnatural drainage, the area along Hollywood Boulevard would burn over maybe three times a year. And when I say burn, I mean that it was so dry, the ground itself, the muck, would burn.

I would be coming home from patrol early in the morning or late at night. And there would be so much smoke that I would have to open up the door, look down, and follow the yellow line to be sure I was in the road. I'd get home, and the vehicle and I would smell like all that smoke—toxic fumes.

I noticed people going to the drugstore, getting all their prescriptions filled because of their lung or breathing conditions. They didn't know what it was, but it was the toxic fumes coming from the ground burning. Some call it "muck smoke." It has a certain smell and a certain toxin that is very harmful to people.

In that area north of Hollywood Boulevard, I imagine after those fires burned several times a year, maybe 2 to 3 feet of top soil was burned off. It was burned down, smoldering for months at a time until it got down to the moisture level in the ground, or we had a good rain that put it out.

When there are fires, the beautiful island hammock islands closest to the canal waterways—extra-dry ground now because the subterranean moisture has been drained into the canals—are destroyed. The ground there would be so dry that the muck would burn right out from underneath a green tree, and the tree would fall right over and be consumed. That's the harm that should be considered when canals are being dug for drainage.

When it gets extra dry, the alligators instinctively dig down into the ground, 3 or 4 feet deep, and make caves 20 feet or longer. Big alligators, small alligators, they would use these caves to get out of drought, bad weather, and fires. But when the muck is so dry, I've seen large alligators, small alligators, just baked, cooked inside the caves because the ground burned and captured them inside what had been their home for years and years. Now even in the Everglades, in certain areas where Flood Control has been at work, even alligators are not safe.

I remember, one year, picking up an alligator about 4 feet long. He'd been burned pretty badly. I picked him up. I looked at him. His eyes were closed; he didn't appear to be breathing, and he looked like he had been baked in an oven—I'd say about medium-rare.

I noticed he moved a little bit, so I brought him with me to see what would happen. So I tried to make things comfortable for him, but he laid there for a week or two, just looked like he was completely cooked. Finally, after about a month, he did finally die, but it was amazing how hardy he was to be burned so severely and still be able to live.

For the deer and other wildlife under normal conditions, fires are not a problem. The animals seem to get away from the fire and know how to deal with it, but when it gets too dry, then the ground begins to dry. When the deer and other animals are searching for water, they go to the gator holes or the waterways. But the ground is burning, so they try to cross over to the water holes, but the ground is so hot, it burns their feet. Their feet become so sore and swollen and infected that they can no longer walk. Then they lie down and die from starvation and lack of water.

It is extremely important that Flood Control officials not let the Everglades get this dry. They are altering the Everglades so much that it is becoming unbalanced, and if these practices are not checked, they will certainly destroy it.

When I was a little guy—I'd say probably five or six—the first time

I heard of a tornado it was a broadcast over the radio. A tornado had struck the south end of town. I remember the paper saying it picked up a whole house and put it on top of an Australian pine tree.

That stuck in my mind. From that time on I had a fear of tornadoes, or I'd say a respect—I knew they were dangerous. Therefore, when I was on patrol or otherwise, I was always looking at the sky, still do, looking at cloud formations and watching for tornadoes.

I've seen as many as five in one day and three in one cloud. It wasn't unusual at all to see tornadoes coming across the Big Cypress, entering the Everglades.

One day in the early 1970s, I had my two boys out on my airboat south of Alligator Alley, and I noticed a tornado. It was off in the distance. It was traveling northward—right where we were going.

I figured, well, I've got enough speed in the airboat. I could beat it before it crossed the trail I was traveling, so I told Tommy and Troy, "Hold on, we're going to try to beat that tornado."

So I full-throttled the airboat, and off we went. We were clipping along pretty good at 90 mph or so, trying to beat the tornado, going toward the airboat trail that we were going to cross.

And lo and behold, I got right in the path the tornado was following—and I ran out of gas!

There we sat!

And the tornado was coming closer and closer.

Luckily, I always carried a 5-gallon can of gas, so I jumped down, poured in a couple of gallons, cranked up the airboat, and we got out of the path of the tornado just in time! That was a close call for me and my two boys.

That particular tornado crossed Alligator Alley and went on northward. It had enough power to pick up a cabbage palm tree from one of the tree islands. It took it about a quarter mile away and dropped it out in the slough!

Not long after, I was traveling down there, and I looked over in the middle of the slough and saw this cabbage palm. I wondered, "Where did that come from? What's it doing here?"

Then I realized it had been dropped there by the tornado. My friend and I tried to stand it up, hoping it would reroot there and grow. We straightened it, packed muck around it, and left it.

Well, it turned out to be a big joke! Al Henschel and other froggers would go out at night. Now, they knew the Everglades terrain like the back of their hand. But then, right out of nowhere, they came across a cabbage palm in a prairie!

"What's comin' off here? I don't know where I am!" It was quite a frightening experience for them.

Then they figured, "That was that damn Tom Shirley again, playing a joke on us."

I was sorry that the lone palm didn't live. But the joke of it all was pretty funny.

One night, while patrolling Betty and Johnny's Levee north of the Tamiami Trail, I went on southward to the fire tower that aided me to see the lights of gator hunters or "jack-lighters" hunting deer or other wildlife at night. It was my favorite spot to see what was going on.

That night while I was up there, I noticed that back south of me, boy, an electrical storm had come up—lightning, bad weather. So I was under the tin roof of the fire tower. I figured I'd be safe here out of the weather. But then a big ugly cloud came my way, thundering and carrying on. It looked kind of bad. Then I saw what looked, even in the dark night, like a big funnel coming down from underneath it!

I thought, "Oh, boy, I hope that's not what I think it is!" But it was. And, with the conditions around me by then, I made the decision to stay there, hoping it would bypass me, go west of me, which it looked like it might.

But it got closer and closer. The wind picked up, got stronger and stronger, and then all of a sudden I saw, when I turned on my light, all these mosquito hawks (large dragonflies) going straight up in the air. There were saw grass plants, their seeds going straight up in the air, leaves and everything going straight up!

The winds got worse, blowing and blowing. The big old cloud got bigger and bigger. Well, for sure this tornado was coming! But there wasn't anything to do by then but stay and wait it out. When I saw all these bugs and limbs and everything being sucked up, I knew it must be pretty close.

Man, this looked pretty bad. The tornado was coming much closer than I had anticipated. But I dared not go down those flimsy stairs because the strong winds would blow me off. So I was captured in that little canopy, which was only about 12 feet square and 60 feet in the air!

The tornado was extra dark, full of lightning, and green inside. It roared like a train coming through the tower. I realized that without my radio, I could be blown far away from the tower into high saw grass and no one would find me. Then here came the hail, just coming down, hitting that tin roof with a roar! Well, I just lay down and held onto the floor and hoped to weather it out, while it blew and blew and blew.

Finally the roar passed on southward and faded away. Just like that, from trauma and wind, to dead calm. But that was sure one close encounter!

Later on, someone stole some of the wooden steps to the tower, so we had to be trapeze artists to get to the top.

Another time that I had an experience with a tornado, I was driving in the Commission car coming down Okeechobee Road entering Hialeah. There at Okeechobee Boulevard I was looking up at all the clouds. I could see that they were perfect clouds for tornadoes, so I'm watching, watching. For some reason, I leaned forward right over the dashboard, and looked straight up—and there was a big cloud forming a tornado right over me!

I looked about 30 feet to the side of me and everything was being sucked up out of a park area. The tornado was right beside me, and I was stuck in traffic in the Commission vehicle! I turned out of the traffic, going in and out of the cars as fast as I could, because the tornado was going to touch down right there!

I ran up to the 7–11 store about a block away. I stopped the vehicle and hollered, "Tornado! Tornado!"

All the Cuban people just looked at me like I was crazy. They didn't even know what was happening.

By that time, it had hit the Hialeah Police Department and the UPS building. I saw parts of the roof coming off.

I just watched the whole thing. I turned on the regular news broadcast, hoping they would say something about it. Then I watched as it traveled northeast.

I got into my vehicle and tried to keep up with the tornado to see all the damage. I followed it as far as I could until it crossed the railroad tracks. I couldn't go any farther, but I heard on the news that it went all the way up to Perry Airport in Pembroke Pines and tore up a bunch of airplanes. Then it went all the way from Hialeah to Broward County and did a lot of damage there.

Another close call!

It's strange being so close to a tornado. The tornado funnel, the cloud, is black, so black, as dark as night, and it is alive with lightning—green lightning. In fact, the whole sky within that cloud keeps flashing with lightning. It was a terribly awesome sight, but in a way, it was a grand experience that I cherish.

My Everglades Camps—1984

As I have mentioned, in the early years of my employment with the Game and Fresh Water Fish Commission I camped out under the stars on a tarp and bedroll or jungle hammock, usually at the Grapefruit Head. While I loved roughing it, this situation was not nearly as desirable as that of my friends such as Al Henschel or Ray Rotenberger, who had built nice permanent camps complete with wells that gave them running water. They could stay out for weeks at a time.

It was hard for me to compete with them energy-wise because at the end of the day they could have a warm shower, prepare a nice supper, jump into a soft bed, and be ready to go the next morning. There was nothing for me to do but build myself a permanent camp soon, before the Glades got too dry. It would give me a place to store my supplies, and I wouldn't have to be so mobile all the time.

There was an ideal location in the farthest hammock northwest in Conservation Area Number 3, one of the highest hammocks in the saw grass. Not many airboaters ventured that far west because of the rough terrain.

I stockpiled my supplies at Mack's Fish Camp. I made two long airboat trips a day carrying cement blocks, dynamite, 2 × 6–12 × 14"-long rolls of tar paper and tools. It was about 30 to 40 miles each way, so I hauled building materials and supplies around 160 miles a day. Working by myself—loading, driving, then unloading—made for long and tiring days. Then several of my friends helped me gather up other material, and during a drought period we began to construct my camp.

Over time we added more rooms, a bath, a hot-water heater, a

In 1955, I began to build my Sawgrass Camp. At Mack's Fishing Camp, I loaded up building supplies, concrete blocks, dynamite, tar paper, and tools on my airboat and made the trip 30 to 40 miles to the site out in the Everglades wetlands. (Photo by George Eddy.)

shower stall, beds, and bunk beds that the kids grew up with. In time we had all the comforts in our Sawgrass Camp!

This camp became suitable for the Game Commission post, so it was used not only by my family, but by other Commission families as well. And, it was never locked because we Gladesmen never locked our camps. The Everglades wetlands was a rough enough environment, and camps remained open and available for anyone to seek refuge from weather or hardship, like when I swamped my airboat and spent the night at Sig Walker's camp.

Back in our home in the city, I'd go to my boys' bedroom and say, "OK, you guys, hit the floor—we're going to the camp!" And I was reminded again of what a blessing it was to have my two eldest sons once again with me to share in my Everglades adventures.

Tommy, Troy, Ray Parks, Melanie, and young Barney would jump for joy. Even the dogs outside knew what was up. I didn't have to tell them.

The other kids in the neighborhood, such as David Kinder, Phillip Murphy, they were all excited. They were part of the Shirley gang, going to the camp.

Ray Parks had come to live with us when he was around twelve years old, and at that point I became his father. My sons had been

By the late 1960s, the Shirley household always had a wide variety of exotic animals. This Bengal tiger paid a visit to my children Tommy, Melanie, and Troy at Christmastime one year. (Photo by Tom Shirley.)

most persuasive in getting him settled in, originally in a red tent in the backyard, as we didn't have room in the house. They took an extension cord and ran it out there so he could have a TV and a fan. They put carpet down and picked up discarded furniture and made it real nice. Then, realizing that it was much more exciting camping out, Troy moved in with Ray!

And Phillip Murphy, now some forty-odd years later, told me that when he was a little kid in the neighborhood, living a block or so away, he dreamed that maybe sometime he would be asked to join with the two Shirley boys and have all of that excitement.

Boy, what joy going to the camp gave them! Of course, it didn't take them long to gather up all their goodies, get packed up, and off to the Glades we'd go. All of them piled on my airboat. We must have looked like a Christmas tree, cutting across the Everglades plains or coming down the trail.

So finally we'd hit the landing at the camp, and the kids would scatter like a covey of quail—jumping with joy. We were going to have a good time that weekend!

As I sit here, I think of what a rich life I've had. I love my wife, Naomi, and my children. We've had some wonderful times. We've had some beautiful memories. We have traveled to exciting places, and here in the Everglades wetlands the kids had the opportunity to use airboats, buggies, three-wheelers, four-wheelers. You name it, we've had it.

The kids learned to do chores, how to cook well without all the niceties of home. Sometimes we had to mow the lawn without the best equipment. We all got cut, bruised, stung, bitten, thrown off ATVs, got dirty, but it all washed off at night with a nice warm shower. Out there we allowed them to be boys!

My sons Barney Shirley and Ray Parks pose on a full-track with Lab the dog in 1977. (Shirley Collection.)

We all looked forward to the various seasons. Winters were for hunting deer, duck, or snipe. I was there when each of my sons shot his first deer, which is important for a father. In spring, the does began to drop their fawns, and the Shirley family always seemed to have a cute little spotted faun to take to the Dade County Fair. Summertime, when all the Glades were dry, was the time to crank up the three-wheeler, buggy, or full-track. The gator ponds and holes always got our attention, and of course we had to investigate each gator hole to find the largest gator. We always seemed to have a metal pipe handy to rod out the gator and maybe take its picture. I taught the kids how to avoid the snakes that were so prevalent during the drought periods. Our family looked forward to being in the Everglades every season of the year.

It was a good life away from the distractions and busy life in the city. At this camp I guided and taught my sons right from wrong. I showed them the mysteries of nature, shared experiences and adventures around a campfire under the stars. This is when a family is *really* together.

We would look out the window and see deer, hogs, raccoons, bobcats, and all the other critters, right in our front yard! How boring it would have been if we had not been fortunate enough to have all of these experiences.

Then, around 1984, I purchased some acreage back in the Big Cypress swamp. Well, it was really way back in the wild woolies, and there I made a camp. It's in a beautiful hammock packed with oak trees—a beautiful piece of property. And I would sit there and think. I had all that I wished for in life. I had a nice house; a good, moral woman, which my wife, Naomi, is; a job that I enjoy; and I had been able to travel to the far reaches of the Amazon, Alaska, Africa, and Antarctica to whet my appetite for adventure. But I dearly loved my Everglades camp.

I thought it would be good to bring up the grandkids in this kind of terrain, teach them about nature and all that it has to offer for a good, healthy life. All my first grandkids belonged to our daughter, Melanie, and her husband, Rocky Davis. They had four kids at the time: Cody was six, Shane was five, Shannon was three, and T. J. was about two and a half. My son Troy's boy, Taylor, was a baby. Blake hadn't come along yet.

They would all pile into the front seat. They'd always want me to tell them a story. And here's the way I'd pick a story:

I'd tell the kids: "OK, you take turns. You say one word and the first thing that crosses my mind will be the topic and it will always be a *true* story." And I'd begin, "Well, when I was a little guy . . ."

T. J. would be sitting in my lap, because he would want to drive, but in about three minutes he'd be snoring, so he'd miss a lot of the "little guy" stories.

So someone would start off. They'd say, "dog," and I'd carry on with a story about a dog.

But in those stories I would always try to interject some of life's logic or a moral or maybe the power of positive thinking or how important it is to go to school and learn everything you can. Things that would stay with them throughout their lives. This went on and on for years. The Big Cypress camp had a beautiful and relaxing atmosphere for me to sit down and concentrate on my grandkids and tell stories.

Of course, all of my grandkids are adults now, but if I asked them if they would like to hear any "little guy" stories to this day, it would bring a smile to their faces and they would jump at the opportunity. I'd have their undivided attention, I guarantee you.

This gave us a terrific bond that still holds our family together. When kids grow up close to their parents and grandparents, it gives them a good feeling of security. This I highly recommend. And a person who has not had the opportunity to observe nature has not had a complete life experience. The Everglades wetlands is there for us all to enjoy. I can only hope it will be available to future generations in a recognizable form.

Pranks, Grasshoppers, and Skunk Apes

We had a wildlife officer, Butch Shaw, who, if I bought a pack of crackers or a piece of candy or something and put it on the dashboard of our patrol vehicle, he would end up eating more than I did.

I kind of got perturbed at this behavior after so long and thought, "Well, I'll fix him!"

I went to Steven's Food Store and got a can of grasshoppers and a can of crickets. I put the can of grasshoppers on the dashboard. It was night, so he couldn't see the label. And we went out on patrol.

Butch was picking away, and—I'll be danged!—he ate the entire can of grasshoppers!

When he turned on the lights so he could see what he had eaten, he got an upset stomach to say the least.

These are some of the stories . . . things that helped to keep us going, because we officers worked real hard, but we also played hard!

This reminds me of another story. Jimmy Sistrunk was always pulling pranks or whatever. He patrolled with Jimmy Thompson.

Sistrunk had a can of black spray paint that he had been using earlier in the day on a project. They were out on patrol, patrolling the L-5 and L-4 Levees, running without lights. Well, Jimmy Thompson always kept a can of mosquito repellent up on the dashboard. When Jimmy wasn't looking, Sistrunk took the can of bug spray and switched it with the black spray paint.

The mosquitoes were really bad that night.

Jimmy Thompson, not knowing what Sistrunk had done, grabbed the can of spray paint and sprayed it all over his arms, his face, sprayed it on the dash and windshield. He didn't notice it at first. He put the black paint back on the dashboard.

"Boy, it's really getting dark out here," he complained to Sistrunk.

Of course, as I mentioned, they were patrolling without lights, but then Thompson realized that it was *really* dark, he said, "What's going on here?"

He turned on his flashlight, and there it was! Paint all over the windshield. It's black! His arms . . . black! He looked in the mirror, and just the whites of his eyes stared back! Boy, did he raise hell and goddamns with Sistrunk, who reached for the door handle, ready to jump out!

We had a great laugh hearing of the prank that Sistrunk pulled on Jimmy Thompson!

Quite often, we'd get new officers who were afraid of snakes. Why they would put in for Everglades duty is beyond me because the

Everglades in those days was *full* of snakes. I would try to break them of their fears because they were sure to come across lots of snakes during their employment.

Usually I'd just bring out a snake every now and then and kind of scare them with it, while showing them at the same time that it was no big deal, that it wasn't going to hurt them. But one day, I was patrolling Betty and Johnny's Levee when we came up on this girl, Jackie, a real famous herpetologist. She had a croker sack just crammed full of snakes.

I said, "Jackie, let me see that sack of snakes." I looked in there to make sure that there weren't any venomous ones. Officer Wendell Clemmons was with me in the Commission vehicle.

Well, I swung that sack of snakes right over and dumped the whole bag right at Wendell Clemmons's feet! He went berserk! He was hollering and screaming and jumped out of the vehicle.

Well, that was my best and quickest method of helping them overcome their fear of snakes. It usually worked!

But not long after, I was going down the Tamiami Trail. Clem was with me, and I was doing about 65 mph, and everything was fine, but I lifted my foot off the gas. Clem thought I'd seen a snake and was going to stop and catch it. He was so spooked! He was all ready to jump out of the car!

I've also been known to play a few tricks on people out at my camp in Big Cypress. This was one of my favorites.

I made a recording and manipulated the tape so that it would sound like we might imagine a skunk ape might sound! The skunk ape, or "Big Foot," has never been positively identified, but the Everglades is one of the places that harbors periodic "sightings," and the lore has sprung up. So in my recording I created the growls, the calls, the screams, the breaking and snapping of branches . . . It all sounded very authentic when I finished that special tape, which I still use today!

At the camp, I would place the cassette out under a 55-gallon drum so no one could tell exactly where the noise was coming from. I would have guests, and I would begin to tell stories at night before we'd go to bed. I would make up stories about the skunk apes. I'd mention how, over there at Roger Tadlock's camp, "Why, he doesn't even come out anymore, because he saw signs of the skunk ape when he came out to his camp. He had seen where the skunk apes had fed on the rubber tree roots." I'd tell them how the skunk apes have enough strength just to dig down in the ground, pull those rubber tree roots right up and feed on them . . . And Tadlock had found hogs that were killed by the skunk apes. They had just ripped open the belly and fed on the intestines of those hogs!

We had several tales like this to tell before bedtime, to reinforce the fact that our camp was apparently in the territory of skunk ape activity!

Since I was the one who went out at night to turn off the generator, I would go out with the recorder set and turn it on. It had about an eight-minute delay—enough time for me to get back into bed and settle down.

After eight minutes ticked on, we would hear a yowling. It would scare the hell out of everybody, but I would already be supposedly asleep in my bed, snoring away.

There would be several other noises, and everybody would get excited! They'd think, "He's over this way. No, he's over that way!" Then all would be quiet. Next, you'd hear limbs and twigs snapping here and there in different places, with long delays of silence in between.

I've had some tough guys, strong guys, brave guys hear it.

And they'd say, "The next time I hear that, I'm going to go out there with my shotgun. I'm going to see what that is!" But no man has ever stepped outside of that door yet! And believe me, I've played this trick on many, many people.

Jack and Johnny were two of my favorite people that I played this trick on. They spread the word that that, "Out there in Big Cypress was the baddest and meanest panther" they'd ever encountered. "He must be gigantic!" They spread this word all over town. Well, I never revealed the secret. Those guys died still thinking they'd heard a huge panther at Tom Shirley's camp!

Dick Lawrence, one of my wildlife officers, was at the camp. I got out the tape and I played this prank on him. Once again, I was back in the bed innocently snoring. He jumped up: "Tom, Tom, the skunk ape's out there! Get your gun! Hurry! Skunk ape's out there. You've got to get up! Get up! Get up!"

But I lay right there, snoring. It scared the fool out of Dick Lawrence.

I'll never forget it. I never revealed to him that it was just a tape. As far as he knows, he really did have an encounter with the legendary skunk ape!

Domestic Violence—1985

Shortly before I was to retire in 1985, maybe a couple months before at the most, I was on patrol west of Medley on the west side of the Miami River and out beyond that into the Glades.

There was a head there, a hammock in the middle of the saw grass, and there was an old still out there, a copperhead kettle with equipment that belonged to Gedson Ford. He had really put out moonshine heavy at one time. In fact, his still was operational on and off for a number of years. He was also a gator poacher, into lots of things.

I was approaching this area. Walking through the Everglades I saw that a car was parked, oh, about 100 yards from me. And I saw a man and a woman there, standing face to face. Then, he reached up and slapped the fool out of her. I saw her hair fly! That's how I knew for sure that it was a woman from that distance.

So I began to get closer and closer, and he was hollering and screaming at her. Then he turned around and opened the trunk of the car and got out an axe.

By that time, I had gotten pretty close. He reached back with the axe poised and said, "I'm gonna' bash your motherfuckin' skull in if you don't tell me!"

I stepped from behind the bush. She saw me and whirled around. His eyes were big as saucers. Here he thought he was there out in the middle of nowhere all alone with the woman! As he whirled around, he had the axe over his head, still cocked.

So I drew my pistol and said, "Put the axe down."

He didn't do it.

I said, "You'd better put the axe down immediately."

He still didn't do it, so I shot couple of inches from his foot and blew stone up into his face.

He immediately dropped the axe, and I began to talk to him, "Is this girl your wife?"

And he said, "Yes."

And I said, "What are you fighting about?"

"I'm not gonna tell ya," he said.

So I got his license, identification, and tag number. Then I asked the woman, "Do you feel safe to go home with him?"

She said, "No."

"I'll take you home then," I said.

I was in a jeep at the time, and to take all three of us would have had us at uncomfortably close quarters, considering the situation. So I allowed him to get in his vehicle. The woman and I walked on toward mine.

Then he hollered, "My car won't start."

The woman whispered out to me, "Watch out, he's gonna do something to ya."

I said, "Don't worry. I'll take care of it."

So I went back and got him out of the vehicle, and I made him stand about 15 feet back. I got in and turned on the ignition, and it started up right up—no problem—so I let him get into the vehicle and drive on off.

Then, I asked the woman, "Is this man your husband?"

She said, "Oh, no."

I asked, "Well, what happened?"

"Well, I went to Georgia for a couple of weeks, and I came back, and he was all mad," she said. "While I was gone, he went to a fortuneteller, who told him I was hung up with another man! I told him I wasn't, but he beat me for several days," and she grabbed her head and moaned.

I said, "What's the matter?"

"Well, he hit me beside the head with the butt of an ice pick," she said.

I said, "Well, are you going to press charges?" and she said she would.

I took her to the Hialeah Police Department and told them what I'd witnessed and shared the information about the man.

I was never called to appear as a witness, so I imagine she failed to bring charges against him. This is an example of the domestic violence situations that I sometimes ran into and had to handle in the rough, isolated areas on the fringe of the Everglades.

5

After Alligator Poachers

Alligator Poaching—1955

In our Everglades District, we wildlife officers spent hundreds of hours and our constituents' tax dollars patrolling and searching, second-guessing alligator poachers. For the poachers, alligators represented the most lucrative business to be made off the Everglades wetlands. An officer could easily catch a poacher with $1,000 worth of gator hides, as the going price per foot between 1960 and 1980 was between seven dollars and twenty-two dollars a foot, and Florida's tanneries were going strong! If a poacher was caught, went through the court process, was actually proven guilty, and fined by a judge, he might lose $250. Once given this legal slap on the wrist, that poacher would be right out there in the Glades again and up to his usual, very lucrative activities.

To make the job of wildlife officer even more difficult, it was very hard to make an arrest that would stand up in court. Primarily that was due to lack of evidence. Numerous times, like the monkey fishermen, the poacher would jettison evidence (in this case, guns and gator hides) overboard in deepwater canals in the dark, during pursuit. With the goods gone, no case could be made.

There were also large operations of major hide buyers who traveled down through Florida to make purchases. We sure would have liked to have caught them!

Gator poachers themselves were for the most part friendly and colorful characters. It seemed to me that you could usually recognize a poacher when he first introduced himself, saying, "I am going to tell you a true story and it's the truth." I would then brace myself for the great lie that was about to be told, while appearing to listen with great interest. Poachers came in small, medium, and large, and we heard stories when they boasted to friends, acquaintances, and informants. Some poachers threatened the law enforcers face to face, saying things like, "I'll cut your belly open. I'll tuck you down in a gator hole and nobody will ever find you!"

These kinds of threats have been made throughout history. Fortunately poachers seldom made threats to my face, and remarkably there weren't too many people who gave me serious trouble. I think that's because I've always tried to treat each individual with kindness, as if he were a gentleman. It seemed to work well for me, even with the toughest old alligator poacher, because he was treated with respect.

I felt that I was fair in making the cases. I always ran through check points before I made an arrest: "Is this going to impress the judge? Is it a good and sound violation? If I make this arrest, is it going to be positive, to profit the Commission, or is it going to go against us in some way?" That was very important to me in every case.

I very seldom put people in jail. If we could maintain contact with the perpetrators and they weren't going to skip town, we would release them on their own recognizance. The only time we'd put them in jail was when we thought they would skip out. Our intention wasn't to embarrass them or penalize them. It was up to the judge and jury to find them guilty and to serve up the punishment and embarrassment.

The poachers outfitted themselves with an airboat, outboard motorboat, a small skiff, or even a canoe. They would use a headlight on a hat to spot the red eyes of the gator reflecting in the dark, rapidly shoot the gator in the head before it submerged, then grasp the gator with a gig and hack it with a hatchet or a machete just behind the head to kill it. That would sever the spinal cord and render it immobile.

The gator could be skinned in a few minutes. It was deftly cut on each side of its back and under its throat, cut on top of each leg, and the tail section was cut to the very end. The bony skin and bony platelets, the scutes, were not marketable. The belly was cut open so the carcass would sink, not float and alert the law to the poachers' nefarious activities, and the turtles and fish would feed off it until it disappeared. And last but not least, the poacher might wrap a few of the smaller alligator hides around his body. That way, if he was questioned

The lengths to which alligator poachers would go to smuggle their hides out of the Everglades wetlands were unbelievable, but at some twenty-seven dollars per foot, poaching was a lucrative profession. Poachers knew all the tricks, including wrapping the alligator hides around their bodies to conceal them, hiding them in butane tanks, secreting them in their cars, and stashing them in trees. Often posing as legal frog hunters, they went through all kinds of nighttime maneuvers to conceal their nefarious alligator-poaching activities from the wildlife officers. Around 1975, Wildlife Officers Jimmie Thorp and Jimmie Sistrunk made this bust on alligator poacher Carl Docton on Highway 27. Docton was owner of a gun shop on Eighth Street in Miami. (Photo by Tom Shirley.)

by the law, his hides would not be lying out to be seen, and he wouldn't have to jettison them overboard to get rid of the evidence.

Even though we in Law Enforcement patrolled such a vast area and our officers were few in number, it was not so very difficult to locate violators or patrol the wetlands during hunting season. This was because there were only a few points within the Wildlife Management Areas where the hunters could easily launch their boats and airboats. They also utilized the few private wetlands recreation areas along canals such as the popular Mack's. So, by patrolling these launching sites, we had a fairly good chance of seeing what was going on and hearing all the gossip.

After many years of working with the Commission, Tallahassee sent out a list of all the wildlife officers in the state and gave the number of arrests that they made on an annual basis. I was shocked and also embarrassed to find that I was at the top of the list! I didn't want to leave the impression that I was trying to impress Tallahassee, so I purposefully dropped down on arrests. I didn't want to be the lead man, to have that reputation. That was not my intention at all. I just knew what illegal activities were going on, and who was committing them, and I had an instinct that let me know how and when I could catch them at it!

Also, when I began in Law Enforcement at the Commission, the definition of "making a lawful arrest" was that the defendant had to have the *intent* to break the law, so I was lenient when the situation warranted it. Today, however, they teach all the officers to make arrests and cite for all of the charges possible in order to cover "bargaining power." I strongly oppose this method.

Camping on Patrol

When I was on patrol for alligator poachers out northwest from Mack's Fish Camp at my old Grapefruit Head, near the Palm Beach County line, I camped underneath that old huge fig or "rubber" tree. It's maybe 60 feet tall with a trunk root structure of 20 feet. The figs are small and red. They provide food for the birds and other animals, worms, insects, and mud puppies. The eating and grubbing around for the figs by all of the wildlife aerates the soil. The roots and trunk of this tree have many holes and crevasses, affording refuge to rabbits, snakes, turtles, bugs, and honeybees. There are many rabbits here, which provide food for the bobcats and the Florida panthers. This is a good high island and one of the refuges for the animals during times of seasonal high water. It was my refuge, too, my base camp when I was patrolling at night for alligator poachers in my early years with the Commission.

I have mentioned that in the Grapefruit Head hammock were wild oranges, rough-skinned lemons, key limes, and grapefruit. These citrus trees were left behind by various earlier Native American inhabitants. There was also an abundance of Indian pottery embedded in the soil, and large conch shell tools were left behind. These shells have two holes punched through them where the Indians secured a stick handle to make a hoe for farming their crops. Some of the human activity on these hammock islands dates back as far back as five thousand years ago.

I liked to pull into the Grapefruit Head before dark so I could be on the northern end of the Glades by 1:00 or 2:00 a.m. That way I didn't have to ride around alerting poachers that I was in the area.

What I needed at camp when I was on patrol were two military rocket containers, one telephone company box for clothing, pots and pans, and canned goods. I had a kerosene 500-watt Coleman lantern. I brought a 10 × 10' green carpet from home. I set up my jungle hammock between two wild orange trees under the big rubber tree. I put my 30-inch-wide mattress inside the jungle hammock, making the hammock extra wide. The width keeps the mosquito netting farther out. It worked out beautifully. I even had a tent-type roof to keep the dew or rain off me. With a soft, fluffy pillow, what more could I ask for?

As I lay there watching the fire burn down to the coals, it put me into a kind of trance; to me it was better than watching TV. As always, I could just lie there looking at the coals burn down and meditate. It's good for the mind, good for the soul. I recommend it for anybody.

On nights like this at the Grapefruit Head, I never get too lonely. After all, there was that old 12-foot alligator about 12 feet from me.

And as I lay there in the evenings, I would hear the lonely, beautiful calls of the whippoorwill. They'd call for hours, calling for a mate—one male, trying to call out prettier than all the others.

Then you hear the limpkins in the early evenings. Theirs is the loneliest call of all. They sound awfully mournful, like a woman hollering for help, and they call all night long.

Occasionally various great blue herons and blue cranes call out with their big squawk. It's an ugly sound. You don't know whether it's a bear or a gator charging them or what? So in the Glades you can never feel lonely because there are constant sounds from lots of animals all around you.

The raccoons come in. You no sooner get camp set up than here they come, around the fire, looking to see if there are any handouts. You can throw out a little twig that's burning, and they'll pat it out with their paws. It's instinct. They don't like fire. They recognize the danger and pat it out every time.

Then there are the deer. The deer come in snorting. They're curious. Usually you're not in the camp more than two hours and you hear the deer splashing, easing around you, snorting—curious, curious animals.

But I'm always on edge when the big boar hogs come in. At breeding time, the females are in season, and the big boars fight among themselves. They run around, scratching and biting and throwing each other around, doing the tussle. I lay there hoping that they didn't stampede over me. The fights usually go on all night long. They could sure make for some long and restless nights!

After getting up to track a suspicious airboater, I went back to my camp, climbed back into my hammock, put another log on the fire, and slept the rest of the night (what was left of it!). At 5:00 a.m., my alarm clock went off!

I walked out to the edge of the hammock, and there was the beginning of a wonderful sunrise. The fog was just lifting and the beautiful color began to change from bright orange to yellow to blue.

Flocks of all sorts of bird life began to travel from east to west, flying right over my head. They were en route to a slough that was drying up on the west side of the Grapefruit Head. The ibis or "curlew" were flying in their "V" formation. The mature ibis have a curved orange beak and orange legs, while their head, body, and wings are snow-white. The wood storks were much larger, with a wing span of 4 feet. Then, most beautiful of all, the bright-pink roseate spoonbills. All were all anxious for breakfast. With the slough drying up, they had easy access to dying fish, crawdads, shrimp, frogs, and even snakes in the breadbasket of South Florida, the wonderful, the perfect, Everglades wetlands!

I looked to my left and smelled the delicate white blooms of the spider lily. With their long, curled petals, there is a resemblance to a spider. Nearby, in the new grass and scrub, tiny delicate spider webs hang suspended. They are covered with dew, and as the sun shines through the moisture-laden web, it reflects a glistening rainbow. Big drops on the webs glisten and shine like diamonds out 100 yards or more from the island.

I know the wetlands like the back of my hand. I know how each fraction of an inch of water depth will establish a different type of plant life. This is why the Everglades wetlands are *so* fragile. The wetlands produce more types of wildlife than any other terrain. What a shame that people can't see what it was like in the early times before man ruined it in the name of "progress," ruined something they could not comprehend.

I took a good, long breath of the fresh air. It was moist, fresh, clean, and pure. I breathed in again and got a whiff of coffee. I looked back, and my coffeepot had boiled over!

"What a wonderful life. And I get paid to do this!"

Bobo's Smokescreen

One evening, about eight o'clock, a little bit after dark, I launched my airboat south of the Loop Road in Monroe County. This area is near the tip end of Florida. On farther south of the marsh, where it gets into brackish water and mangroves, is a place where poachers like to hunt the really big alligators.

The sky here is beautifully clear; clouds are puffy white; the terrain looks red, and the ground is a fire of colors at certain times of the year. The skies at night with the stars just twinkling make you feel like you're at the end of another world. It's a very secluded, vastly lonely, but very peaceful area.

Anyway, I was sitting there one evening in the dark. It was about midnight. I was probably about 15 miles south of the Loop Road launch. I was sitting there having a little cup of coffee out of my thermos when I heard an airboat start up about 4 miles away. Apparently it had been sitting there doing something in the dark, because I hadn't seen a light all night. So I cranked up my airboat under the cover of his engine noise.

He ran a while and turned his engine off. Well, this kind of operation gets to be a cat-and-mouse game because you don't want the other guy to hear your engine, so you've got to turn your engine off before he turns his off.

This went on for the better part of forty-five minutes or so. The minute he turned his engine back on, I'd turn mine on, and off we'd go. By then I was probably 50 feet from him. But he must have turned around and seen my exhaust pipe with the flare of blue and red flames coming out of it. I figured that he knew the law was on him, and he struck out at full bore, heading back eastward toward the rocky area.

This was right in that area I've mentioned before called the Tentacle Rocks. And I kept thinking, "Be real careful, because if you crack up and get thrown out here on that coral, there isn't going to be any sewing you back up!"

This fellow was heading right for those rocks and I knew it, so I was trying to get up close to him to see who he was, so I could at least recognize him. But I was catching his prop blast and all of the water mist. I couldn't see too well, and we were both still going full bore.

He made it in into a channel through the bed of rocks, and in and out he went.

Well, my boat was a little bit wider than his, and my airboat slid a little bit. I couldn't turn quite as sharply as he could. He was in and out of those tentacle rocks like lightning. Boy, was it a mad chase!

We pushed on and I realized, "This place is going to open up and there won't be any rocks!" So I floorboarded it, and I came upside of him, and boy, I looked ahead and there's a big, big, long rock standing about 2 foot out of the water.

Boom! I hit that rock and almost flipped the boat.

OK, I gathered things back up and off we went again. It was a wild chase that seemed to go on and on and on. I was pretty proud of myself, as so far I had followed him through all those rock channel obstacles, and *he* knew them very well, let me tell you.

Next he headed northwest and looked like he was going full bore back to the cypress area, so I was trying to get around all the prop blast and everything, the trees, the bush, the cabbage palms, as the wild chase continued. Finally I was about 50 feet behind him, and he was headed to a particular cypress strand.

This cypress stand had a trail through it that was made many years before for little airboats about 4 feet wide. Well, at 6 feet across, mine was extra wide, plus the trail was so old that the cypress trees had grown and expanded, so it was really close quarters for my airboat.

But there we went, racing on through. I was trying hard to catch up with him. Then, all of a sudden, "Poof!"—there was this big cloud of smoke.

I couldn't see anything—not even my hand in front of me!

I cut my engine. I bumped into one cypress tree, then another, before the boat stopped. Luckily, it didn't tear the whole top cage off the bow while I was crashing into those trees.

In that cloud of smoke, all I could do was to sit there in complete blindness, with my adrenalin still simmering, cussing my dilemma, and breathing in kerosene!

Kerosene!! Well, here's what this fellow had done. Some of the poachers rigged up a failsafe, a little trick with an oil pipe and a pump. By pumping kerosene into the exhaust, you get a dense cloud of smoke. Well, I had heard about the rigging, but this was the first time anyone had pulled that trick on me. It really worked very efficiently, let me tell you.

So I had to sit there in the still of the night, and it must have been about a half hour before the cloud of smoke disbursed a bit. Even then, as I could still barely see, it took me about 200 yards to get out of it because that poacher had kept the smokescreen on for quite a while. That's one fellow who got away from me. But I guessed that it was Bobo, the old famous gator poacher. Just like our Commission airplane, I had gotten so I could tell whose airboat it was just by the sound of their engine. And it sure sounded to me like old Bobo Redding from the Blue Shanty! Bobo may have gotten away this time, but I'm sure looking forward to trying to catch him another night real soon!

On the Trail of Sig Walker

The Commission purchased an old Army weasel. It's a full-track arrangement, like a small swamp buggy on military tank treads—very effective for much of our patrol area. We were going on patrol south of the Loop—Officers Dave Bowman, Jimmy Jordan, and me.

It was going to be a real journey. It was a dry season, but our vehicle was only about 3 feet off the ground. My officers and I departed Loop

Road early one morning and traveled southward to investigate the half-dozen airstrips made by the Homestead Outlaws.

As we traveled southward, we checked each landing strip, looking to see if there was any fresh sign of aircraft activity and checking inside the various camps for any type of evidence.

Making the rounds westward, we went down around the mangroves, then continued on westward to what they call "Camp Coconuts." It's a pretty nice camp, made in the mid-1950s by Ed Mitchell, a major avocado grower from Homestead. We made camp there, ate lunch, and rested awhile. We didn't see any sign that people had been making use of the camp for several days.

So after lunch and a quick nap, we headed on farther westward on the edge of the mangroves checking for vehicular activity. We were careful because when you get too close to the mangroves and the west coast, you get into a very soggy-type terrain. You can very well get stuck and be there for days.

Traveling the area, we checked other camps such as "Camp Crack-Up," named for M. C. Lowe, who comes in there with his plane. He can make a plane do just about anything he wants it to. Lowe was a very, very efficient and popular pilot, especially among the violators.

We worked our way around Gator Hook Strand, which runs north and south. The cypress strands are very beautiful there, festooned with orchids and bromeliads, a wild country full of alligators, deer, and a bird rookery. It's a very, very beautiful area.

We worked on around northeast to Sig Walker's camp. Arriving, we began to check it out. Usually when I'm checking a camp to see if there's any illegal contraband or whatever, I go out from the yard area. Then I step back into the bush and walk in a circle completely outside the lawn area. That way I can see if there are any trails that leave the campsite.

Well, in making this circle, sure enough, I came across what I considered to be a sign of a fresh trail. So I followed it out, and it went to a big tree. I looked up in the tree, and there's a croker sack hanging just full of something. I got up in the tree and pulled it down. Sure enough, it was a sack of alligator hides! Oh, boy, I'm going to make a catch on Sig Walker now, and he was a rough, rough poacher to catch.

So I put the hides back. I went back to the camp and told Jimmy

Jordan and Dave Bowman what I had found. (That proved to be a great mistake!) I figured, well, we'll be going back into town with the weasel so I'll contact my helicopter pilot, and he can fly me back out there and drop me off. I'll just sit out here and wait for Sig Walker to come back and pick up the alligator hides!

Leaving Sig's camp, we were careful not to leave any signs and took his main route out. I marked the trail with particular twigs and sticks that would let me know if anybody else had come back into the area after we left.

I got back in town and contacted our helicopter pilot and told him I'd like to get back out there immediately. Unfortunately, the pilot was in the shop making repairs on the helicopter. He wouldn't be through until the next day.

Well, I was upset. I knew time was against us. But I had no choice but to wait until the following day.

We took off early the next morning. We flew over Sig Walker's camp, but as we were setting down, I saw these little tire tracks. Apparently Sig had gone out to his camp in a little old scooter of some sort. He had picked up those alligator skins and left before I got back out there!

I felt a strong suspicion that someone had tipped off Sig. Could it have been one of *my* men? It seemed like everybody worked with Sig, tipping him off, giving him information. As a result, it was very hard for me to make a good case against my old friend Sig Walker. So I just had to chalk up another one for Sig. We'd just have to try again.

One night soon after, Jimmy Jordan and I went to Loop Road to check the airboats that go out there frogging and sometimes engage in illegal activities as well. When we identified the tags on one vehicle, they checked out to be registered to Sig Walker!

We stayed back in the dark. The procedure was that I would go ahead and check the airboat when it came in. And I told Jimmy, "Now you go on down there farther east down the road and you stay in the bushes. Probably what will happen is that Sig will let somebody out with the alligator skins and you'll see him. I'll check out the airboat when it comes in, and, of course, I'll find nothing. When Sig drives on down the road, then the fellow with the skins will jump in the vehicle and they'll be home free." That was our plan.

"SIG WALKER"
The Hunted

Sigsbee F. Walker Sr. was an acquaintance of mine who had supported me in becoming a game officer. Sig had been a game warden himself. Then he worked as a stand-in for the star of the popular TV series *Lincoln Vail of the Everglades*. But Sig became a notorious alligator poacher and head of a lucrative organized poaching and moonshine operation. He proved to be a most elusive opponent during my employment, as he had so many friends and tipsters that it was difficult to catch him red-handed for prosecution. He became number 1 on my "most wanted" list. (Shirley Collection.)

Sure enough, Sig Walker came in, and I politely checked out his boat. We talked about old times, mutual friends, and so forth. I eventually left to walk to my vehicle, which was parked farther west.

Meantime, Jimmy Jordan came back, and I saw another fellow with Sig. We walked on down the road, and I asked Jimmy where the other fellow had come out of the bushes.

He said, "About 50 yards from the landing. Well, right about here."

And I said, "Well, that's where the skins are."

So I shone the light down there, and sure enough, there was a sack full of alligator skins; and there was also positive proof—a .22 rifle with Sig Walker's initials carved into the butt!

But just to cover all bases, I wanted to get the fingerprints on the gun checked. So I gave it to Jimmy Jordan to take to the crime lab in the morning, as he lived closer to it than I did.

Great! We had a strong case now. With a firm fingerprint check, we'd have Sig Walker nailed!

But two days later, I asked Jimmy, "What about the gun?"

"Oh," he said, "We just got it back from the crime lab and they couldn't find any prints on it."

I said, "Oh, hell!"

Sometime after that, I got a call in the night from my other wildlife officers, Gary Phelps, George Eddy, and one of our Game Management employees, Wayne Cohen. They claimed that they had just had a run-in with Sig Walker and Ed Westbrook. The officers had stopped them on Highway 27 after they'd watched them load up their airboats and so forth. They were sure that the men had been alligator poaching.

They wanted to look inside the trunk of Sig Walker's car. And Walker had first given them a lot of static, but when they gained access, there weren't any gator skins. The officers felt that Sig must have stashed them and would probably come back the next night to get them.

I thought, "I think I'll get involved this time!"

So I went out to what they call Joe Moe City. It was a little gas station at the junction of Highway 84 and Highway 27. I pulled in there to get fuel. I had my gun and gun belt unfastened and lying in my front seat.

But as I pulled up I saw Sig Walker's wife and Westbrook's wife in a vehicle there. I figured something was going on.

And I thought, "I've got to get out of here fast!"

So I got out of my car, left my gun and gun belt, and ran on foot all the way down to the airboat landing about three-quarters of a mile north.

I stayed in the dark waiting for somebody to come to the landing and pick up some hides or drop off some hides. I waited there for quite a while.

Well, along came Sig Walker in the car with the two girls, Tommy Williams, and Ed Westbrook. They were looking for me. They would drive around and look. This kept on for the better part of two hours. Meanwhile, Gary Phelps and Wayne Cohen were up on Highway 27 watching to see what Sig Walker was going to do.

Well, Wayne Cohen had a problem back then. He stuttered pretty badly. He came up to the landing where I was hiding in the dark, and I said, "Did you see Sig Walker go?"

And he was trying to tell me which way he was going. He just made sounds like, "Dat, dat, dat!"

I said with some frustration, "Tell me which way he was going!"

He was excited and stuttering so bad that he couldn't get it out.

Frustrated, I said, "Hell, just point!"

So he pointed south.

Well, OK! I told him to go ahead and leave. So I'm continuing to hide in the bushes, and sure enough, after a while (and by then it was getting on, about two thirty or three o'clock in the morning), somebody pulls up and gets out of a vehicle, walks down to the airboat landing, and picks up something out of the bushes!

Well, I figured this is it, so I jumped out. Meanwhile, Sig rushed back to the car and slammed the doors!

I said, "OK, you all have to get out. You're in a Management Area. And I have authority to check your vehicle. I suspect you might be in violation."

They said they weren't going to get out at first. Then after talking, they decided OK, and they opened the doors.

I went around to the driver's side. The door was open, but then Sig hollered out, "All right, lock it up, quick!"

So they slammed that door. Well, my hand was in the doorway so they had slammed the door right on my hand, which was now hung up in the door! They opened the door a crack, so at least I got my hand out!

They just sat there. They weren't going to get out; they weren't going to pay any attention to me.

Well, I was in a bind. They could just drive off, and there was nothing I could do. But I sure wanted to see what they'd picked up from the airboat landing. So I just raised the car's hood and took the coil wire out! With no recourse, after a while, they let me search the vehicle. But there wasn't anything but a raincoat. They had just baited me out.

So Sig and his wife made a comment that they were going to file suit against me for pushing them down the levee! Pushing them down the levee?

I said, "OK, if that's what you want to, that's what we'll do. I'm going to go ahead and put you under arrest for "resisting arrest!" which I did.

I took them all and put them under arrest, and to save myself from any other problems, I took the two women to the hospital. I demanded that a doctor examine them to show proof that there were no bodily injuries whatsoever! Boy, they didn't like that. They gave me a bunch of static, but that's the way I followed through with this incident.

Finally, this case came up in court. I explained what had happened to Judge Lambert, a Broward County judge who knew me personally. He was upset and quite concerned when I had told him about the consistency of illegal activities in which Sig and these other fellows were engaged.

When I was nineteen years old, I was involved in an accident involving a 12-gauge shotgun that went off and blew off two fingers on my left hand. So, during my testimony in Broward County Court, I was telling how I attempted to search Sig Walker's car and how in the ruckus they slammed the door on my hand.

The judge asked me, "Well, did it hurt?"

I innocently raised up my left hand, the one missing two fingers, and said, "Nah, it didn't hurt."

The jury gasped and got wide-eyed, then looked at one another as if to say, "My goodness, it must have been awful for him!"

The judge rolled his eyes, but nothing more was said. And Sig and company were found guilty as charged!

Buyers and Sellers

Alligator poaching continued to be the number-one priority of my job. I had enlisted a friend to be one of my informers. He worked with the other poachers, was around them all the time, heard their discussions, and reported their violations to me. He was invaluable to my work.

Well, he met with me and told me about a hide buyer named Regan. Regan came from Ocala, and he traveled south through the state picking up alligator skins from various poachers. He was going to be coming down to our area on the following Thursday.

Regan had a brand-new white Cadillac. He had it undercoated inside of the back trunk area. And he had airlift shocks put on it so he could carry a heavy load. We figured we'd be waiting for him.

I acquired his tag number, vehicle identification, and a description of the white Cadillac and reported it to the Highway Patrol. Troopers put out a bulletin with instructions not to stop him unless he was going north. If he was headed north, that would mean he had the gator skins with him.

I gathered up my officers and stationed some on U.S. Highway 27 and some way out on the Tamiami Trail, Highway 41.

We waited all day for word from the Highway Patrol. When we sent out that bulletin, I thought sure we'd pick him up in a short time, but late that afternoon, we got a call from my informer, telling me Regan was pretty tricky. He had evidently changed auto tags, so the tag we had given out on the bulletin was incorrect.

By this time, Sig Walker was not only one of the most notorious gator poachers around, but he was heading up an entire organization! And, it was quite effective because he had so many friends who were willing to work with him as he was just a friendly, cordial, and kind man, very likeable. He was also successful because of all of his knowledge as an ex–game warden.

Well, this one particular night, the poachers had launched an airboat out from Andytown. This was a little place, west of U.S. Highway 27, north of the junction of 84. They put in the airboats and went westward, hunting the Everglades' western canals.

They had pretty good luck. They killed about a dozen or so alligators and skinned them out. Everything was going pretty good. They could skin a 6-footer in an average of seven and half minutes. That's pretty fast.

Well, this was exactly what happened one night. All was clear, and the poachers were going down U.S. Highway 27 in Tommy Williams's vehicle, which was a '49 Chevy convertible, heading south toward Miami.

Wildlife Officers Gary Phelps, George Eddy, and Wayne Comb went to pull them over and search the vehicle, having the authority to search any vehicles leaving or entering Wildlife Management Areas. When they finally stopped the vehicle and the officers began to search it, the presumed poachers began to give the three officers a lot of static.

Well, years after I retired, I interviewed Tommy Williams and found out just what went on that night. Quite a story! They had actually had the alligator skins lying on the floor in front of the backseat! Meanwhile, the wildlife officers had been adamant about getting into the trunk, where they assumed the hides would be hidden! Tommy Williams had stayed in the car. He'd pitched the skins into the front seat while the officers were at the back. Then, anxious to get the officers away from the vehicle so he could hide the skins, he told Sig Walker and Eddy, "Get back there and start a fight; get them away from this vehicle!"

So Eddy Westbrook went back and started a fight by pushing Officer George Eddy around. It had the right effect as a diversion, taking all of the attention away from the vehicle!

Just the day before, Tommy Williams had taken out the floorboards in order to repair the transmission. He'd taken the floorboards out and just put the screws in finger tight. Now, he was real busy because he had the idea that he could take the alligator hides and wrap them up around the transmission! He finally got the floorboards out, but here came the game wardens back again!

So Tommy said, "Go back there and start another fight, I've gotta have some more time to hide these skins, I gotta have more time! You've gotta get 'em back there. Start another fight!"

So Eddy went back there and continued where he'd left off, pushing another of the officers around. Tommy was able to wrap those skins around the transmission and put the floorboards back!

Then, as soon as the ruckus in the rear settled back down, the officers came up and searched the car, but they couldn't find any skins.

The search over, the poachers were allowed to leave. They pulled off down the road, but as they did, one of the skins fell off the transmission right onto the highway! The wildlife officers had their backs to it, as they were going back to their vehicles. Tommy saw the skin lying out on the highway. He slammed his car into reverse, backed over it, and just sat there with the vehicle over the skin until the officers left.

That was sure a real close call for those poachers! But Sig Walker and his buddies got away with the skins, about a dozen of them at $27.50 per foot!

Getting Tough—1963

In total frustration over the Sig Walker situation, I made up a list of the ten poachers I most wanted to catch. You can bet that Sig

Walker—past president of the Everglades Conservation and Sports-man's Club and all-round great guy; handsome stand-in for TV star Ron Hayes in the popular 1961–62 season show *Lincoln Vail of the Ev-erglades*; and notorious alligator poacher and moonshiner—was near the top of my list!

I had become gradually more suspicious that it might be my own men who were alerting Sig of future busts (as you may have guessed from some of my previous comments). Like I've said, Sig was real like-able. And he was running a big, lucrative operation—surely a tempta-tion for my men.

So that day in court I was real pleased when Judge Lambert had found Sig, Tommy Williams, Ed Westbrook, and their two wives guilty as charged for "resisting arrest" in the pre-sentence investigation. The judge was so enthused, in fact, that he invited me to meet his wife af-ter the court session, which I felt was an honor and certainly seemed positive for the outcome of our case.

But later, after Judge Lambert read the pre-sentence investigation report, which noted that Sig had been a stand-in for the TV star Ron Hayes (as Constable Lincoln Vail), he took it upon himself to rule on a lower sentence for Sig.

Man, I just couldn't win!

Now, with my "most wanted" list in hand and a good group of hand-picked officers behind me, word got back to Sig that we were really out to shut down his operation. Apparently, he began to feel threatened, worried that sooner or later Tom Shirley was going to get him. Rumor had it that he was sweating it out.

I guess Sig was trying to protect his fine public image, so he decided he would do something about it. In August, he spoke to my superiors, Lou (Louis F.) Gainey at the regional office in West Palm Beach and also to Tom (W. Thomas) McBroom. Then he sent a formal letter of complaint to the director of the Game and Fresh Water Fish Commis-sion, A. D. Aldrich, in Tallahassee. In the letter he complained about the "unlawful Gestapo methods . . . still being used, under the direc-tion of your Lt. Tom Shirley" and asked for "an immediate investiga-tion into the matter."

His detailed description of the fictional "violation" incident was pure fabrication. Sig closed the letter by threatening the Commission.

He said he would get "an audience with the Grand Jury," and "an appointment with the Federal Bureau of Investigation on the matter covering violation of Civil Rights."

On September 7, I fired back a letter to the Commission's assistant director, Earl Frye. I reminded him how in 1962 there had been a major shakeup in the Naples area that broke up a gang of wildlife officers who had been actively selling wildlife to commercial interests. I noted that those "non-dedicated" officers had been terminated. I further reminded him that, "Now, a year later, we have the good fortune of having hardworking dedicated officers who are bringing an end to this illegal organized group of commercial violators." I continued: "Mr. Sigsbee Walker has influenced both Commission employees and ex-employees to participate in his illegal operation during the last seven years. Mr. Walker has the reputation of being the slickest operator around with the right connections, who will never be caught and this is why our own personnel have joined him.

"Mr. Walker now knows that we are aware of his organization and activities and knows that if he cannot successfully discourage, transfer, or knock out our opposition in any manner, that his operation cannot exist. Therefore, the closer we get to him the louder he will scream. Mr. Walker is using and will continue to use all possible influence knowing that these moves will make or break him. This is the price the Commission must face and pay if they wish to exterminate his influential power which has caused corruption within our own Commission personnel."

The Commission was upset enough over Sig's letter to make the decision to order lie detector tests for some of my men. I was incensed over this, and in that same letter, I questioned:

"Are the investigators or the Commission willing to ask Mr. Walker to take the polygraph test [as] to his activities contrary to the Game Commission's rules and regulations? I realize this movement may embarrass Mr. Walker as it did our officers.

"There is not one man in my area who would refuse to take this polygraph test if I requested him to, but I find it unnecessary and against principles without cause."

I concluded:

"I would hate the sportsmen within my area to know that this request was made of my officers as we have been stressing the importance of teamwork among our officers and sportsmen club members to become better organized to do a better job. Wildlife in the Everglades will someday be history and we are trying to extend this period which is invaluable and we need all phases of support possible."

The Game and Fresh Water Fish Commission's Law Enforcement brass were very concerned about whether they were going to have to deal with the FBI investigating Tom Shirley.

Well, the next thing you know, Sig Walker gave me a call!

He said, "Tom, you know, I like you. I think the world of you, but I have to sue you and the Game Commission for $2.5 million."

I said pretty much what I always did when people told me what they were going to do. I said calmly, "Well, do whatever you think is necessary."

But what was comical—well, not comical, ridiculous—was that Sig started spreading the word about what a good guy he was and how that bad Tom Shirley was trying to catch him with alligator skins!

He began to make the rounds at the sportsmen's clubs, bad-mouthing me. His wife went to the Dade County Airboat Association club meeting, which in those days was basically a "redneck" airboat meeting, all dressed up in fur and high heels. That seemed sort of comical, too, as if she was trying to put on airs and make a very good impression. She also was repeating the story that I pushed her down the levee that night when they resisted arrest!

Well, for the better part of two years these rumors circulated that weren't favorable to me at all. The big questions were, "Is Sig Walker a gator poacher or not?" and, "Why is Lt. Tom Shirley saying that he is?" Even though it was widely known that Sig was a major poacher, I needed indisputable proof to take to court. And I didn't have it!

A heartfelt offer was made by another friend, Paul Ledbetter, who said, "Tom, if it comes down to it, if need be, I'll go and testify that I have hunted alligator with Sig Walker. So that will clear your name. You can depend on me going straight forward and helping you out on this deal, because you don't deserve this." Well, that was a kindly offer, but I really wanted to get the goods on Sig myself, once and for all.

But it sure was hard to do, with all of his informants out there. And years later, after I had retired from the Commission, Sig's poaching buddy Tommy Williams leveled with me: "Hell, Tom, Sig had more personnel working with him than *you* did!"

Of course, this situation made for a very stressful time for me and could have created serious problems for both me and the Commission. It was hard enough to realize that I couldn't trust my own, the Commission's own, personnel. There could be no teamwork among us, as I had to keep my guard up and work alone. And as you can imagine, even obtaining solid proof of my men's disloyalty to the Commission was a difficult enough task. And once I had the proof to fire them, I'd then have the difficulty of making sure that I could hire fellows who also wouldn't let the Commission down. What a dilemma!

Getting Tougher

We had an interesting thing going on. I continued to try to obtain undercover information on individuals who were working with other poachers, such as Sig Walker. We managed to get one individual out of jail up in Palm Beach County through the efforts of Lt. Elliott Lott. He was able to get the individual and send him south to me in the Everglades, where I knew him as "Bob Craig." He was an exceptionally good alligator poacher. He had done most of his hunting up in Palm Beach County but often came down throughout the Everglades region as well.

The Commission had a supply of alligator skins that we had accumulated over a period of time from taking nuisance alligators. So I supplied Craig with alligator skins to see if he could find individual buyers. And so he did. He even went to Sig Walker, who purchased a few of the alligator skins.

But Bob Craig was always getting into trouble. I would get calls from the Sheriff's Department that they had caught Mr. Bob Craig speeding and engaging in other illegal activities. He would tell them that he was working for Lt. Tom Shirley on an undercover mission, and they'd call me for confirmation of his stories. I was getting too many of these calls and couldn't tolerate many more.

I knew this operation was unique and questionable, so I called the regional manager, Lou Gainey, and told him about the plan, and how

I now suspected that my undercover agent Bobby Craig was also probably out killing alligators and selling them to the highest bidder.

Mr. Gainey could not approve such activity himself, so I went ahead I called the Game and Fresh Water Fish Commission's executive director, Earl Frye. I explained the situation to him. He gave me approval to go on with my operation as planned. That was a relief since it eliminated the risk of my getting into trouble myself.

So Craig made several sales and looked into doing business with various individuals. He was able to detect suppliers of alligator skins and buyers. Sig Walker had quite a few in his freezer.

I also got in contact with the State Attorney's Office in Miami and talked to Mr. Steadman, a solicitor I trusted. I explained to him about my plan. I wanted to go by legal procedures, such as getting a search warrant. Steadman told me that I could not get a legal search warrant for alligator skins. The warrant had to be for various types of drugs or contraband, such as moonshine. Well, Sig Walker was also in the moonshine business.

Steadman reiterated that I couldn't go in unless the lawbreaker definitely had the products that he mentioned. So I went about trying to plan a set up where I would have proof that Sig Walker had moonshine in his house. Then I would be legally safe.

At the time, I had no information on who around town bought or sold moonshine. I contacted Alcohol and Tobacco. They put me in contact with an informant. I met this man, a large individual who was blind in one eye, at his home in Hialeah's Colored Town section. We sat out in folding chairs at a round metal table in the grassless front yard; extremely friendly girls were constantly coming and going in and out of the house.

I told him about my plan, that I needed somebody to go purchase some moonshine. He said, "Well, I know Mr. Sig Walker. I've purchased moonshine from him before."

Well, that was great! My next move was to obtain information that would assure me that Sig Walker would have moonshine *and* alligator hides at the same time. Bobby Craig was at Sig Walker's house that evening. While they were talking business, lo and behold, Bob Thompson, one of my undercover officers, came in and was talking very friendly with Sig Walker.

Now, I had hired Mr. Thompson months before. It was top secret that he had been hired to go undercover for me. He would write monthly reports, sending them directly to me and to nobody else. It was such a top-secret mission that even my wildlife officers didn't know that he was working for me. He wore no uniform and drove a plain vehicle. But I was getting information from him that I wouldn't have been able to obtain any other way.

However, while Craig was there with Sig Walker, he reported to me that Thompson proceeded to tell Sig Walker the locations where we were patrolling! So Thompson was a "double agent" informing for both me and Walker! Well, that really upset me—another problem in a long line of problems I would have to deal with.

I went to another informer's house in Colored Town, where my first contact had referred me. This guy was known by his first name, Buck. As with my first contact, we also sat in his front yard, making final plans for him to try to purchase moonshine from Sig Walker. As we were sitting there, he had his portable radio on.

While we listened to the radio, the news came on that President Kennedy had just been shot. "Shots were fired!" was what they said at that time. The news media said everybody was pointing toward a sand hill where they heard the shots.

Buck and I just kept talking. But as time went on, Buck began to get very nervous, very upset. It really blew his mind when he heard that Kennedy had been shot. He said Kennedy was the blacks' "last hope for freedom."

He told me that he was a member of a body of four hundred to five hundred individuals scattered throughout the country. Buck talked like he was very involved with this private club. The only thing I could think of was that he was talking about the Black Panthers, which I had heard about in the news.

As time went by, he got even more agitated. He went into his house and brought out a gallon jug of moonshine. He sat there and poured himself a healthy glass.

We were listening to the radio, very tense—both of us. We didn't know whether Kennedy was going to die or whether he was just wounded, but as we sat there Buck got more drunk and more angry.

Then, he went back in the house and he brought out a chrome-plated

.45 automatic, slammed it down on the table and said, "The mission of the club . . . We have people scattered out through the United States . . . The mission is to kill two white people for every one of us. If we carry out that mission, the mission would be complete." He picked up the .45 and slammed it down again. He was steadily getting more and more violent as the moonshine took effect. And, he kept looking at the .45 automatic.

At that point, we weren't talking business any more. We were totally wrapped up in the media reports. Buck kept saying that Kennedy was very much aware of their good membership in this organization and that they were capable of being extremely violent. He told me that they had all of the equipment to do a great job within the United States.

He kept repeating, "All I have to do is kill two people."

Well, since he kept repeating that, and seeing his condition deteriorate as he got more drunk, I figured my best bet was to just ease out of there before he decided to shoot me and somebody else.

I was going down the Tamiami Trail—I remember that quite well. I was headed west on U.S. 41 at about 107th Street, and it came over the radio that President Kennedy had died.

Receiving that horrible information upset me terribly, as it did people throughout the nation. And considering all of the events of the day—including the shock of finding that my friend and associate Thompson was also an informant for Sig Walker—I figured it was best to just scrap the whole operation!

And so Sig Walker walked away again, a free man.

I fired Officer Thompson. I went by his home and told him to report to West Palm Beach and turn in all his equipment, his vehicle, and his airboat. He was highly upset, of course. He actually went so far as to contact a well-known attorney, and they went to Tallahassee for the purpose of getting me fired! There they met with the director and Earl Frye. But the director and Earl Frye backed me up for having Thompson fired. So everything worked out well, considering.

Not too long after, I understand that Sig developed a heart condition and was not going out into the woods anymore. He ended up moving to Immokalee, building airboats, and living close to the reserve—Fakahatchee Strand, I believe it was. I wondered if he was still operating his alligator hide business. But I had not heard any rumors that he had. I think he just decided to get out of the poaching business.

Then one night I received a phone call that Sig had been struck by lightning and had almost been killed. So I called him up immediately to see how he was doing. The odd thing about it was that his airboat had lightning strikes painted on the side of it. That was the name of his boat, *Lightning Strikes*!

Well, unfortunately, this accident affected Sig's mental abilities. His health began to fail, and he died. I went to his funeral. It was sad to see him lying there. He had a lot of friends, and I know a lot of people miss him to this day.

Big Alligators

One of the most memorable big alligators I've known was that 12-foot alligator that pulled the 1⅛-inch pipe down into his den, rolled, and wrapped it tight as a wet rope around his snout (see cover photo). Some real power there! When I talked to various Gladesmen as I made my rounds, the question inevitably came up, "What's the biggest alligator you've ever seen?"

Well, Joxey Redding at the Blue Shanty on the Tamiami Trail had an awful lot of experience with alligators, and he would venture way on down south, around the Ten Thousand Islands, to a place where there were a lot of them. He told me that some of them just died of old age there. And he claimed the biggest alligator he'd ever seen was 17 feet. Now that's a big alligator! There was another individual by the name of Ray Kramer. Ray did a lot of fishing in a particular area in the mangroves and the brackish water, which opens up into the salt water. He said that he saw an alligator that he knows was 20 feet long. He also said that he got on an alligator's back that he knows was 20 feet long! He straddled it, sat on that gator's back, and his feet didn't even touch the ground. That was a huge alligator!

There are reports of alligators that did exceed 20 feet in the very early years. But the largest one that I've ever experienced myself, we caught and measured on an alligator complaint.

A hysterical woman had called us from Plantation, Florida. That morning she was all ready to go to work. She walked through her

I'm looking down the throat of a 15-foot alligator. (Photo by Toby Massey.)

utility room to get to her Volkswagen, which was parked in the garage, and when she did, a huge 14-foot 4-inch alligator came alive! It had come into her utility room through the carport. He began thrashing about, knocking into the washing machine, the drier, the freezer! He was as scared of her as she was of him. She phoned the Game Commission, gathered up her three children, and took refuge in the bathroom.

Meanwhile, the huge alligator made it back to the carport and hid underneath the Volkswagen. When Officer Conley Campbell responded, he saw a huge and very scared gator under the little car. The gator was so large and so powerful that he picked up the little Volkswagen. In fact, they thought he was going to run off with it on his back! Conley had never seen such a monstrous alligator.

Conley called the Fire Department for help. It took four officers to get the gator into Conley's Game Commission truck. This "problem" gator found a new home at Aquaglades Tourist Attraction on State Road 84 in Ft. Lauderdale. They had alligators and other animals, and the owner, Bill McCullough, also wrestled alligators there.

This story has an interesting side to it. Officer Campbell had been called out just the day before on an alligator complaint. He caught an aggressive 9-foot black alligator in very good shape and delivered it to Aquaglades. Bill McCullough released the 9-footer into a pool.

So Conley and Bill put the 14-footer in the pool with the 9-footer at Aquaglades. The next morning, I went to see Bill at his home for a morning cup of coffee, and then we went see the alligators. We were surprised to see the 14-footer all alone in the pen. He had *eaten* the 9-footer, which now was a lump in his belly! This enormous alligator had then crawled up on the cement platform by the pond and did not move for two weeks while he digested his meal.

He was truly huge. It looked like his back stood up maybe about 30 inches off the ground. This was an enormous alligator with much too much power.

While taking my airboat out on night patrol, I would travel up the Mud Canal about 15 miles north of Mack's Fish Camp. At the entrance to a willow strand that crosses the Mud Canal, the props of the many airboats that passed that way over time had cut a pathway that looked just like a tunnel that went for close to 100 yards.

There was a big alligator that stayed right at the entrance of that tunnel. I guess he caught different animals that came walking through the shallow ditch. He was one of the biggest alligators I've ever seen. On numerous occasions I would approach that tunnel, and sometimes I'd be clipping along pretty good at 60, 70 miles per hour or faster. Either he'd be underwater or maybe I just didn't see him until I got there, but as I approached, he'd come raring up out of the water! And I mean, he was enormous. His head looked like he'd be about the size of a hippopotamus.

Why he would jump out of the water like that, I don't know, but if my airboat had struck him, it would've been like me running into a concrete wall. So, ultimately, I remembered to be cautious each time I went through there. He could have surely torn up my airboat, or if he was really in a bad mood, he could've ripped the cage or the grass roll right off! I hate to think what he'd have done to ME!

I remember one night, Gary Phelps was with me, and I approached the willow strand entrance real easy because I wanted to show that alligator to Gary. As I approached, sure enough, there he was. He was lying on top of the water. Well, as I pulled up there, I saw there was another smaller alligator about 4 feet, and he was lying on the back of the large alligator.

I said, "Here, Gary," as I pulled up there. "Look at that alligator. See how big it is?"

So as we were looking, he said, "Well, Tom, that ain't very big. He's not very big at all. I'd say he's about a 4-footer."

"Look closer," I said.

This alligator was *so* big that Gary couldn't put it all together. Finally I pointed out the head of that alligator, and Gary just about fell over! He'd never seen an alligator that big!

I never had the opportunity to measure that gator, but the airboat was 12 feet plus 2 or 3 feet for the grass roll. The alligator was easily longer than the whole boat put together. He was enormous—my estimate would be 16 feet.

Then there was another one, truly the biggest I'd ever seen. A helicopter pilot and I were patrolling. We were headed south by the Miami Canal again, which was a real heavy alligator hangout. We were just about 2 miles south of the Broward and Palm Beach County line. We were headed south in the helicopter, and I was looking down.

At first I thought I saw a great big boulder, so I told the pilot to whip around there. "Was that a boulder or an alligator?" I wondered.

So we whipped around, and this alligator, I mean, he was a monster. He could've gone at least—and I say "at least"—17 feet. I've never seen one so gigantic. We turned around twice, but he went down during the last circle. He was a monster!

Something else that was sort of peculiar and strange . . . When we'd be patrolling by helicopter up and down the Mud Canal, as I looked behind the helicopter, I could see all these alligators bellowing. You should have seen the water just dancing off their backs 6 to 7 inches high! There's something about the noise, the frequency level of the helicopter engine or blades, that really set the males off, really turned them on. It was always a sight to look behind and watch the water vibrating off the gators all along the canal.

I had to keep a fire at the Grapefruit Head all night as it helped keep the alligators away. There was one 12-footer that in my early Commission days hung out right at the junction where the Weasel Trail crosses the Mud Canal. He stayed there throughout the duration of my employment.

During the mating season, the alligator males start bellowing. That's a deep, rumbling sound. You can hear it for miles; it's really something to hear. During the mating season, along the Mud Canal, there were hundreds of alligators, of course, and they'd be bellowing all night, so heavily that it would be hard for me to sleep.

After I retired from the Commission, letting bygones be bygones, I talked to Tommy Williams, Sig's poacher buddy and my former officer. I said, "Tommy, how about telling some of the old stories? What's the most alligators that you guys got in one night?"

He said, "Well, Sig Walker and I, we got 70 in one night. Our favorite time to hunt was in hurricane season, just before a hurricane hit! We knew that everybody was going to be busy making preparations for either before or after the storm. Well, that was our favorite time to go poaching."

That they did. They took their airboats south of the Tamiami Trail. They knew the route in the area of the Tentacle Rocks, and they knew it fairly well eastward. So as night fell, they entered the western part of the Everglades National Park, knowing that the park personnel would be busy taking care of preparing the buildings, vehicles, and boats, or would have left to see to their own homes and families.

They had the two airboats and the whole place to themselves like never before. There were a lot of alligators to the south. They went on back into what they call the Eleven-Mile Road that goes farther into the park. There's an observation tower and a pond, where the state had piled up an awful lot of alligators for the tourists because there was water there year-round. I was there myself one time, and I counted 110 alligators while I was just standing in one place. It was truly an alligator's paradise. I imagine that's one of the places they hit.

I asked Tommy, "What's the largest alligator you've ever killed?"

He recalled, "Well, north of Tamiami Trail there's a canal that runs parallel east and west. Just east of Betty and Johnny's Levee. There's an awful lot of alligators in there."

So they were running one night. They shot one, killed him, and he was 14-foot 3 inches long! Tommy was in good shape, but that's an enormous alligator. He was too big and heavy to get him in the boat!

So he had to skin him and take care of all of the preparation while he was still in the water. A lot of times, you've got to get in the water, depending on how deep it is, to skin a heavy gator.

Anyway, they skinned out the big 14-foot 3-inch gator in the water. Then they looked a bit farther, and there was another big alligator, so they shot him. He was even larger, 14 foot 6 inches! A hide that big is very cumbersome to handle—at 4 feet across it would be heavy, hard to hide from a game warden, maybe even hard to sell. There's a lot of work to skin a big one, and it's not really worth the effort. Their hides aren't worth all that much because their hide is full of "buttons."

They would shoot for a while, peel some gator skin, and then go back to shooting again. They sure had a good night's hunt. Seventy gators in one night—that's a lot of skinning to do! But figuring $27.50 per foot, that's a lot of money for one night's work!

Wild Bill

This evening turned out to be one of the busiest evenings I ever spent. I had gator poachers running out of my ears. I pulled up to Mack's Fish Camp, and I saw this vehicle from Monroe County. I knew that meant problems.

I ran its tag, and sure enough, it was one of the major gator poachers out of Everglades City, so I knew my hands would be full with him. Well, I left there, as it was early in the afternoon, and I figured I'd check around and see what else I could find.

I went to Betty and Johnny's Levee (named for a nearby honky-tonk), which runs from Tamiami Trail (Highway 41) all the way northward to Mack's Fish Camp and joins with the Miami Canal. Along Betty and Johnny's Levee there's a canal that produces much, much wildlife—rabbits by the thousands.

So much game and wildlife was found there—bobcats, coons, possums, deer, hogs; even panthers were reported. And it was an excellent place for the gator poachers because along the shallow canal bordered by the spoil road, there was an abundance of alligators.

On this levee, there was also the fire tower that I was stuck in during the tornado. I'm guessing that it was put there by the Graham Corporation. Ernest (Cap) Graham in the early years grew sugarcane on his Pensuco Sugar plantation, which in later years, became Graham's Dairy.

There was a canal running from the Graham homestead westward to this levee. I had a key, and as I mentioned, I used this fire tower quite often as an outlook to see across the Everglades and spot the alligator hunters or whoever was poaching or hunting with a light. This evening, after traveling up the levee, I got to the tower, climbed up, and looked eastward. I saw a couple of lights working in the canal there.

The way they were working their lights, it sure looked like they were hunting alligators. In order to get the poachers closer to me, I used Ballantine Ale cans as decoys. Those were my favorite because when you "shine" them with a light, they have a real red tint to them, the exact color of an alligator's eyes. So I took two of those cans and stuck them into the soft muck just above the waterline in the canal. Hopefully, those poachers would shine the light on those cans and, thinking it was an alligator, come on up to it.

Well, sure enough, I no sooner got those cans placed than boy, they opened fire! I had to run for cover! They were only about 100 yards off, and they were working closer and closer, and when they finally got right up close, I stepped out of the bushes. I was planning to put them under arrest for hunting with a spotlight. But it was only a couple of kids! This experience shook them up, of course, but it shook me up, too, because they almost shot me!

So I showed them the beer cans that they were shooting at, and we all had a big laugh!

I said, "Why don't you all just clear out of here? I've got business to take care of here tonight. There's some activity going on here that I want to check out."

After the kids left, I went on ahead and climbed the fire tower again. I waited up there about forty-five minutes or so looking southward. Sure enough, I saw another light sweeping across the canal in the Everglades area.

So I climbed down, went back around, and drove down the Tamiami Trail. I found their vehicle and checked out the tag and looked inside. I saw some old hooks and lines and so forth—same type of equipment that alligator poachers use. Then I saw where somebody had tied up a boat and slid it into the canal. So I got in my vehicle and rode down the levee with my lights out.

It isn't easy trying to creep up on poachers in a situation like this, but I did it very slowly and quietly. And as I neared them, I watched a man kill about a 6-foot alligator. He shot it and pulled it into the canoe he had built. It was a little kayak-type boat, with an open hull, that he poled. In fact, he was one of the best boat polers around. I was hoping he would come to my side of the canal to skin the alligator, but he kept moving on down the canal.

Then he turned down a canal that branched westward off this one. Well, that kept me from getting to him at all.

I thought it was best to wait for him back at the landing and catch him when he returned to his vehicle on the Tamiami Trail.

That gave me time to race home and get my personal vehicle—a '49 Oldsmobile that wouldn't be recognizable—change my clothes, grab a fishing pole, and race back as fast as I could. I got there just before sunup and began fishing not too far from where he was going to put in.

Here he came! I cast out my line again. And he watched me for a while, but it worked. He wasn't expecting any trouble so he walked down the levee with his sack full of alligator hides and began to load up his boat. I was waiting for the last moment in case he was working with another fellow. When he finished, I walked over to see what he had.

I took his alligators, his gun, and so forth. I put him under arrest. His name was Bill Schoelerman, known as "Wild Bill." He was one of the most famous poachers around the Loop Road and in Monroe, Dade, and Broward Counties. I took all of his equipment, including his homemade boat.

So we went to court. Before my case came up, my boss, J. O. Brown, had a previous case stemming from his arrest of Bill for possession of a crocodile. And we were both surprised when Schoelerman got up and acted as his own attorney!

He did a great job. He was like a Philadelphia lawyer, but he was dressed in a cowboy hat, dungarees, and cowboy boots. And I tell you, he acted and sounded like a great attorney presenting his case, pacing up and down. Any pioneer attorney would have been proud of him. So he fought the case, and he was quick to point out how he was a good fellow. How he worked with the National Park Service and was a member in good standing of the Audubon Society. Why, you would have just thought that he was a wonderful guy!

And he pled "not guilty"!

Well, the judge found him "not guilty"!

OK, my testimony came up next.

Well, I had taken pictures of all the items that I confiscated from him: seven alligators, his .22 rifles, and all of his equipment, including his boat. Of course, he knew that I had all the evidence and pictures to prove my case for the Commission. So, after my testimony and the presentation of evidence, the judge asked him, "Are you guilty or not guilty?"

Wild Bill said, "Judge, I'm guilty as charged."

So it went from one extreme to the other. I thought that was pretty amusing.

The judge found him "guilty" and sentenced him to sixty days in jail, which was a pretty stiff penalty in those days.

So Bill went to jail. But he wasn't in too long—just about ten or fifteen days. He was a real sweet talker. He talked the judge into releasing him on his own recognizance for the Christmas holidays. Well, Christmas came and went, but old Wild Bill never showed up again. I don't know what happened.

Next, Bill sweet-talked the National Park Service. They got behind him and wanted me to support him to become a wildlife officer. But I knew that when people go gator hunting, it's just something in their blood that they can't seem to get out. I didn't need any more problems than I already had, sometimes catching my own officers killing alligators and then having to fire them, so I couldn't support Wild Bill.

Sure enough, Wild Bill went on back to gator poaching. He poached until the federal regulations were passed in the 1970s that prohibited the taking or manufacture of crocodilian goods and so knocked out alligator hunting altogether. Wild Bill was then out of a job, because gator poaching was the only trade he knew—and he was a good at it. I don't know what he did for a living after that.

Dugan Yates

Dugan Yates was a longtime alligator poacher and hide dealer. He was the individual who had complained to Tallahassee about my Gestapo tactics when I made that surprise check on him, swooping down in the dark in my new, aerodynamic airboat!

Well, two of my officers, George Eddy and Wendell Clemmons, were out patrolling one night. They came across a light working, so they went and checked it out. The fellows were froggers, so they were clean. The officers came back to camp. They were in camp for a few minutes when we heard the engine of an airboat, running to the north of our camp.

Well, that was Dugan. He was still frogging, now in the area where there was a dike. This dike was built to contain a break in the 74-mile-long oil line that ran from the Sunniland/Felda oil fields in southwest Florida across the Everglades to Port Everglades.

I warned George, "When you go out to check him, be careful, because he'll suck you into that dike."

They said they would be careful. So George Eddy and Wendell Clemmons got into the boat, and off they went in the dark.

But Dugan was clever. He knew that territory and he knew those officers of mine were pretty green.

Dugan was on the north side of the dike, and Wendell and George went driving straight to him. They had let Dugan suck them right into that dike!

They hit the levee and almost turned the airboat over. As it was, it turned over on its side. The accident banged up George pretty bad, and he also got a black eye. Wendell ended up in the cage some way, and the prop was banging off his ankle as the engine idled.

They managed to turn the airboat upright, but they couldn't come back to camp because they were so banged up. The rudders were bent and so forth, but at least they lived through that episode. And it sure worked out for Dugan Yates!

It was just lucky for him that George and Wendell didn't get chopped up bad that evening!

I was always anxious to catch Dugan. Once, I received word from an informant that Dugan had a cache of salted hides waiting for market.

With some of my best Game and Fresh Water Commission law officers. *Left to right*: Wendell Clemmons, Jim Sistrunk, Lt. Tom Shirley, Conley Campbell, George Eddy, Rich Albury, Archie Manard, Lonie Bill, and Bud Marcus. These wildlife officers were active during the progressive years, 1966–76, prior to the institution of the forty-hour week. They doubled their forty hours per week because of their hard work and dedication. (Shirley Collection.)

It was eight hundred dollars' worth. But someone tipped him off, and I missed him by minutes! That kind of thing was just some of the frustration in my job.

Earl Dickson the Tracker

One night, I was going out on routine patrol, leaving from Mack's Fish Camp, going west of Highway 27.

Well, to go on that patrol out there, it would be about 55 or 60 miles out, and I would have to run without a light to let the poachers think the area was clean, that there were no game wardens out there, no lights flickering anywhere. So I'd go out there with no lights in the dark.

Well, sure enough, I saw two lights out there working.

And I thought, "I'll try to sneak up on them."

So I cut my engine every so often to see if they were still running; and they cut theirs off every so often for the same reason. It's the usual cat-and-mouse game. I ran a bit, then cut off, and I heard them cut off . . . Uh-oh, they know I'm here!

There was this old fellow. He was a big dude, Earl Dickson. He was a heavy equipment operator, mainly bulldozers, but he loved to gator hunt, just couldn't stop doing it. I'm sure he made more money running a bulldozer than he did hunting alligators, but come the season, he'd just hang up the bulldozers and off to the woods he would go. Gator poaching was in his blood!

Well, I realized that while I was trying to sneak up on Earl Dickson, *he* was going to try to see who I was. So I'm doing all kinds of curlicues in the marsh, running in heavy saw grass strands, wax myrtle thickets, and then I'd shut off. He'd pick up my trail!

And here he came. He was picking up on me. I was going in circles. I was running all sorts of maneuvers, but Dickson was very good. He was one of the best trackers I'd ever run across. So our game went on and on. Now he was tracking for real, getting closer and closer. And now I was really trying to get away!

Well, now he knew for sure that it was me since I was the only one that patrolled that north end of the grass. So I just turned my back and struck out another way. I went on ahead and checked out another airboat.

I pulled alongside of Joxey Redding, catching him totally by surprise. It was real quiet, and I was talking with Joxey. All of a sudden, the lid on the big cargo box mounted on his airboat opened . . . scared me at first! I didn't know what was coming off. Were alligators coming out of there or what?

And out comes the tousled head of Joxey's ten-year-old son! He'd been laying down in that cargo box taking a nap while his Dad was frog hunting.

I was only with Joxey a short time, and here came Earl Dickson. He had tracked me right down! As he pulled up beside me, he said, "Now that I've tracked you down, Tom Shirley, you've made my night!"

Dickson was the first person to make a very large front deck on his airboat. This extra-large decking made it much easier to skin out gators! He was some poacher, but as a tracker, he couldn't be beat!

The Oil Pit

Late one afternoon, I was driving down Thirty-Sixth Street way far west in Miami. I noticed a lot of buzzards not too far off the road. The way they were circling and going down, I felt that they were on some feeding program. So I figured I'd go and investigate.

I found an old, sandy road. I got in among a bunch of old buildings—it looked like a ghost town!

Well, I found the buzzards. They were feeding on a gator carcass. It looked fairly fresh, as if maybe it had been killed the night before.

This place had an unusual set-up. It was an old roundhouse repair place for the steam engines from the early years. I decided that this was the locomotive shop used when laying the railroad tracks for Henry Flagler's railroad to Key West. Just sitting there abandoned. Looking around, you could visualize how busy this place had been in the olden days with its workhouses with stacks, and big, big buildings. The 1935 hurricane had come across the Keys and killed a lot of people, torn up the tracks, and changed the history of Flagler's railroad to Key West—maybe that was why this place had become a ghost town.

I saw recent tracks of vehicles that went up to a dilapidated building. I went inside and could see there was a big oil pit. Apparently this was where the railroad workers had discarded many gallons of oil. The pit was about 10 feet wide and 15 feet long. No telling how deep it was, but it had been here all those years.

Well, I could tell that the poachers had dragged the alligator carcasses in there to dispose of them. Alligators, maybe deer too, were pitched into this big oil vat where they submerged. It was indeed a great place to get rid of the evidence of the carcasses. And it looked like it was used fairly frequently.

There were fresh pieces of gator flesh and blood around. And that proved to me that the poachers had actually been there just the night before, so I figured I'd come out and stake it out. They probably wouldn't hunt two nights in a row, but I'd stake it out anyway. It was Friday night.

So late in the afternoon, about sundown, I came in by another route so I wouldn't leave any fresh tracks where they could see. I scouted around, looking over the perimeter for signs to tell me what route this poacher used, which way his vehicle's tracks came in and exited. It looked to me like they'd come in several different times and from several different directions.

Well, I figured that I'd sit there almost all night, so I had taken my bedroll with me to make myself comfortable. I'd just wait them out. Night came. I just lay there watching the beautiful stars and the clouds and the moon pass by. The owls were really attracted to this place. They knew I was there, and the old barn owls would fly right up over me. I was under an old pine tree, and the barn owls would hoot and carry on. Then they'd leave, and those old screech owls would come. Even a great horned owl appeared. It was very entertaining to see the variety of owls. And they sure kept a close eye on me! So it helped me pass the long hours at night waiting for those poachers to arrive.

Well, no luck.

So I thought that Saturday night might be busier. So the next evening, right after dark, I came out and got myself comfortable, hoping those fellows would come tonight.

Well, sure enough, I guess it was about four o'clock in the morning, and this truck came winding in and out of the countryside, coming closer and closer.

My heart began to pound. I didn't know how many men there were, how many gators they had, or what their agenda was. But here they came to discard the carcasses.

They pulled to a stop about 80 feet away from where I hid in the bushes watching.

I heard one of them say, "Well, we'll just go ahead and skin 'em out here."

They had fourteen alligators to skin out. They were talking all the while.

Eventually, I decided it was as good a time as any to jump them, so I stepped out from behind the bush, turned on my flashlight, and told them that they were under arrest.

But there was one fellow still in the truck. He cranked it up and began to drive off. As I ran to get him, the other two fellows jumped on the back of the truck. As they turned, I was hanging onto the door, but they swerved sharply, and the centrifugal force threw me off.

So there went all my poachers, getting away. I ran to my truck and off I went. OK, we were going to have a wild chase! This was a real sandy area full of pieces of steel and chunks of railroad ties scattered around those dilapidated buildings. It was a good area to really get bogged down and stuck in the white sugar sand.

So I chased them around and around for about fifteen minutes. Finally, I was almost getting stuck, but the next thing I knew *they* hit a sand dune and got stuck. That was my break!

I pulled up. I got to the three of them and told them that they were under arrest. "Don't make any false moves," I said, "or somebody is going to get hurt. I don't want it to be you!"

I collected their guns and their drivers' licenses.

Their truck was buried down in the white sand. So I said, "Well, you all had better get busy and dig your truck out of there, because you all are going to be on your way down to the Sheriff's Office. You fellows are under arrest for poaching alligators, and I've been waiting a long time to catch you!"

Finally, they got the vehicle unstuck, and we drove back by the oil pit. We drove off to downtown and the Sheriff's Department, where I booked them in.

The individuals were Tommy Lee, Joe Brown, and Jim Thompson. I'll always remember them because they were out of Everglades City. It was always a challenge to get guys from there. I gathered up all of the evidence: guns, head lights, knives, gig and brazing rod (used to run through the alligator's spinal cord to the tail). I kept their driver's licenses until I left them at the booking desk. I loaded all fourteen gators in my truck.

About a month later, we went to court, and they were found guilty as charged. I was hopeful that this might be their last time, at least using this location!

A Sticky Mess

One evening I was driving near Dade County Prison west of the airport in no-man's-land, and I decided to take a look at the oil-pit location again, just to make sure that it wasn't being used again for illegal activities. Besides, I thought it was just the most interesting place, with all of the owls and all.

I left my truck a ways off and walked in, and sure enough, I got there in time to witness three men pulling seven gators off a truck!

I made my way back to my truck to get my mosquito bar camouflage net. I put the net on and returned to a wax myrtle bush about 40 feet from the concrete building. The 10,000-gallon oil pit was high near the ceiling. I had a great view of all that was taking place. The three men picked up the gators that they had skinned out and began dragging them toward the oil pit vat in the building to dispose of them, passing within about 30 feet of me. I could hear the rocks rolling under the carcasses as they dragged them along.

I thought, "Man, are we going to have some excitement tonight!"

They dragged the gators up the stairwell into the building next to the oil pit. Then one of the men went to the truck, then back upstairs with a gasoline lantern. He began pumping up the lantern in preparation for lighting it.

Well, there was a shelf up above the oil pit, and there were these four barn owls—some folks call them "monkey-faced" owls. They were just barely old enough to be flying.

As the guy tried to light the lantern with a match, one of the barn owls came flying from the shelf right into his face! It frightened him so that he yelled, falling backward down the concrete stairs! The other two men came running, thinking for sure that the law was there! It took them about ten minutes to regain some composure!

They relit the lantern and went ahead skinning the gators by the oil pit. I eased in closer for a better view. The lantern cast their large shadows on the white wall as they worked. I waited for them to skin all of the gators but one. Since the hides could be put in the evidence freezer, that left only one for me to skin.

Those three poachers were now bragging among themselves on how many gators they had killed and how they'd never been caught! They said, "If old Tom Shirley could see us now!" and I almost laughed out loud! I kept easing on up until I was only about 30 feet from them.

So by that point I was sizing up the situation for the bust. I knew these guys. Buck was the largest, at about 275 pounds. The other two, Leroy and Steve, standing in a corner while Buck skinned, were of medium build, around 185 pounds. They had a rifle within reach, and each man had a pistol on his side. I thought, "Man, if I jump up and arrest them now, all hell is going to break loose!"

By now you know how I like catching poachers by surprise. I asked myself, "What is the best way to put the fear of God into them? How can I best control the fear and excitement? All the while, I was sizing up the men and their weapons! Hopefully they wouldn't be so surprised that they would fall into the burned oil pit because I wasn't sure how we'd get them out!

I eased up the stairway, still in my camo, and jumped in the doorway, yelling as loud as I could, "HEY! You're under arrest for taking alligators!"

They began screaming, jumping, and falling over dead alligator carcasses! As I quickly took their guns, all hell really did break loose! The four owls came off the ledge and began flying around the small room, screeching and flying into all of us. And they became even more frantic because I was standing in the only open doorway, so they couldn't get out into the night!

Then one of the owls somehow flew into the oil pit! And that's when the mess really started. He managed to get out, but as he began flying, his wings threw oil in all directions! It didn't take long for all of the men to be drenched with oil.

Meanwhile, Buck was running in circles hollering, "What the hell is going on?!"

As things calmed down, I asked for their driver's licenses. They asked if they could smoke. Well, I was a bit leery of that since they were covered with oil, concerned that they might catch fire! But I said, "OK."

Oil was all over their hands and faces. And they were so shaken up that as they were trying to get their licenses out of their wallets, their cigarettes kept flipping out of their mouths! It was quite an ordeal just to collect all three licenses!

Next, I wondered how I was going to haul these guys in. If I called on my Motorola for the sheriff's wagon, there was no way they would find their way to this remote location. I just told the poachers that they'd have to follow me to the Sheriff's Office. I told Buck to go ahead and dispose of the gator carcass as usual. He took his knife and cut the gator's stomach open and threw the whole thing into the oil pit. And I wondered just how many gators lay at the bottom of that pit.

The guys asked if they could go home and change their clothes, but I told them that they'd gotten themselves into this mess, so they'd have to ride it through. I got my small tarp for Buck to sit on in my truck. The other two men used their raincoats to sit on in their vehicle.

Picture us walking into the Dade County Sheriff's Office. All four of us looked like hoodlums. The jailer was astonished, "You guys must have struck oil somewhere!"

"What do you want us to do with these characters?" he asked.

"Anything you want to do. They're all yours." And I left for a hot bath.

Many years later, Buck, Leroy, and Steve told me that I sure broke up their poaching days. After the oil pit episode, they never poached again!

Chico on the Job—1965

I had a Rhodesian ridgeback dog named Chico. I used to take my little sons out to Opa Locka Airport, where jack rabbits had been imported from the Southwest and turned loose many years before. I broke that ridgeback into chasing down those jack rabbits, and what a race it was!

So I put Chico to work with me. I'd take him in my airboat when I'd go on patrol. If I was going to a camp or to check out possible violations from deer or alligator poachers or anything else, I'd turn old Chico loose while I was out there socializing with the hunters. He'd be sniffing around, searching for anything that might be covered up—dead or otherwise.

Many times, he found covered-up deer hides or doe heads hidden underneath the campfire! The poachers would dig a hole and build the campfire on top of it, thinking that would be a safe way to both secrete and dispose of the evidence.

Well, I made about six or eight cases with Chico. But I had to watch him. One time, I was checking out a camp, socializing, getting ready to call Chico and turn him loose, but I'd left the engine running in the airboat.

All of a sudden, I heard the engine revving up, gunning, gunning, gunning. I looked up to see the boat driving off! Chico was sitting up there on the gas pedal, just sitting on the footrest. He looked at me as he passed, like he knew what he was doing.

Well, I hollered at him, but I wasn't fast enough. He drove on off, but after about 200 yards, the boat finally hit a cypress tree. I had to go down and fetch out my airboat.

The people in the camp thought that was pretty funny. Well, I did too as long as the airboat didn't get hurt, which it didn't. But that taught me a lesson. Next time I left my airboat, I'd make sure to take Chico with me.

One cold, dry winter morning, Chico and I went on a patrol south of the Loop Road in my truck. I went and checked on a camp. There were five fellows in there and I began to talk to them.

I told Chico, "Go ahead and do what you do."

As I was talking to the five individuals, I noticed that Chico went over behind their generator shed and stopped. I knew there was something there. I went over and sure enough, there was a whole bucket full of gator hides.

So I had to go ahead and put these five guys under arrest. Even though it was early, they were liquored up pretty bad; anything could happen. My radio didn't work half the time anyway, but I walked over to my truck and acted like I turned on my radio and was talking to the Sheriff's Office in Hollywood. Then I came back and told the guys that I was going to put all of them under arrest and to produce their driver's licenses.

With the licenses, I went back and acted like I was on the radio again, giving all of their information—names and addresses and so forth to the Sheriff's Office so they would think that their information was being processed. We were in a real isolated area, and with five of them to handle in their condition, I wasn't taking any chances. Also, I was going to have to take all five of them all the way down to Marathon in the Florida Keys to finish the arrest procedure because they had been poaching in Monroe County.

Well, I rounded them up. I put some of them in my truck and some in their truck with Chico. We drove to Marathon, fortunately without any complications.

The Blue Shanty Group

About 30 miles west of Miami on Tamiami Trail was the little old juke joint, the Blue Shanty Restaurant, owned by Joxey Redding and his brother Bobo, those pioneers in airboats and frogging—as well as major hide buyers and gator poachers—who I talked about earlier. It was at the Blue Shanty where froggers and Gladesmen hung out—especially gator poachers.

Bobo always went barefooted. I don't think he ever worked at anything except poaching alligators and frogging. He was a tough old booger. But after many years of frogging and gator poaching, Bobo went to work with a construction crew. During that period, a crane fell over, collapsed, and caught Bobo underneath. It smashed his face in, broke his collarbone, caved in his chest, collapsed one lung, and, I think, fractured his skull.

I didn't know how in the world he lived through that, but I understand it went like this: It took them a long time to get the crane off of him. Bobo was just lying there, still alive, barely breathing, and his lungs and his rib cage were smashed together. They couldn't get them apart. They thought it would kill him for sure. The doctor bent over him at the crash site. Bobo could hear the doctor saying, "Well, if we don't get these ribs off from his lungs, he's gonna be dead in a little bit of time."

Bobo couldn't see, but he could hear. He was praying they would get those ribs off of his lungs, and he managed to speak up, "Pull them ribs off, you guys. I don't want to die."

The equipment guys around there—they made some sort of device to pull his ribs off his lungs and heart.

Well, to make a long story short, though he should have died, Bobo had the will to live. He went through a lot of torment and so forth, but he came back to life, strong and well, roaming again, poaching alligators.

And he was hard at it. He was one of the guys who was on my "ten most wanted" list, so I made up my mind that I was going to try to catch him.

Bobo hunted way south of Tamiami Trail. The Tower Road goes into a section that the Everglades National Park manages, and at the end of that road there's a dead-end, and sometimes that's where Bobo did his alligator hunting.

"OK," I say, "I'm going to set aside two or three weeks, and I'm going to go down there every night until I catch Bobo gator hunting."

So I went down there all by myself at night, and I hid my vehicle in the bushes, and I walked on down to the end there, and, with the camouflage netting, I got all set up, and sure enough, here came Bobo.

So he was gigging frogs and gigging frogs, and there was an alligator right at the end of the dike in the canal there. I could see him. I figured this was a perfect place for me to catch Bobo catching and killing alligators. So I was there and hidden, watching Bobo come up there. Actually, the alligator was inside the Everglades National Park on the east side of the levee. So he killed the alligator and got it in his boat and then sped on off into the national park. Well, I didn't have a boat so I couldn't catch him, and he got away from me that night. I figured I'd think up another plan.

So I went to my friend Bill McCullough's Aquaglades on Highway 84, where we delivered the "nuisance" alligators that we sometimes had to catch. I went by to see if I could borrow three or four of his Aquaglades alligators. I gave aspirins to two of them, making them real docile and non-mobile, and I gave the other ones a shot of nicotine, which does the same thing.

My plan was to take these gators out as bait—to put them at the water's edge for Bobo to come along and kill. I thought that I might be able to catch him in the act.

I took the long ride, about 7 miles, down south of the Trail and went inside the national park on the road that separates it from the east to the west. I took those alligators from my vehicle and positioned them at the water's edge. I would be right there, so I could get in the water and apprehend old Bobo before he got away.

Then I drove my car back a quarter mile or so. Then I walked back and lay out there on the dike.

I did this for three or four nights. Bobo was around, but he never came close to those alligators. It got kind of lonely out there at night, so I figured I'd call one of my wildlife officers, Jerry Powell.

We gathered up our sleeping bags, and off we went to get everything set up. At night, we'd lie out there, listening to the frogs croak, looking at the sky, and watching the shooting stars. It was really beautiful. We spent several nights out there and ate up the better part of a week, week and a half, only to realize that Bobo was ranging farther south in his airboat, to the track through the Tentacle Rocks.

But then he came back our way! He came back within yards of where I had put the comatose borrowed alligators. Our hearts were pounding, and I thought, "I'm going to catch Bobo tonight." He cranked his engine off, made a cup of coffee. He stayed there a while. We were anxiously waiting.

But he finished his cup of coffee, cranked up, and headed on back where he came from! So there we were, we'd lost our chance to catch old Bobo again.

But not too long after that, we got lucky!

Bobo and Joxey were apparently out "frogging" one night north of the Trail off from Betty and Johnny's Restaurant near the levee. Officer Jimmy Jordan and our pilot were out flying that night, and they recognized the Reddings' vehicles parked there at Betty and Johnny's.

So old Bobo and his brother, they're out in their boat. Jimmy Jordan and the pilot could see their activity, and it appeared that they were poaching.

Jimmy Sistrunk, who later became one of my good officers, was still a civilian and was with me on patrol. The Reddings' airboat was just coming in, so I got in an airboat that was docked there, and my men were hiding inside of a boat.

I was going to observe him unload.

Well, Jimmy Sistrunk headed down the levee in the dark and hid in the trees and the bushes.

And in the dark, here came Bobo. He had a sack full of alligator skins. He walked by Jimmy Sistrunk, and Sistrunk said, "I'll take those alligator skins."

So there we caught Bobo after all! We put him and Joxey under arrest, took them downtown, and wrote them up a citation.

Only every now and then did I stop in at the Blue Shanty for a Coke. So many poachers drifted in there that they felt uncomfortable, and so did I. Joxey sure didn't take kindly to me coming around.

Joxey's wife was Baby Doll. Well, Baby Doll was a shotgun-packing woman—a rough-and-tough gal, let me tell you, a very hell-raising woman. She had a baby, and she would come out there tending bar with a breast hanging out, nursing that baby. I thought that was sort of unusual.

Her husband had always held the record of never being caught by a game warden. Then here comes Tom Shirley and caught him fair and square! It was a highly embarrassing situation for Baby Doll, and she let me know it. She got all over my case every time I saw her! I'd a whole lot rather deal with Jox than with ole Baby Doll!

A Real Surprise

Warren Siciliano was a well-known martial arts instructor, a fascinating man who traveled throughout the world studying all styles of hand-to-hand combat. He took parts of all these techniques, especially karate and judo, and combined them into a martial arts technique that he marketed as "Karado." He was one of the most famous instructors to utilize these new techniques.

So starting in the early 1950s, I decided I would take some training under him, which I did for many years. I became his top student, captain of his Karado team, and worked my way to an eighth-degree black belt, of which I am very proud.

While training, you fall into a habit, a schedule of training. For me, it was every Thursday night.

I hated to break training, but I knew very well I'd better go out on patrol this particular night because I'd heard about a group of fellows coming down from Sebastian to Everglade City. That was bad news, for when these guys came down to South Florida, there were always a lot of gator poachers mixed in.

We knew who the poachers were: Craig, Yates, Osborn, Brown, Lopez, and others, and when the gators began their breeding season, the poachers simply could not resist the temptation!

So I took off that Thursday night and put my airboat in across from Andytown on the west side of Highway 27. I drove out all the way without lights to be sure that I wouldn't give myself away. I stayed up several hours, waiting to see lights of airboats, listening for engines way off in the distance.

I checked all the airboats in that particular area. They had no guns, no sign of harpoons. There were no blood stains, and my most important observation was that there was no "smell" of alligator on the boats.

About midnight I went back to my usual camp spot at the Grapefruit Head near the Palm Beach County line.

Well, about three o'clock, I heard an airboat running way off in the distance. Well, time to go check it. Time to go to work!

So I put my shoes back on, got in my airboat, and off I went, as always, keeping the lights out so I didn't expose myself. Then, way far off southward, I see this boat—airboat. It looks like he's frogging right now.

So I spent about an hour or so trying to get in closer to him. When I got about 200 yards away, I turned my engine off. I watched him for a while, and I noticed that he was going around in circles—same circles, same pattern. This was very unusual.

So I got a little bit closer, about 50–60 yards from him, and turned my engine off again.

He was still going in circles. This was strange . . .

Ok, I flipped my engine on. BOOM! I went firing up close to him. I went to check him and looked at him. This fellow, he was all slumped over with his head down around his knees. He didn't have his hand on his steering stick, no hand on his gig. He was just sitting there going in circles with his head on his knees.

So I had to jump into the airboat while it was still moving. I looked at his face, and it was old Bobo Redding!

Well, old Bobo was all slumped over unconscious.

As I mentioned before, Bobo had been in that terrible construction accident, and it was just a miracle that he lived. But here he was, out here in the middle of nowhere frogging!

He was still unconscious. So I patted him on the arm and said, "Bobo get up! Wake up here! What's going on?"

So Bobo pops his head up and kind of comes around, moaning.

"Hey, Lieutenant! How are you doing? What are you doing out here?"

And I said, "Well, what are you doing out here, all tied into your seat here? What's going on?"

He said, "Well, Lieutenant, when I come out here sometimes, because of my accident, I just collapse. I fall unconscious in my seat, and I'm so fearful that I might fall out of my airboat and drown or get in the crop. So I tie myself to the seat! I pass out every now and then, but I'm OK so long as I tie myself in."

I said, "Well, how long do you coast around?"

"Oh, it might be an hour or two. I never know for sure," he said.

So I didn't untie him. I just let him stay put. He already had about 60 pounds of frogs so he wasn't doing too badly.

I said, "OK, go on about your business then and have a good night."

Old Bobo. He was a tough son of a gun. I went to his funeral several years later, and his old arms looked like gator hide itself. He lived off the Everglades—gigging, trapping, fishing, killing gators, a real Gladesman. You name it, as effective a hunter and trapper as I have ever seen, a real legend in his own time.

6

Everglades Floods

The Altered Everglades Wetlands

The Flood Control District and the Wildlife Commission held a lease agreement on 3,998,930 acres, larger than Rhode Island, that comprised the Everglades Wildlife District. This land had been contributed by more than 150 landowners who, as announced in the January 1959 issue of *Florida Wildlife* magazine, entered into a lease agreement with the Game and Fresh Water Fish Commission to manage their land.

In 1964, the U.S. Corps of Engineers built dikes for the Central and South Florida Flood Control District east of Highway 27 and north of Highway 84 that enclosed Conservation Area 2. Neither Flood Control nor the Wildlife Commission realized in those formative years the dire impact that these future Water Conservation Areas would have on the ecology and wildlife that existed within the Corps of Engineers' dikes. But, with a lifetime in the Everglades wetlands, I was very concerned that Flood Control should understand the Everglades hydrology as well as I understood it. They needed to be cognizant of the effects of their proposed high water levels, the effects of the duration of those levels, and the limits that deer (as a benchmark) could tolerate in depth and time period. The deer could not withstand 15 inches of water for more than six weeks. They simply could not survive. But my concern fell on deaf ears.

The Conservation Areas were built in stages. For us in Everglades Wildlife Management, Conservation Area 2 was our first lesson. The area was flooded and overseen by technicians with no understanding of the hydraulics of an Everglades wetland. The pumps were opened,

Legend

1. Andy Town
2. Aquaglades
3. Betty & Johnnie's Rst. & Dade-Broward Levee/Tower
4. Blue Shanty Restaurant
5. Cap Graham's Rock House
6. Chokoloskee, FL
7. Coconut Palm Camp
8. Cooperstown
9. Dade Co. Airboat Assn.
10. Doral Country Club
11. El Rancho
12. Gator Hook Strand & Sig Walker's Camp
13. Grapefruit Head
14. Homestead AFB
15. Iron Curtain
16. Joe Moe City Gas Station
17. L-Four Levee
18. Lone Palm Slough / Cabbage Island
19. Mack's Fish Camp
20. Medley, FL
21. Miccosukee Res BC, Truck Stop
22. Miccosukee Res HQ
23. North Airboat Trail
24. Ochopee
25. Oil Spill Dike
26. Perry Airport, Pem. Pines
27. Pinecrest
28. Polock's Tavern
29. Radio Tower
30. Ray Rotenberger Wildlife Mgmt. Area
31. Rotenberger Landing
32. Sands Point Landing Strip
33. Snake Creek Canal
34. Tentacle Rocks
35. Tom Shirley's Big Cypress Camp
36. Tom Shirley's Sawgrass Camp
37. Tom's Fish Camp

Map of southern Florida, showing key landmarks and destinations. This illustration gives some idea of the vast area across which we wildlife officers were responsible to protect wildlife and uphold Commission laws. Features such as the canals and conservation areas 2 and 3 are evidence of how the irreplaceable Everglades has been (and continues to be) devastated by man. (Map created by J. Brian Dalrymple.)

and the high water levels were reached, but no one was accountable for checking weather conditions, the water's effect on the overall Everglades ecology, or the water's effect on specific wildlife.

The 1964 hunting season opened. Because of the high water, the deer and all the other animals had by then been forced to retreat to the dikes to escape the floodwaters! The hunters had a field day, as thousands of deer were waiting for them like sitting ducks. By 9:00 a.m. on the morning the season opened, all of the deer hunters had their limit. It was an awful sight.

So, after this experience, along with my assignments as a wildlife officer, I also assumed the role of an Everglades advocate, gathering data and feeding the sometimes horrifying statistics to the media and to organizations such as the Florida Wildlife Federation and the Everglades Coordinating Council, who were in a leadership position that could challenge the system and hound Flood Control at every turn.

The reality of the Everglades wetlands, as I have pointed out, is that it was *not* a river or a storage compound. It was a natural wetland dotted with high islands that had existed since the time that the waters receded from Florida some 3,000–5,000 years ago. In the Everglades, the shallow sloughs, deeper flows, saw grass, and peat bogs all had a purpose in the hydrology and the support of plant and animal life. And the ecology of the high islands was something that the wildlife depended on, that was integral to their existence in periods of natural high water. In Conservation Area 2, these islands were quickly and completely decimated by Flood Control through the practice of allowing too much water to stand for too long. Even the huge ficus trees on those islands could take high water for only so long; then the roots rotted, and the trees fell over and died. The conservationists, sportsmen, the Wildlife Commission—we were all stunned at how rapidly this destruction took place.

And this was how all of the historic habitation, agricultural, ceremonial, and burial sites on the Everglades islands in Conservation Area 2 were destroyed, and of course all of the animals with them, from the terrestrial insects to the carnivores who didn't make it out in time. They died. These were animals that Florida's Wildlife Commission and every Commission officer like me had taken an oath to protect!

Many organized conservation groups—the Florida Wildlife Federation, the Everglades Coordinating Council, Marjory Stoneman Douglas's Friends of the Everglades, the native Gladesmen, wildlife officers, hunters, the Seminole Tribe, the Miccosukee Tribe of Indians of Florida, all persons and agencies who were intimately connected to the Everglades ecosystem (some for centuries, others for generations)—attempted to offer sound advice and statistical information on how to balance the drainage operation in the Everglades. But Flood Control's engineers, scientists, and computers ruled the process, and as a result, huge sections of the Everglades and its occupants died. Conservation Area 2 and later Conservation Area 3, representing 750,000 acres of the Commission's Wildlife Management land, became lifeless while we watched, helpless to stop the process.

Saving Deer from the Flood—1966

For Flood Control, Conservation Area 2 was just the beginning. By 1966, Flood Control had finally managed to encircle with their dikes all of the area north to Palm Beach County, east to Dade and Broward, south to the Tamiami Trail, and westward to Collier County. This system also enclosed the traditional island camps of a number of Miccosukee Indians who happened to live within the boundary.

This was Conservation Area Number 3. I knew that with no structured opposition to fight Flood Control for the health of the Everglades in Conservation Area 3, it would suffer the same fate. And the deer herd, once estimated at around ten thousand, would all die.

I had written to the Wildlife Commission's regional director, Lou Gainey, but the Wildlife Commission's hands were tied. They had *no* power to stop what was going to happen, as all of the state's agencies were mandated to get along. The Commission was not in a political position to be adversarial, and it ignored what I saw as our inherent responsibility, to put pressure on Flood Control.

In too many meetings, Flood Control would say, "We haven't heard anything from the Wildlife Commission. None of their reports have said the Everglades deer herds are being harmed."

I was frantically trying to get some help, appealing to anyone I could think of to stop the devastation that would result. I vented to

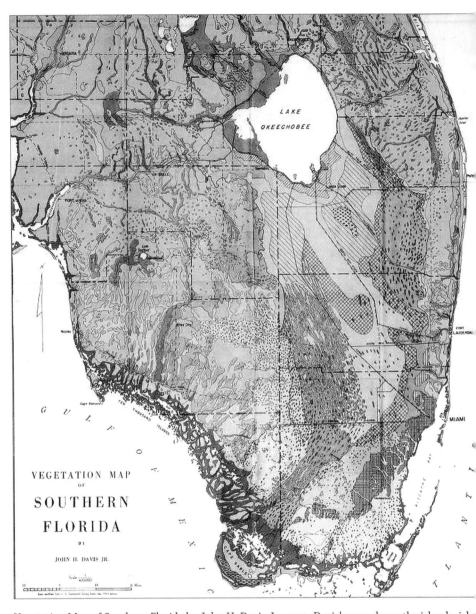

Vegetation Map of Southern Florida by John H. Davis Jr., 1943. Davis's map shows the islands, isle and wetlands of various kinds that once ranged across the Everglades. Since 1947, the Flood Contro District's "water management" projects have flooded over these lands, killing millions of animals, obliterating habitat and valuable early human artifacts and settlement history, and wreaking havo on the Everglades ecology. Because vegetation is so sensitive to water levels, this map, as a compre hensive blueprint of the Everglades wetlands as it was in its "natural state," should be utilized as a guide for future restoration. (Davis map modified from U.S. Geological Survey state map, 1933 edit University of Florida Map and Imagery Library, George A. Smathers Libraries.)

John Pennekamp, who had been a major supporter of Everglades National Park, telling him, "There are things that I know are true, but I can't print this information or they'd fire me!"

By spring of 1966, Flood Control was ready and eager to try out their dikes and see what would happen in Conservation Area 3. So they turned on the pumps, and gradually, over a period of weeks, the water flowed up—up and up and up.

I witnessed it from a plane flying over Everglades National Park. The park hadn't protested, either, I assumed because they were a federal entity. However, as I looked down at the floodwaters rising in the park, their deer herds were already moving westward, looking for higher land.

But the sportsmen remembered the debacle within Conservation Area 2. This time, the sportsmen decided that they weren't going to lay back and let the deer herd die like before. However, the organizations still did not comprise an organized front, so group leaders approached this immediate issue on an individual basis.

Franny Taylor (of the Francis Taylor Wildlife Management Area) and Paul Ledbetter had a half-track, so they rigged it up with a bulldozer blade. They went out into the Everglades almost every weekend when they got off from work. They would go out and use the half-track to push up these little islands, which proved extremely effective. When the water came up, the deer would search for dry ground, and at least the islands would save them from drowning. It was a great project that these two individuals created north of Alligator Alley.

But when I called Ed Dale, the director of Flood Control, to try to get the water down, he said, "Tom Shirley, I'll tell you, I would rather have every deer out there dead than to have them use those islands that Franny Taylor pushed up!"

As the water began to rise, photographer Toby Massey took a series of fantastic, poignant photographs that illustrated the plight of the deer in this flood. The pictures were picked up by the major newspapers in Washington, D.C., headlined "Man-Made Flood!" One photo that really got Flood Control's attention and called attention to the plight of the Everglades animals across the nation showed my officer George Eddy carrying a newborn fawn over his shoulders while wading through water up to his chest.

Left: In the flood perpetrated by Flood Control in 1966, the wildlife in the Everglades wetlands was decimated. Even if the deer could find a dry island, they soon ate all the vegetation and starved. Here Officer Bruce Lawless examines a deer carcass. (Photo by Toby Massey.)

Below: During Flood Control's 1966 flooding, the Game Commission opted to remove deer to higher ground. Here a captured deer is loaded onto an airboat. *Left to right:* Tom Morris and George Eddy. (Photo by Toby Massey.)

Then, with the Wildlife Commission's hands tied and Flood Control uncaring, I began reporting to the news media. This got me involved and gave me a platform to voice my frustration and concern. In May 1966, I was interviewed by Vic Saling for *Gator Tales*, the Everglades Conservation and Sportsmen's newsletter. The front page carried the Massey photo of the newly born fawn clinging to a rock in a sea of water. I reported on the imminent destruction of the deer herd: "As it stands now there is so much water in the area now that they'll not get enough to eat to see them through the rainy season."

Because of Toby Massey's photographs, the plight of the Everglades deer became a big news item with the Associated Press, making my publicity campaign even more effective (and solidifying Toby's career with AP). Wildlife organizations throughout the United States became very concerned about the animals being killed off in the Everglades. I was surprised to realize that people throughout the world knew and loved the Everglades wetlands and didn't want to see it destroyed.

Meanwhile, the Wildlife Commission's Biology Department, our *own* department, said there was "no problem" with the deer herd. That was really upsetting, because for me and the sportsmen it's very easy to determine just looking at a deer running across a slough whether that deer is in danger of dying. Instead of having the light, slick, white coat that reflects, they look like their hair has become more like fur and it stands straight up. Then we know that a deer is seriously affected and in mortal danger. The deer's "general health" is at risk. For us, no scientific necropsy studies would be needed to determine that obvious fact.

As the conditions in the Everglades wetlands escalated during my rounds in Conservation Area 3, I saw hundreds of deer just standing on the high spots, marooned on the dikes and in the hardwood hammocks. Certain areas smelled like feed lots. There were so many deer in the area you could count them at night, hundreds of shining eyes.

I had a plan. I wrote a letter and sent it to all state and federal agencies, inviting them to a tour of the area so they could see for themselves. I had eight or nine Commission airboats and friends available to take them out and show them firsthand what was going on. Twenty-five people showed up: Ed Dale, director of Flood Control; the Humane Society, the Wildlife League, the U. S. Fish and Wildlife

Flood Control just wouldn't listen when I told them that their scientifically calculated water levels would reach flood levels and kill off the wildlife. During our rescue work, a newborn fawn swam to a tiny outcropping above the floodwaters. It then crawled up out of the water and posed. Toby Massey created these headliner photographs that illustrated to the nation the plight of the Everglades animals. (Photo by Toby Massey.)

In yet another award-winning Massey photo, my officer Bruce Lawless's rescue of the fawn from the chest-deep floodwaters poignantly illustrated Flood Control's disastrous error in judgment. (Photo by Toby Massey.)

Commission, and Art Marshall from the University of Miami's Biology Department. Harmond Shields, the powerful director of the Salt Water Fish Commission, was also there, and the media.

Shields said, "What are we doing out here? You know, Lt. Shirley, *this* is a Water Conservation Area!"

I replied, "Well, then what are we doing out here acting so concerned over the dying animals?"

Freddy Fisikelli, president of the Dade County Airboat and Half-Track Club, was extremely active in fighting this crisis. While I was very busy recording the water depths, keeping track and making notes of what was taking place in the Everglades, Fisikelli was talking to the media, keeping them abreast of the conditions, making reports, and coordinating with other sportsmen's groups in Palm Beach and Collier Counties.

We raised such a fuss!

The island El Rancho, which I've mentioned before, south of present-day Alligator Alley (I-595), was one of the larger Everglades islands and where I would stay at night when I was on patrol in that area.

During this flood, I would venture to say almost two hundred deer migrated there to die. At the camp on the island I had an electrical cord, about 30 feet long with a light bulb that I would attach to the battery on my airboat. I used the light at night at El Rancho. I moved it out to the area where the deer would often come up to the base of a big rubber tree to die. I'd watch one come in, then various animals such as hogs would pick on it until it was dead. Then they would feast on it. It was not a pretty sight. But it was inevitable.

This went on for two to three months while I camped there nights on patrol. The deer would come in from long, long distances because they could smell high ground. They would come in with the hair rotted off their legs. Their hooves were all swollen to where it looked like they were ready to drop off. What a sad, sad sight it was . . .

By noon the next day, the animals—the bobcats, the raccoons, the possums, the beetles, buzzards, and everything would come in and feed on the deer. The only thing that would be left would be hair on the ground and maybe the skull cap. The body would be completely gone, hardly any sign that a deer had been there.

The fawns were the first to die, then the yearlings, next the does. The bucks were the last to die. And I did watch around two hundred die at El Rancho.

But Flood Control was still pumping at No. 8 Pumping Station at the north end of Conservation Area 3, which supported Broward and Dade Counties. Again we pleaded with them to turn the pumps off and to quit flowing water into Area 3, but they wouldn't agree and kept pumping.

Our wildlife commissioner, W. T. McBroom, was very proactive, aggressive, and not afraid to jump right into the middle of things. Also, he was always looking for ways to improve the Commission's Game Management programs. Game Management had, over the years since I joined, become a stronger, separate division of the Commission's programs. Game Management still wore the green Commission uniforms, but by now, those of us in Law Enforcement wore blue.

So I reported to Commissioner McBroom what was taking place.

I also told him of the conflicted information that was coming out of the Biology Department. Then I invited him to go out with me on the airboat. We took a daylong tour.

We were out for a little while and counted twenty-two deer carcasses. He became upset, mad! Obviously Game Management was down on the job. He called the Tallahassee office, and they suggested, "Call Tom Shirley. Ask him what's going on!" At least the red tape trail had begun.

But it wasn't fast enough for the sportsmen's organizations. They were becoming totally impatient as the situation worsened, and they began to raise a bunch of hell! I even heard rumors that some of the sportsmen had acquired 500 pounds of dynamite. Their intention was to blow up No. 8 Pumping Station if Water Management didn't turn the station off and quit flooding the area. This event never took place, remaining just a rumor. But sure enough, years later, the stored dynamite was actually found!

All this death and trauma, both for the animals and those of us who cared for them and their habitat—and all it would have taken to end the crisis would have been for the Flood Control Manager to get on the telephone and call No. 8 Pumping Station to turn off the water!

And while the Commission was still trying to decide what to do about the deer situation, Bob McDonald of the Palm Beach County Airboat Association personally led a rescue effort to retrieve deer, going against the Commission's directives!

He told the press, "We're going out there whether the Commission likes it or not," and the airboat brigade entered Conservation Area 3 in force! They made headlines as saviors, while the Wildlife Commission looked really, really bad.

But it was due to this bad press that the Commission entered the picture the following week. They determined in hindsight that the best thing to do was to go along with the wildlife clubs, who had recommended going out and catching the deer and taking them to areas of dry ground in the first place. From then on, the Commission was actively carrying out this plan—with the world watching!

Commissioner McBroom put me in charge of this project. The Game Commission joined with the county conservation groups, who were now working with *US*! During the operation, we caught and removed more than four hundred deer. It was a greatly beneficial project. Almost all of the wildlife officers within the Everglades Region were involved in capturing or removing the deer to higher ground.

Again in *Gator Tales* I put out the urgent message, "All air boaters are urged to aid the Game Commission in this emergency."

Ray Rotenberger from West Palm Beach, who owned land north of Conservation Area 3 (the Ray Rotenberger Wildlife Management Area), helped by flying over the inundated area south of Alligator Alley with his Piper Cub. He would locate the deer and by radio, direct us to them.

Rory Looney had an Everglades camp and landing strip for his Piper Cub. He called me and told me he would lend us the Piper Cub to use in the deer-capture operation. I met with Mr. McBroom and told him of the offer. The deal was that if we damaged the plane, we would have to fix it. The deal was agreed to, but wouldn't you know, a short time after the operation got under way a helicopter pilot crashed Mr. Looney's Piper in the canal!

We would pull up beside the deer in our airboats, jump out, and bulldog (wrassle) them down, hog-tie them around the legs, gently pull them in the airboat, blindfold them with scarves and cloth handkerchiefs (as that seemed to make them less afraid), and take them to Alligator Alley. We had a volunteer veterinarian to tranquilize them.

We had to really be careful in handling the deer while they were awaiting transport from Alligator Alley, keeping them in shade so they wouldn't get too hot and being sure to turn them over every so often to get the gas out of their intestines, which could prove fatal. Last, a Game Commission truck would arrive to take another load of deer to areas eastward or northward where they would be released on dry land. Most went to the Ray Rotenberger Management Area and to Holey Land Wildlife Management in Palm Beach County. While deer are fairly fragile to move, we kept records of the deer that died and figured that we lost only 10 percent.

Interestingly enough, in 1964, the Commission had restocked the deer population in Conservation Area 3 with deer from Louisiana. We found that those Louisiana deer were stronger and better adapted to the Everglades than our own native deer. The deer herds should

These deer were captured by airboat by the Commission, conservationists, and sportsmen to whom we appealed for emergency help. They are lying on the swale of Alligator Alley trussed up, tranquilized, and blindfolded to lessen the trauma as they await transport to a dry area. We moved about four hundred deer, saving them from death by drowning or starvation. (Photo by Toby Massey.)

continue to be built up with the Louisiana stock, but unfortunately, the Commission is no longer involved with restocking.

During this crisis, the news media were most effective in providing coverage. *American Sportsman*, an ABC television series not on the air until 1965, came down and wrote up the capture effort for a future show. It was a great program, spreading the word on what was taking place with the Everglades wildlife worldwide. As a result, I received correspondence from China, Japan, and Africa.

Eventually, the water level dropped to a safe 15 inches. The deer who had survived came off the islands where they had congregated and once again began to feed out in the sloughs. Another crisis had passed! But since the 1966 flood, the deer herd in the national park has not recovered.

Meanwhile, for their efforts that year, the Flood Control District patted themselves on the back for pumping 700 billion gallons into the reservoir and saving the southeast coast $20 million dollars in flood damages. And in an ironic twist, Governor W. Haydon Burns gave the annual Conservation Award that year to . . . Flood Control! What a joke!

Flood Control inundated Conservation Area 3 again in 1968. By this time, the sportsmen had organized enough to file a federal lawsuit against Flood Control. A federal judge was taken out to inspect the dead deer and check the high water levels.

But the situation continued. Politicians (and certainly the Flood Control engineers) still had no clue that the Everglades wetlands was created by natural water flows, droughts, and fires. That the interruption of any one of these cycles would destroy the system. Even to this day, the engineers and the computer-model people don't have a grasp on that simple fact. They just want to flow water.

But in the aftermath of the flooding of Conservation Area 3, the Everglades wetlands began to change forever.

What is 100 years to a computer?

The preservation of the animals is only possible through the unequivocal restoration of the Everglades to its natural state. That has been my goal for many decades. Because of my job with the Florida Game and Fresh Water Fish Commission, I kept records on water tables. They show the facts about drainage, flooding, and pollution. I have seen the terrible damage done in the name of Everglades restoration. Its equally disastrous results were not accomplished by basic common sense, but by the ignorance of individuals with their heads in their computers who never get their feet wet long enough to actually understand the mechanics of this ecosystem firsthand. We know, for instance, that certain types of vegetation exist only in certain depths of water, from inches to feet. Thus, knowing the type of vegetation will tell the relative water depth. If the water depth is altered drastically, the plant dies.

Unfortunately, at this date, only a *very* few of us know and understand fully what the "natural state" of the Everglades wetlands was before drainage, and why.

7

Public Policies, Private Disasters

The Governor's Conference

Fidel Castro came into power in Cuba in 1959, and sugar imports
to the United States were cut. As a result, sugarcane cultivation in
southern Florida was escalated. Between 1963 and 1998, the acreage
devoted to sugar production would double to cover 400,000 acres
from Lake Okeechobee south into the Everglades wetlands. In time,
the wetlands suffered a severe ecological decline because the introduced sugarcane produces phosphorus. Unfortunately, one plant that
thrives on phosphorus is cattails. I pointed this out to a reporter, who
quoted me in "Sugar's Sweet Deal," a 1998 *Reader's Digest* article. "You
see those cattails?" I said. "A few years ago none of that was there. No
wildlife can live in that" (Fitzgerald 95).

But those cattail forests continued to take over and supplant the
native vegetation. They squeezed out all other forms of animal life, as
the water where cattails grow contains zero oxygen and cannot support the smallest minnow.

All of this happened because by 1981, Florida and Washington had
begun to embrace the émigré family of Cuban sugar barons. The Fanjul
family planted their sugarcane on the drained wetlands south of Lake
Okeechobee. Congress made it easy by restricting imports of sugar
and guaranteeing a high minimum price for both growers and proces-
sors of beet and cane sugar in the United States. They also guaranteed
loans to sugar businesses.

No one in the United States wanted to go without low-cost sugar,
and the southern Lake Okeechobee location was perfect for growing

sugarcane. Florida thus became the major U.S. producer, while the Everglades wetlands was dealt another blow, this one even more dangerous than the up-and-down water levels.

Michael Grunwald summed up longtime Everglades advocate Art Marshall's assessment of the Everglades wetlands' plight in *The Swamp: The Everglades, Florida, and the Politics of Paradise*:

> The C&SF project [Flood Control] had sliced up the organism into a disjointed marionette, and the water that was its lifeblood no longer flowed . . . Lake Okeechobee was imprisoned by its dike, so it no longer flowed into the upper Glades, except when the sugar growers demanded water for irrigation. The upper Glades was becoming a sugarcane monoculture, so it no longer flowed into the central Glades, except when the growers dumped water during storms. The central Glades was divided into five compartments that only flowed into the southern Glades when water managers decided to flood the [Everglades National] park; the water in these "conservation areas" barely flowed at all, collecting in stagnant pools where sawgrass decomposed into ooze instead of muck. Inside the park, Shark Slough and Taylor Slough no longer carried much fresh water to the Ten Thousand Islands and Florida Bay, which began mutating from brackish estuaries into salt water lagoons.
>
> The entire system was broken. (265)

As if this wasn't enough, in 1968 it looked like the Everglades was to be compromised yet again—this time, by big-city business. Some investors in Miami decided that the booming metropolis could use a state-of-the-art "Jet Port" way out in the Everglades wetlands on the north side of the Tamiami Trail. This was a joint effort between Dade and Monroe Counties. But, at the last minute, with millions of dollars already spent on plans, prep, and runway, Florida and national sportsmen and conservation groups, including my friend Freddy Fisikelli, banded together for the first time to squelch the absurd project. Of course, neither the Everglades National Park nor the Game Commission had taken a strong opposing position, even though this project would have had a severe impact on both agencies and the wildlife.

Out of the Jet Port controversy, however, came a new weapon that could be used to fight on behalf of the Everglades wetlands—a unified front called the Everglades Coalition. The coalition was made up of state and national chapters of the Audubon Society and the Wildlife Federation, the Sierra Club, and Marjory Stoneman Douglas's Friends of the Everglades. It also included the important conservation and sportsmen's clubs that used to be so gung ho and active in policymaking and sponsorship of the Florida Game and Fresh Water Fish Commission's programs.

Then, in 1971, there was a drought like no other. Miami had only 3 inches of rain in six months. Despite seeding clouds by airplane in the hope of stimulating precipitation, the Everglades wetlands burned—on and on. Things were so bad that Florida governor Reubin Askew called the Governor's Conference on Water Management in South Florida on Miami Beach on September 22, 1971.

I attended the conference. Charlie Loveless, the biologist who was responsible for the initial deer studies made when I first joined the Commission, was there as well.

In his opening remarks, Governor Askew explained the stakes.

There is a water crisis in South Florida today. This crisis has long range aspects. Every major waterway in the Everglades basin, Everglades National Park, the conservation areas, Lake Okeechobee and the Kissimmee Valley is steadily deteriorating in quality from a variety of polluting sources . . .

The quality of water, though potentially adequate for today's demand cannot now be managed effectively over wet/dry cycles to assure a minimum adequate water supply in extended drought seasons.

Of course, all of the professional people attending acknowledged the major problems in the Everglades wetlands. In fact, so many people attended the conference that the participants had to be broken up into three different groups. The event lasted three days.

We all knew that the water crisis in the Everglades wetlands was caused by uncontrolled growth of cities as well as of agricultural interests, which put burdensome demands on Flood Control. But this conference was a first in that it called for a new responsibility from city and town planning, which would result in infrastructure and regulations for such things as water usage. In the future, the Flood Control Districts would be called Water Control Districts, which required the agencies that needed water to be regulated.

All of the information gathered from the many participants during the conference was collected into a summary. The summary's final analysis targeted the issue that the State of Florida had made a major mistake in allowing the large agricultural interests to move out onto the floodplain. It further recommended that the state should repurchase the floodplain and return it to its natural state as Everglades wetlands. This was great news that we saw as big step toward the recovery of our Everglades!

However, the political powers watered down the summary considerably. During the conference, the summary was rewritten three different times, and each time saw another watering down until the final summary did not represent the truth. But the conference was ending, as was the endurance of the attendees. Even Charlie Loveless was pressured. He finally gave up and went along with the third report.

And business continued as usual. Now, four decades later, we are faced with the same battle, but a much smaller Everglades wetlands.

The 1970s also brought federal interest to the area. The government wanted to establish a national park within the Big Cypress. The land would be withdrawn from the State of Florida, hundreds of acres that had been under the jurisdiction of the Game and Fresh Water Fish Commission. It was left up to the citizens and sportsmen to say whether this large section should be placed in the hands of the government.

Calvin Stone was vice president of the Florida chapter of the National Wildlife Federation and also the Everglades Conservation Club at this time. He called me and asked me to come to his home. He was going to call Washington with the recommendation to approve or disapprove the federal legislation to set aside the land for the Big Cypress National Preserve. During his call, Mr. Stone stated that I was the law enforcement in that area. They asked for *my* recommendation.

Well, the fight over Big Cypress was between the conservationists and greedy real estate interests. The recommendation for the preserve would assure that the land and the wildlife would not be disturbed so I said that I would approve it . . . IF, the government would turn the

Big Cypress Preserve over to the Florida Game and Fresh Water Fish Commission to operate as a Game Management Area!

It was written up as agreed, but the feds slowly took over in force. They eased out the Florida Game and Fresh Water Fish Commission, and eventually, they even went so far as to restrict our "traditional use" of the land.

Eastern Airlines Flight 401—1972

It was December 30, 1972. It was a dark night. I was driving down a levee to park my vehicle. For the New Year's holiday I was going to my Sawgrass Camp at the north end of the Big Cypress Seminole Indian Reservation, about a 4-mile walk through the marsh. But, just as I parked, got out, and was closing the door, a special news bulletin came on my little juke box radio that an air crash had just occurred in the Everglades near Miami.

I got back in the vehicle and listened to the report. A commercial airline had crashed in the Everglades west of Miami International Airport. It was Eastern Airlines Flight 401.

Well, I raced the 65 or so miles back home, got my airboat, and headed south. I kept trying to get information about where, in the Everglades, the crash site was.

But nobody knew. It was the New Year's holiday, and apparently everybody was out partying and not their normal selves. I couldn't even get any sound information from the Florida Highway Patrol. I understood that the information had to come out of Atlanta, but I couldn't wait. I took my airboat and headed south to the Everglades and out the Tamiami Trail.

There's the levee there, L-67D.

Well, I didn't know which side of the levee . . . northeast or southwest? So, on a hunch, I took my airboat down the northeast levee. I went down, oh, probably about 8 miles, and by that time, I saw lights.

There was an Air Force helicopter hovering there. The crash site was not too far off the levee.

I launched my airboat and immediately went out and started rescuing people. They were crying, screaming, and hollering, of course. There was one group all singing together, trying to keep themselves calm. Before the rescue was really under way, people were just sitting there in the Everglades dark, many injured, traumatized, afraid of the water, fearful of imagined snakes and alligators, and with dead people all around them.

The wreckage was strewn out for a quarter mile.

When I came on the scene, my light was like a sign from heaven to those poor people. It really lit up the area. I began carefully circling around picking up the injured and taking them to the dike. At least I was getting them out of the water which was covered with jet fuel. Luckily it wasn't combustible. I worked through the night picking up the injured.

An Air Force helicopter, a big Huey, was trying to help, but the wash from the blades was picking up big pieces of metal from the wreckage and slinging them through the air. It was very dangerous, actually killing survivors! So we got word to the Air Force to call their Huey away. The Air Force was very good after that point.

In the meantime, I'm in and out of the water loading up all these people on the deck of the airboat, which worked out wonderfully for such rescue work.

The next morning I began searching for the dead. I would locate a long path about 6 feet wide that looked just like a lawn mower had cut through the 10-foot-tall saw grass. I would follow the path to the end. There I would find two dead people still strapped in their seats. Those paths were about 50 to 70 feet long, and there were many of them.

The Game and Fresh Water Fish Commission called in about thirty additional personnel to assist, which was extremely helpful. Of course, we weren't afraid of alligators or snakes like some of the other rescue workers. But it was doubtful if any were left in the area anyway with the spill of jet fuel covering the area. We worked the better part of thirty-eight hours without sleep. After thirty-eight hours of working in jet fuel, I began to blister. So I went home, got some rest, came back, and worked another twenty-four hours straight.

The rescue officials were real tight on security. I asked the person in charge from Eastern Airlines, "How many people were on board?"

His answer was just, "All the people are accounted for."

But they were still finding bodies three days after it happened! I must have asked him six times in the two days, but I always got the same answer. In fact, there were 101 killed and only 75 survivors.

It was an awful experience that I shall never forget. It bothered me greatly for some time. I kept wondering what the people had been thinking just before the crash. Because of my reoccurring thoughts on life and death, I held a meeting with all of my officers. One of the things I covered was the subject of life's choices, specifically regarding cooperation and respect for others on the job. When given the option, I said, they should work *with* one another, not *against* one another. This doomed flight and our labors to aid others, living and dead, seemed to provide a good life's lesson about being positive and caring, with love!

Alligator Protection

During the latter 1960s and early 1970s, Flood Control was digging a new levee and canal (L-31) on the west side of Highway 27 to Everglades Holiday Park. It would run right through the heart of one of the most prolific alligator nesting and habitat areas in the world.

When they dug this canal, it dried up the area west of Highway 27. It dried up so much! It dried up the alligator holes and the caves, which provided a home for many of the smaller alligators. So as a result, literally thousands and thousands of alligators had to migrate eastward to a canal where there was water.

Water Control Management had totally upset the whole environment for the alligators. It was unbelievable . . . the numbers of alligators that moved eastward. To give you an idea, take a measurement of 100 feet . . . in that distance there might be as many as 800 to 1,000 alligators. Most of them were small, 2–4 feet, but they came in all sizes.

I recall one morning, Gary Phelps and I received a call. There was an airboater broken down in the Everglades. So we got in my airboat and went on patrol to search for the individual in that area.

But on the way, I recall going down the canal about 9:30 a.m., a perfect time for the alligators to be sunning. There were literally thousands of alligators, just thousands of them, jumping into the water and swimming off. They were *so* prolific! I doubt there was a place in the world that had a greater concentration. But those alligators don't exist any longer. The word spread, and this area became a popular place for alligator poachers to hunt.

We wildlife officers spent a lot of time catching alligator poachers in that vicinity. Jimmy Sistrunk and Jimmy Thompson made an arrest on Highway 27, catching an individual by the name of Carl Docton who had in the neighborhood of twenty alligator skins and hides.

But times were changing. In 1960, New York State passed a law called the Mason Smith Act that banned the sale of endangered species or their manufactured products. The Lacey Act— which had been passed in 1900 to stop trafficking in domestic bird plumage (birds such as the snowy egrets of the Florida Everglades)—was amended by Congress in 1961 to also prohibit interstate trade in crocodilian hides. That was a grand moment for the safety of our alligators. But with this new law, the price per foot shot up to an all-time high. Alligator shoes cost $70 to $350 per pair and handbags $150 to $250. Alligator luggage sold for up to $1,000 per piece.

When domestic sources of alligator and crocodile hides were outlawed, dealers turned to caiman and crocodile hides from Central and South America, Africa, and Southeast Asia. Most of the species in these areas are now endangered.

Well, about this time, Patricia Caulfield was managing editor of *Modern Photography Magazine* based in New York. She had a strong desire to do a picture book on the Everglades, including some of the nature writings of the famous author Peter Matthiessen. She contacted Lou Gainey, the regional manager of the Game and Fresh Water Fish Commission, Everglades Region, and asked for his help in working on such a book throughout the Everglades.

For a while, I was assigned to work with Pat. We worked very hard, putting in long hours, long days, while she took photographs of all the beautiful scenery, the sunsets, the birds, the eagles, the alligators, all the wildlife, for the fantastic book called *Everglades.*

We spent three days working in the Big Cypress staying at my Sawgrass Camp. In one phase of shooting, Pat was trying to get just the right image of an eagle coming in to its nest in the Big Cypress. But the lens that she was using was not adequate for her needs. So she left the Glades, drove back to town, flew back to New York, purchased another lens, and flew back the same day! Up early the next morning, she shot the picture that she wanted!

I told her of my love for the alligators. I told her how the alligator plays a major role in the Everglades wetlands habitat for the fish and other animals by creating ponds of water for them during drought times when there is so little water available. How sometimes these tunnels go back 20 feet and some are even fed from underground springs. I told her how I could feel it if I checked the water temperature in a gator hole with my hand. If the water feels cooler, I know it's connected to a spring.

I described to her how the fish that live in the gator holes would survive the drought and be the breeders for the following season. That very soon after the seasonal water levels return you would see thousands of fish-spawning sites throughout the Everglades. And I used to wonder where all of the fish came from so fast to repopulate the Everglades wetlands? This is the wonderful part of nature, a wonderful part of the Everglades ecosystem that many people don't know anything about.

The alligator holes also provided for birds and mammals during droughts. Birds nest in the willows ringing their ponds and have a supply of fish, too, while the mammals come to drink and eat the smaller animals that congregate there. I impressed on Pat that it's very important to remember that the Everglades wetlands is made of water, drought, and fire. Take away one of the three and the Everglades will be destroyed forever. That is a fact that the engineers and computer scientists at Water Control must accept and act on accordingly or the wetlands will die.

Pat listened and truly fell in love with the alligators, particularly. She understood how hard we game officers worked trying to catch alligator poachers. She saw how I was working with various reporters and authors concerning chronic problems that we had with alligator protection. She went back to New York and told wildlife experts the difficulties we were up against.

She made arrangements for the New York Zoological Society to make a trip down here to interview me and to investigate the problems we had protecting the alligators. They were very serious about our problem. They investigated my activities, the problems I encountered while out on patrol, taped all of our conversations. They were very thorough in trying to get to the bottom of our needs for thorough alligator protection.

Then they went back to New York and met with the state regulators. With the great influence of the New York Zoological Society, New York City passed a law that made it illegal for importers or any company whatsoever to have any commercial market whatsoever in any crocodilian product. That covers caimans, crocodiles, alligators . . . and that covered all stores, Sears to Macy's to high-end boutiques.

The New York law was extremely effective. It was so effective that the U.S. Fish and Wildlife Service copied it and made it a federal regulation. When that law was passed, it nipped alligator poaching in the bud.

That was a great reward for me, knowing that I had had some influence in saving the alligators I cared so much about. And, it certainly made our job in Law Enforcement much easier, not having to worry about chasing poachers around the Everglades day and night! But, the State of Florida—the Game and Fresh Water Fish Commission—wasn't in favor of such stiff regulations on alligator protection!

In fact, Dr. Frye, the director of the Game Commission, with whom I was on pretty good terms, called me aside. He said, "Tom Shirley, I've got an idea you were behind this, and if I ever find out that you were, we've got serious problems."

I took that to mean what he said. It could have been just a warning to keep it quiet. But, nevertheless, the State of Florida didn't want such stiff regulations.

After the law passed, about a year or so later, famous Florida herpetologist Ross Allen tried to get special regulations set up so he could have several alligator compounds. He wanted to be able to handle all of the alligator complaints. He attended a Wildlife Commission meeting and even proposed to have the alligators he would keep in captivity on a perfectly natural diet!

He was trying to convince the public and the Commission that he would take proper care of them, by feeding them their natural food, meaning raccoons, possums, gar fish, and the like.

I said, "How are you going to come up with all this food?"

"I'll raise it," he said.

So I told him, "Well, you'll have more money racked up in feeding coons and possums than you'll make profiting on the alligators!"

Well, he sold the Commission on his idea, but he didn't sell me. I really got on the wrong side of the Commission at this point, I'm sure. But nonetheless, the alligator farms, exhibits, and so forth became organized businesses.

Once the alligators in the United States appeared to be making a comeback, approaching the "carrying capacity" levels, the U.S. Fish and Wildlife Service changed their category on alligators from "endangered" to "threatened." I got a call from the Florida Fish and Wildlife Commission's chief of law enforcement, Brantley Goodson, who said, "Tom, you guys down there . . . Don't take alligator poaching so seriously. Just kind of let it slide."

As years passed, the public began to be told how good alligator meat tastes and what good products the skins make. Here we go again!

Touching Base with Water Management

It was 1975. Under the state's new growth management, the newly created Water Management District was accountable to the state. Regardless of the name, though, like their predecessor, Flood Control, they were *still* going against regulations and holding water in Conservation Area 3 north of Alligator Alley. However, with my data in hand, our game commissioner was now able to bring this up at a state cabinet meeting. It embarrassed Water Management.

My records showed that the water was 2 inches above regulations, but by the time Water Management checked it, it was 2 ½ inches over. So, finally, Water Management had to acknowledge that I, representing the Game Commission, was on top of the situation and looking out for our interests, the wildlife!

It was then determined that I should produce a monthly report on water levels or other problems for Water Management. Up until then, no one had really shown interest in my statistics on this aspect of water management so vital to the well-being of the wildlife and ecology of the Everglades wetlands. I was delighted!

However, this was not a good deal for Water Management, because now all of my monthly records on Water Management's overages were documented information. Besides problems with water levels, I was also responsible for reporting dangerous hazards, such as the debris left over from their drainage projects—huge boulders or AA steel pipes sticking out of the marsh that could be very dangerous for airboaters. So it wasn't long before they told me to quit sending in my reports. I'm sure they feared being sued for any accidents resulting from those "documented" hazards.

But with all of the years of adversarial concern over water levels, I didn't have anything against the Flood Control/Water Management personnel themselves.

In fact, I used to stop by Pumping Station No. 171, L-28 Levee at Alligator Alley to have lunch with some of the guys. And I tried to support one of the men who showed interest in becoming a wildlife officer.

It's just too bad that for so long Flood Control had such an attitude, coupled with the political power and control, that no other agency could coordinate with them and that it was the helpless wildlife that bore the brunt of their actions.

Of course, seeing Flood Control's evolution since their creation in 1949, it's also obvious that the "wildlife," originally an important part of the equation, ceased to be their concern. Flood Control was mandated to focus their efforts on flood protection for towns and agriculture and the storage of water in times of drought, while we at the Wildlife Commission were simply fighting a losing battle.

8

Law Enforcement in
a Failing Ecosystem

Mercy Deer Hunt—1982

In the later 1980s, Water Management had constructed two weirs in the Miami Canal. The weirs were designed to save the Everglades soil from burning in the bad drought periods.

In 1982, one of our Commission biologists had a meeting with Jim Shortmeyer of Water Management. They had decided to try out the new weirs. "We're going to have 18 inches over the whole area!" he said with enthusiasm.

I said, "What's so good about that? That will be a total deer kill!"

This biologist didn't know any better. He was fairly new. He didn't know anything about the Everglades water table, didn't understand that the water couldn't go over 15 inches or the deer and the islands would be jeopardized, or how rainfall could further cause adverse effects combined with Water Management's suggested water levels.

So here was a new biologist *trying* to communicate with Water Control but who was so new that he didn't know any better about their concepts of water levels and the wildlife. Well, Water Management went ahead and closed the weirs, both of them. And the water came up just as they planned, 18 inches, and it began to kill deer in the whole area.

The situation was so horrible that the Game Commission decided that they should call an "emergency hunt" (called a "mercy hunt" by the media). There was a lot of adverse publicity over this "mercy hunt," as the hunters were to kill all the deer they found, including does, fawns, and yearlings under the auspices of the sanctioned emergency hunt.

I was terribly upset about this hunt and the stranded deer. I spoke my opinion at the Commission. I also commented to the press, "The deer are dying like flies!"

My boss, Lou Gainey, was really teed off. As we passed in the hall, he said sarcastically, "Tom, how does a fly die?"

The papers were reporting in high gear. *Miami Herald* "Outdoors" reporter Jim Hardie noted that the establishment of "deer islands" could "prevent a repeat of this fiasco . . . The noble Everglades deer unfortunately doesn't merit consideration from the Corps and the WMD [Water Management District] . . . Scapegoats in this tragedy are the hunters and the Florida Game and Fresh Water Fish Commission. They are in a Catch 22 situation."

Finally, someone who saw and reported it as it was. Hardie went out and witnessed the wildlife's predicament in this man-made flood himself and wrote: "The levee is alive with activity. Armadillos; a big sow hog with a litter, pushing helpless fawns out of the way; a bobcat bounds by and rabbits scatter . . . adult deer were standing in the water while . . . snakes, opossums, field mice, raccoons, birds, turtles, frogs and other creatures make up the menagerie."

The media were really ramping up on the radio, newspapers, and TV. I thought, "This time, I'm going to stay out of it." I was a bit concerned about my job, as my director had made the decision! I went to a Wildlife Federation Meeting with my friend Freddy Fisikelli, who was then the president. Freddy was going to leave the decision of "save or kill" up to the Wildlife Commission.

You recall that in 1966 our Game Commission had put a lot of effort and zeal into saving the deer in Conservation Area 3, albeit only after being shamed into it by the sportsmen. But this time, the Game Commission was promoting the slaughter!

There was an argument. I told the Commission that in 1966 we had moved four hundred deer and only 10 percent had died. Regional Manager Gwynn Kelley said that my estimates were not accurate. I reiterated that they were indeed.

Kelley said, "Tom, if you hold your ground on that, you'll be finding another job."

Well, because I was so upset, during the emergency hunt, they assigned me to the Tamiami Trail.

"We'll keep you off the Alley; then things can work much smoother," I was told.

That was the best thing for me because I knew better what we could do to save the Everglades, other than kill off the deer herd.

The media were still full of the story. Finally on July 18, 1982, the decision of "kill" or "save" was left up to U.S. District Judge Eugene P. Spellman. The judge "reluctantly reversed his decision to stop the 'mercy hunt' for 2,000 deer" following a daylong hearing. The *St. Pete Times* further noted, "This case at least has taught us one lesson. Some long look must be made at the water levels in these conservation areas."

Meanwhile, a group of conservationists tried to illegally remove deer south of Alligator Alley. Unfortunately, they had no experience in driving airboats or in catching deer. Their efforts met with poor results. The Commission was very pleased when the group had poor luck. They didn't want successful efforts to make the news and cause additional public outcry that would make the Game Commission's decision for an emergency hunt look worse than it was.

However, my two sons, Tommy and Troy, happened to be listening to the radio covering the conservationists' unsuccessful deer-capturing project. They came home and grabbed an airboat and headed for the Glades. They wanted to help with the conservation work because *they knew* how to catch deer!

Troy was recovering from a hang glider accident at the time and had both feet in a cast, so he drove the airboat while Tommy and their friend Phillip Murphy caught deer. They hog-tied and blindfolded four of them and then dropped them off on an island, while they caught four more. They then loaded up all the deer and took off toward Alligator Alley, where the media and conservation groups had their headquarters.

Gwynn Kelley received a radio message that the Shirley boys were coming in with a big load of deer. He ordered the helicopter pilot to head off the boys and tell them to promptly release the deer. A pursuit ensued with the chopper and Officer Jim Sistrunk chasing them. Finally, very frustrated and furious, the boys were instructed to release the deer back into the very deep water where they found them, knowing that they would most probably die. Those were two very angry young men!

So the sportsmen went out on their "emergency hunt." It was a shameful thing.

After the hunt, on August 3, 1982, J. Walter Dineen, director of Environmental Sciences Division, Resources Planning Department of the South Florida Water Management , answered a letter from Marjory Stoneman Douglas.

Called the "Mother of the Everglades" for her 1947 book, *The Everglades: River of Grass,* and founder of Friends of the Everglades, Douglas had written to the department asking what was going on with Water Management that they would initiate a situation that would so jeopardize the Everglades deer?

In his response to her letter, Dineen confessed, "The water over the majority of [WC Area 3] considered as 'deer range' is only 12 to 27 inches deep. That is not too deep for Everglades marsh, it is obviously too deep for 5,500 deer."

After the hunt, the chief biologist, Frank Hayes, came down from the Cooperative Wildlife Disease Study Group, University of Georgia, Athens. Frank was conducting a study on what was killing the deer . . . besides the high water! This was a duplication of the same monitoring study done on the deer in flood conditions in 1966! At that time they blamed it on the cattle industry. Next they blamed the deaths on the "barber pole" parasite that attacks when deer become stressed (stressed in this case, because of the high water conditions!). It appeared to me that the "powers that be" desperately wanted to put the blame on anything *but* high water!

As I was taking off in the helicopter to fly over the inundated Conservation Area, the Wildlife Commission's biologist Vic Heller said rather jokingly to me, "If you see any deer, shoot me some for our studies."

Well, there weren't many out there, of course, but I shot two from the helicopter with my .44 Magnum pistol. We strapped them on the struts and flew back to the lab.

Vic knew that I was a good shot, but he was amazed that I had shot the deer from the helicopter, from the air, *and* with a pistol, not a rifle!

But, after looking the deer over, Jim told me that one of them wasn't any good for their "organ study" because I had "shot it in the body."

"OK, Jim," I said, "where should I shoot them?"

Jim put his finger on the dead deer, right on the artery at the side of the neck. Sure enough, when I returned with two more, they were shot exactly where Jim had showed me. Now that really blew them away!

They wanted more deer, but we searched and searched, and didn't find any. Since there were hardly any deer left to be found, I sent my officers out at night and said, "Go ahead and fire hunt" because we desperately needed a dozen deer for Jim and Vic's studies. But in the end, after going out night after night, the men had to go outside of the area to kill enough deer to satisfy the biologists.

Then the Game Commission got some correspondence from Tallahassee—from Governor Bob Graham's Office. The governor wrote in his letter that the "emergency hunt" had been really bad publicity for Florida. Therefore, the state would benefit by bringing down the deer herd and other animals in this floodplain, so that there wouldn't ever be a repeat of this adverse publicity.

So the Wildlife Commission did. And that's why there's so little animal life left in the Everglades. Further, the next deer hunting season, they opened up the season in Conservation Area 3 to does from the Broward County/Palm Beach County line all the way to Tamiami Trail (Highway 41).

During that season I think there were fewer than nine deer kills, which usually numbered around 1,000. And more than half of that number were does, so there was clear evidence that they were successfully carrying out the governor's directive.

From that time on, hunting season after hunting season, we opened up the season for does. This procedure clearly almost wiped out the Everglades deer herd. Since then, it has never recovered. And in a few years, because of the depletion of the deer herd, the Commission began to endorse a more comprehensive management approach that focused on "non-game" animals, such as birds.

During his period in office, Governor Graham was lauded by the news media as the governor who "saved the Everglades." He's known for that to this day. But I don't agree with his example of "saving" the Everglades.

I repeatedly asked the Water Management District heads, with all their computers and scientists and studies, "What are you going to restore the Everglades TO?" I looked into blank faces, and I haven't gotten an answer yet. And to this day, the wildlife, plant life, ecology are still being destroyed, not "restored," because enough priority has never been given to the wildlife and habitat.

Seminole Indians and Hunting Laws—1983

In 1955, shortly after joining the Game Commission, I was tipped off that an Indian on the Tamiami Trail, Pete Osceola Sr., was in possession of a live fawn. Being new to my profession as an officer of the state, I asked legal professionals at the Commission how to handle this situation. They advised that I would probably not get a conviction because the man was an American Indian.

I took the time to write Washington, D.C., and asked if they could forward information concerning the Indians' rights in such cases. They promptly sent a book concerning the legal status of various Indian tribes going back to the early 1800s. Their reply was basically, "Leave the Indians alone. It would not be to the Commission's benefit to attempt prosecution." So, from then on, when dealing with the Seminole or Miccosukee Tribes, I have always followed the advice of the federal government.

Many times while on patrol, I'd come upon Indians who had killed deer—sometimes as many as six: bucks, does, and yearlings—but they were within their rights by Florida law. One evening in December 1983 at the remote Big Cypress Seminole Reservation, James E. Billie, chairman of the Seminole Tribe of Florida and a medicine man in training, chanced on a Florida panther. It was an auspicious encounter with an animal of family legend and the promise of powerful medicine. The panther was shot and skinned. Some of its meat was eaten in accordance with traditional customs that were considered necessary to preserve the spiritual welfare of the Florida Seminoles. And then all hell broke loose when a tipster, a fellow Seminole with a grudge, alerted the authorities.

I was by then bound to the Regional Office, and two wildlife officers were handling the investigation concerning James E. Billie's shooting of an "endangered" Florida panther. When I heard of the incident, I was more than willing to let it ride. I suggested that to my new superior, Captain James Reis, newly from Chicago, a person who knew nothing of the Indians at all. I lent him my book on federal regulations that I had received some twenty-three years earlier from Washington and told him that my advice would be to let the panther kill go.

I said, "Save the Commission money and court time, and just let it go. If you prosecute, we'll all lose, whether Seminole chief James Billie is found guilty or innocent."

I told Reis that the Miccosukee Tribe of Indians of Florida (another federally recognized tribe and close relatives to Seminole Tribal members) held a lease on many thousands of acres within our Game Management Area in Conservation Area 3. If the Commission followed through with prosecution against Billie, there was an almost certain chance that the Commission and the public would be posted off the Miccosukee Reservation.

But Captain Reis wouldn't hear of it. He decided to see it through. And he did, with all the whistles and the press, and it was picked up not only in the local papers but in the *New York Times*! It was the biggest trial, the hottest news. The State of Florida in appellate court reinstated a criminal charge against Billie in October 1986. Then it was the Marine and Wildlife Resources Office of the U.S. Justice Department vs. James E. Billie. And this case was still going strong until October 1987, when a "not guilty" verdict in the state trial changed their minds. Then, the U.S. Justice Department declared a mistrial and dropped its case.

Billie had told the court that he had killed the panther because it would bring him religious status. Well, I had a friend, Frank Weed, who raised panthers over on Highway 29 near Immokalee. Frank was also a close friend of James Billie's. I had a very old Incan relic that I had picked up on one of my trips to Peru, a knife with a panther totem on the handle. I had been told in Peru that some Indian tribes worshipped the panthers. I gave it to Frank Weed to give to James Billie. I thought that it would help him prove in court that other Indians worshipped panthers for religious purposes, too.

But the charges against Billie by then had become questionable, as experts admitted that the bloodline of the Florida panthers had been adulterated. Years earlier, wildlife experts had infused Florida's wilderness with pumas imported from the western United States in order to "bolster" the Florida panther bloodline. So there was every chance that the panther Billie killed was *not* a pure-blood endangered Florida panther of the genus *Felis* [or *Puma*] *concolor coryii*.

However, as a result of this trial that challenged native rights, as I predicted, the Miccosukee Tribe posted their reservation and took over the management of thousands of acres themselves. The state's wildlife officers were told "not to trespass." And now people have to pay a lease each year for their camp sites within reservation boundaries.

Captain Reis could not conceive of the Florida Tribes' increasing political power, which stemmed from an exploration of their inherent sovereign rights. Ironically those rights were explored and tested most successfully by Billie himself, which also ushered in the tribe's new economic windfall, gaming. Reis's handling of the panther situation cost the Commission and Florida sportsmen dearly.

FBI and Killers from California

By now, I was no longer in the field but bound to the Game Commission's West Palm Beach Regional Office. There I had to take care of a lot of office details and paperwork. I didn't care for that too much, but there I was, in charge of the Everglades, the Big Cypress, the Ten Thousand Islands, and the Florida Keys.

I believe in keeping in good contact with my personnel, my officers, and sitting in the "ivory tower" wasn't the best way to do it as far as I was concerned. Nevertheless, that's where I sat. So you can imagine how excited I felt one day when the FBI gave me a call.

They said, "Tom, we need your help."

My ears perked up. I said, "How's that?"

The caller said, "Well, we have four killers who have left California. They're on their way to Florida. They are supposedly going toward Miami, and we have information that they are looking for a woman who owns a fishing camp and has a lot of jewelry."

Nell Jones, the "Queen of the Everglades," was proprietress of Mack's Fishing Camp on Highway 27 and a very dear friend. (Shirley Collection.)

Well, these individuals had already killed a couple of people. They were dangerous subjects.

And, by the description of the woman, I knew that they were definitely headed for Mack's Fish Camp. Nell Jones was known as the "Queen of the Everglades." She owned a lot of jewelry and showed it off.

Nell and I went way back. As you know, Mack's Fish Camp had been my main base for my airboat put-in when I went on patrol. Over the years, Nell had always looked out for me. I had a very special place in my heart for her, as she did for me. She was such an outstanding and wonderful person and was loved by many. Any people who ever bad-mouthed me or made trouble in her place as often as not got a broom or a board whacked across their back! Nell didn't take any foolishness from anybody. And people out in the Everglades would rather bad-mouth the wildlife officer than the president. But Nell was always there to take up for me. I couldn't have asked for a better friend.

Now she might be in big trouble!

So I acquired a picture of the ringleader, and I rushed out to Nell to see if she knew these fellows.

She said, "Yep, they used to come here regular."

So if she knew them, then they also knew she could identify them. After robbing her, they would have to leave her dead! Realizing how dire the situation was, I contacted the Sheriff's Department and got two individuals to assist me. I even kept this secret from the Game Commission because I didn't want to take any chances of information leaking out. So I just took some days off.

But there was another problem with the secrecy of this operation. Nell's husband, Junior Jones, almost always left in the afternoon and went down the rocky road south to the Wagon Wheel Bar and Restaurant, which was owned by his father and run by his brother.

Junior would go down there and drink and have a good time with the boys, and he'd come home sometimes ten o'clock or midnight. He had built himself a little room on the second story so when he'd come home kind of liquored up, he'd climb up those stairs and go to bed.

We couldn't let Junior know what our plans were or what danger Nell was in, for fear he would get drunk and talk! That could blow our whole plan and could get both Nell and Junior killed.

So I had the deputy sheriffs, brothers George and Dave Matthews, and my friend Bill Thompson to help me set up a plan. I was to stand behind the counter at Mack's. One sergeant was going to stand at the front door. When he answered the door, it would be close quarters with the identified killer. If that's who it was, the sergeant would drop to the floor, and I would automatically blow the killer away. For this mission, the officers had bullet-proof vests. But I didn't!

We were all prepared. I went home and got all my guns—shotguns, pistols, I even brought my .458 old elephant rifle, at the time the most powerful gun the United States had ever made.

It was necessary for us to hide from Junior in case he woke up or something. So we all stayed out of sight until after he left. Then we would come in and spend the night, leaving about eight o'clock the next morning before Junior got up. I was extra nervous, as I was sleeping in Nell's bed while she slept somewhere else. I decided if I ever heard Junior coming to the bedroom door, I'd jump in the closet.

Who knows what he would have thought if he had caught me in Nell's bed!

This went on for a week!

Meantime, these individuals arrived in town with a woman and held up the Sonny's Barbecue on Highway 84. There was a disruption followed by a shootout, and a person was killed. But the bad guys escaped.

So we stayed at our positions for another couple of days to make sure they had left the area, which they did. So for us, for Nell, we were relieved, and our mission was accomplished. But that was a kind of law enforcement work I hoped I wouldn't have to experience again. The first thing Nell did was to go out and buy me a bullet-proof vest of my own!

In the Line of Fire—1984

Uncle Steve Roberts, head of the Roberts clan, told me that there was a square stone monument down around Flamingo near the shore. On it is a bronze plaque with the following inscription: "Guy M. Bradley, 1870 to 1905. Faithful to death as a game warden of Monroe County. He gave his life to the cause of which he was pledged. Erected by the Florida Audubon Society." Bradley had been one of us. The first game warden in the Everglades!

Uncle Steve said he had moved that stone back about three times, because the tides would eventually wash out the fill. He went through the effort to move it back, to keep it permanently on solid ground.

The story of Guy Bradley, told in Stuart McIver's *Death in the Everglades*, has to do with the fashions of the 1890s period, when every fine lady's hat had to be lavishly adorned with feathers, sometimes even complete birds, or multiple birds! But the ultimate decoration was a spray of white snowy egret plumes.

These plumes are shed naturally by the birds when they are molting. But the market for plumage was so lucrative that hunters shot the birds when the plumage was at its prime. The beautiful feathers extend from the bird's head down to the neck of both the male and female egrets. Unfortunately their prime was only in the spring during the mating and nesting season.

The birds were killed by hunters who wiped out entire rookeries where the birds nested. Their eggs were left to rot and the newborn chicks to starve or be eaten by predators.

As the birds became scarce, the price of feathers escalated. Hunters hungry for profit slaughtered the birds without mercy, which led to the snowy egrets' decline almost to extinction.

The Audubon Society hired Bradley, a local man, as the game warden to combat the slaughter in the Everglades rookeries. He loved the Everglades and was a great woodsman. I could really relate to him.

One day, he was patrolling the area, much as I did in my job, when he came across a fellow and his two sons he knew very well. Bradley had earlier arrested one of the sons for illegal possession. The father told Bradley if he did that again, he'd kill him. That's what eventually happened. And Bradley was shot.

The supposed killer was taken to court, but due to a lack of witnesses he was acquitted. However, the people of Flamingo, his close neighbors, righteously set fire to the man's house, warning him never to return. A federal law, the Lacey Law, was passed in 1900 and another in 1910 that prohibited the possession of egret plumes. But it was only a campaign of education and a change in fashion that eventually stopped the slaughter. The public outcry, however, had lasting positive effects. It created and strengthened conservation clubs such as Audubon and developed into the first major environmental conservation movement across the nation.

Bradley's story sure struck home to me. In my job the same scenario could play out. I, too, knew the poachers with whom I dealt, and some were friends. They could possibly outdraw me, and I could surely envision that my killer might be acquitted due to "lack of witnesses"!

But my job, like Bradley's, was to uphold the wildlife laws, as we had sworn to do. However, I sure didn't want to get shot doing it!

At one time I spent a lot of time with Jack Storm from the Attorney General's Office in Tallahassee. As I mentioned before, we became close friends when he helped me handle my cases as a private attorney.

In hearing the pressures of my job and how we officers were literally "in the wilderness" apprehending armed men—men with a lot of testosterone, usually liquored up and resenting being apprehended—Jack became very concerned about my safety and that of my officers.

He said, "Tom, why do you put yourself in the line of fire just to save a deer or the alligators? Don't you realize how many very close calls you've had? You're going to get yourself killed. Why do you do that?"

I said, "Well, that's what we have to do. We take an oath to protect the wildlife and the fish for the State of Florida. This is what it calls for. This is part of our job. We swore to do it, and that's what we're doing! Whatever it takes to enforce the law, we'll do it!"

Jack asked me to sit down behind his desk. He said, "Tom, *think* about this seriously! Tell me the number of times that you have had close calls."

I sat there and thought, "Well, there was the night at the Robertses' camp when I had drawn my gun, but there were two guys out of sight on the roof who had their rifles cocked on me; there was Gator Roberts when he attempted to draw his rifle on me during the airboat dogfight; there was Jerry Harris the cop who drew his .38 pistol on me; and, why as a close call, there was even the *Wild Kingdom* cameraman wanting me to roar my airboat in for another 'close shot,' when I almost wiped all of us out with Marlin Perkins in the back seat! . . . Or when I nearly burned up in the fire on the dike, or when I was chasing that 'fire bug,' Snow. Then there was a man getting ready to chop his girlfriend with an axe when I came along just in the nick of time. Why, he was ready to turn it on me, but I discharged my weapon at his feet . . ."

Boy, I was just warming up!

Then I thought, "Oh, and what about Pollock's Tavern?"

It was located around 20 miles from Miami on the Tamiami Trail on a 5-acre tract adjoining the Everglades. It was a popular gathering place for the hunters and airboaters to meet. It was a pretty rough place, especially in the afternoon, because the airboaters who frequented this tavern were pretty heavy drinkers.

My officer Chuck Mann attempted to check an airboat when Pollock came out and told him, "Get off my property or I'll shoot you dead in your tracks."

Officer Mann left Pollock's and notified me of what had taken place.

So the next day I went to Pollock's in an effort to smooth things over. I went inside, and Pollock and I had a conversation.

But Pollock sneered at me, "I have already killed two men and if you come on to my property again, I'll blow you away!"

I informed Pollock that by law I had the legal right to come onto his property to check all of the hunters and airboaters and said, "I'll be back to carry out my duties the next Sunday."

So Pollock spread the word that on Sunday he was going to blow me away with his shotgun. As you can imagine, this threat made for much excitement among his patrons! They were all looking forward to seeing what would happen.

Sunday came around, and I fully expected that Pollock would try to keep his word.

About twenty airboaters showed up and were all prepared for some excitement. It seemed probable that there would be a showdown, that someone might be killed or wounded. As I walked across the field, I saw Pollock standing in the doorway, daring me. But I went about my business checking the airboats, while keeping an eye on the doorway.

Well, everything went smoothly without a hitch, with no more problems at Pollock's Tavern! Still, with his threats, I considered that a "close one."

And I smiled at Jack, "Well, Jack, I could go on and on. It's just part of my job, I can't change it."

He said, "Well, Tom, it's your life, yours and the other wildlife officers'. But I still wonder . . . is your life worth it?"

Not too long after Jack last represented me, he was killed in a private airplane accident out over the Everglades. It was a sad day for me because he was such a great individual.

My personal security on the job was that I felt there was a science to what I did. It was based on my long number of years in the Everglades. I knew the land, the outlets. I knew the canals, levees, the put-ins, fish camps, everything. Especially I knew the temperament of most of the men I was dealing with. Vic Heller, who recently retired as assistant director of the Game and Fresh Water Fish Commission, came on as a biologist while I was with the Commission. He recently commented on my instincts concerning the lawbreakers, "Tom knew what they were doing and he knew how to catch them doing it!" While Johnny Jones, a powerful and influential leader of the Florida Wildlife Federation during my Commission days, recalled, "Tom was a good man—unless you were the bad guys!" But as I have said, I was polite, and I was fair. People remembered and respected me for that, and the news spread.

I had my Karado training. I was familiar with my gun and my holster and continued to practice fast drawing in my spare time. That might be the only reason I'm here today. But since I came up against some pretty big guys, like Jerry the cop, who my pistol might not have stopped in time, I switched over to the biggest pistol made, a .44 magnum. And I felt much safer.

Then we had to consider the reality that, as wildlife officers, we were up against armed hunters. Hunters have .00 buckshot in their shotguns. They've got .30-06 high-powered rifles. If there was to be gunplay, they would have the jump on us. So we were always going to be one step behind, handicapped before we even started into the woods. So I was careful on operations where there would be firearms activity.

But even being as careful as possible, we have been unfortunate to lose officers in the line of duty. Officer Conley Campbell, whom I mentioned, was patrolling L-5 Levee on the Broward/West Palm Beach line with his brother-in-law one night.

While Campbell was making a routine "stop and search" on a station wagon, Oscar Pablo Duran got out with a flashlight. Meanwhile Conley had seen a deer hidden in the back of Duran's vehicle.

To Campbell's surprise, Poacher Duran—a CIA-trained member of the notorious Cuban Alpha-66 unit—pulled out a pistol, crouched, and shot Campbell five times.

Campbell fell to the roadway and opened fire with his .357 Magnum, hitting Duran in his hip. Campbell rolled off the levee into the marsh. Duran drove off at a high rate of speed with one of his tires flattened from Campbell's shots. Campbell radioed for assistance, and Duran was apprehended on Highway 27.

While Duran was found guilty and sentenced to fifteen years in prison, he served only five before he was released, while Conley Campbell spent months in the hospital and in treatment. He eventually returned to work, but the job no longer had the appeal that it had before he was shot, and he resigned.

Then Officer Peggy Park, twenty-six years old, was murdered in the line of duty. She was killed by a paroled felon on December 13, 1984. She was the first female conservation officer to be slain while on-duty.

And there were other hazards on the job. Jimmy Thompson had been set up to be fired by the Commission and then work with me undercover. He went to work at an airboat shop, where he built boats for many of the poachers, who would come in bragging about their hauls. As my informant, this situation was working really well, and I was getting good information.

Jimmy was always afraid of electricity. One day, he was working with an electric drill under the deck of an airboat. He didn't realize that the connection on the cord was faulty. He pulled the cord, and it fell on the metal deck, shorted out the drill, and grounded to Thompson against the aluminum hull, electrocuting him. What a sad day for us all.

I was always cautioning my officers on their safety. One of the Commission's part-time employees, Tommy Taylor, recalled how I would say: "Remember, always be alert. There are outlaws out there that will kill you. You are often alone. If you treat people fairly, they will remember it . . . and if you don't treat them fairly, they will tell twice as many people!" Maybe being as fair as we could helped to keep us safe.

Stalking Deer Poachers at Night

Being in the office most of the time, I was always anxious to spend some time back out in the Everglades. Working with the officers was the part of my job that I most enjoyed.

I kept getting complaints from the Dade County Airboat Association that there were individuals going out at night in their airboats, "jack-lighting" does. So, as complaints kept coming in, I asked the officers in that area to see what they could do to knock this violation down.

Wildlife Officers Bob Douglas and Roy Martinez were in that patrol area. I had apprised them of this situation before. So I said, "Well, why don't we all go out, the three of us, and see what we can do to catch these outlaws?"

So we got in my vehicle. I always carried mosquito bar and a camouflage suit and netting in my car. That makes for beautiful camouflage.

So that night we went down to the Tamiami Trail, and sure enough, those individuals were out in their airboats south of the Trail from the Airboat Association Headquarters.

I noticed that they came in on their airboats and piddled around, coming up close to the road in one place, then going back out and doing some frogging for a while. Finally, they came back to a little cabin that they had about 150 yards farther west from where I'd seen them stop the airboat before.

I put on my camouflage suit and snuck out on the field, pretty close to where they had stopped their boat. I had just reached the area, and here came two of them walking right out of the cabin toward me.

"Oh, boy, here I am," I thought. "I'm going to get caught!"

It was an open field, and there was only one little old bush. It wasn't more than 5 feet across at the most, with hardly any leaves. But that was the only place for me to squat down. Well, I did have on my camouflage . . .

Here they came . . . and they walked right past me, very close. I had to move very, very slowly to get my arm and legs out of the way, so they wouldn't step on me. They went on beyond me about 50 feet, where they picked up a deer and began dragging it back to the cabin.

I lay there very still. I thought sure they were going to drag that deer right on top of me. I saw it was a doe, so as soon as I could, I gave Roy Martinez and Bob Douglas the signal with the flashlight to come on.

When my officers arrived, we walked over to the cabin.

Hunting at night with a light, "or jack-lighting," and taking a doe out of season were both violations of the hunting laws, of course. So we arrested Earl Feldman, Jack Coleman, and Ray Jackson. They had been drinking . . . were feeling pretty rough and tough . . . All of a sudden, Ray went over and got hold of the deer and started dragging it off!

Then Earl Feldman grabbed the deer. He started running for the airboat, dragging the deer behind him!

So I hollered for Roy Martinez to stop him. "Stop him before he gets into the airboat!"

Feldman dropped the deer, but he jumped into his airboat.

Well, Roy jumped into the airboat right behind Feldman trying to stop him! Feldman cranked up his boat, and off he went! He was trying to throw Roy Martinez off the boat, cutting figure eights, swirling 'round and 'round, and Roy was on the front of the airboat, which was wet and slippery. He was falling all over the place.

Well, with that engine running, you know, 3,000 RMPs, if you fall on that prop, it's going to cut you to ribbons.

So this fracas was going on, water spraying all over. Roy was fighting to stay in the airboat, and I feared for his life. I figured there wasn't anything I could do but shoot out that engine. I had to bring it to a stop to save my officer. So I pulled out my .44 Magnum. Bam! Bam! I shot twice. I shot through the engine, knocked it right out, so Feldman was stopped.

We proceeded to place him under arrest. Well, Feldman was pretty liquored up and pretty mad. We were ready to take those three guys in to jail, when Roy Martinez mentioned that he had a friend, a Highway Patrolman, who was patrolling that night. "Why don't we call him to give us a hand?" he suggested.

Sounded pretty good to me! I figured these guys were so liquored up that if they got to scuffling around, one of them could get one of our guns. Help might be real nice. So I said, "OK, Roy, go ahead and call your buddy."

That was the first time I'd ever called for backup!

We took them in and booked them. Feldman was fined three thousand dollars, but he was a pretty wealthy individual who lived down on the Keys. But, as with so many of the guys that I've arrested over the years, we remained acquaintances. We'd talk about the good ole days, and we'd sort of forget the adversarial parts or laugh them off—the poachers knew I had a job to do. They understood that. But old Feldman still holds a bad grudge against me. He never did forgive me for putting that .44 Magnum shell through his 180-horsepower engine!

The Waning Days—1985

I was active in the Everglades wetlands during the period when the wildlife was abundant, but, as my tenure with the Game and Fresh Water Fish Commission came to a close, the wildlife and fish had greatly diminished. Professionals from many agencies blamed the sportsmen for killing off the Everglades wildlife. But I knew better. The hunter had not shot the butterfly, he had not killed off the otters, poisoned the snakes, the turtles, or the birds. He had not kept the eagles from nesting in the Everglades as they used to do. He had not polluted and poisoned the water, nor had he flooded the areas and killed off most of the wildlife population and the islands on which they lived.

In 1966, when I witnessed the Everglades wetlands beginning to change, it was, of course, due to the Everglades being altered by the

In my efforts to show the error of Flood Control's excessive flooding of the Everglades wetlands and to prove to politicians how those excessive water levels were endangering the three-thousand-year-old islands and all the wildlife, I utilized the indisputable proof of photographs. This is the camp of my friend Al Henschel as it looked when I first saw it in 1955, a dense hammock with large banyan trees. (Shirley Collection.)

With the excessive floodwater held in Conservation Area 3 by Flood Control, the trees at Henschel's hammock began to rot at their roots. Even the large banyan trees began to die. This is the water level in 2006, and behind me is all that remained of Al Henschel's camp. (Photo by Stanley Kern.)

network of dikes and canals that interrupted the natural water levels, the creation of man-made floods, and later the introduction of runoff and nonquality water from agriculture.

As I mentioned earlier, when I joined the Game Commission its programs were guided by its constituents—the conservationists, freshwater anglers, sportsmen, and the strong organizations to which these men and women belonged. The Commission's job was to hire Wildlife Management to oversee the welfare of the game: to restock, to preserve, and to regulate hunting seasons . . . to make game laws, with direct input from the constituents and with our Law Enforcement division to protect the wildlife by locating and fining violators. It was really a wholesome, stable, and balanced program.

What happened?

Well, first, the U.S. Corps of Engineers who built the canals and dikes that destroyed the Everglades happened, and then Flood Control/Water Management that operated the Corps systems; next the politicians happened, who so catered to growth that they let agriculture like Big Sugar move into the Everglades and spread nutrient pollution; and then the federal government took more of our wildlife management area for the Big Cypress National Preserve. All of these projects so damaged our outreach and disrupted the long-term goals of the Game and Fresh Water Fish Commission that it lost its momentum and credibility with its constituents.

With Flood Control's policies from 1948, their restructuring as Water Management in 1972, commandeering the Everglades wetlands and moving water with no regard for the harm it was doing to the wetlands or to the wildlife that lived there, everything had changed. It changed for the Commission, and it changed how I felt about the Commission. Since I joined and swore to protect the wildlife "So help me God," *we* were no longer in control.

I had witnessed the destruction of the Everglades wetlands, but I was only capable of yelling against the wind. I sometimes felt that I had fought long and hard for the Everglades wetlands and its wildlife, the deer, the gators, and the islands . . . and lost miserably.

I'd lost mainly because the Commission, my own employer's goals, had been thwarted by not having a powerful voice within the state government. My bosses' jobs would doubtless have been jeopardized if they had not played along with the whims of Flood Control. But how unfortunate that the very thing that made the Commission fresh and wholesome (being nonpolitical) was exactly how we as an agency let the Everglades wetlands and the wildlife down!

I recall being at a meeting with Water Management in the 1970s with my boss, Dr. Frye. Things were really heating up, and I had some significant input to add. He said to me, "Keep talking Tom. We want to hear it from you. Keep talking!" I realized that the Commission, being part of state government, couldn't protest or show advocacy, but it was OK for me to offer my personal, professional opinion . . . to some degree!

In the thirty years that I was with the Game Commission, I saw the agency go through many changes and transitions. In the 1940s, the Commission's budget was less than $750,000, but they were so zealous, such major believers in the restocking of wildlife. With strong backing and support from their greatest fans, the many hunting and conservation clubs, they nonetheless managed to restock hundreds of deer that year. The deer came from the King Ranch in Texas. Later, Louisiana traded us deer for turkeys. But, by the time I retired in 1985, the Commission was avoiding restocking projects altogether.

Indeed, the sportsmen's interest, support, and knowledge were once considered valid as a checks-and-balances system for the Commission to make effective wildlife recommendations and decisions. They were regarded as the Commission's allies, not its adversaries. And the Commission in turn encouraged all sportsmen to unite and form conservation clubs in an effort to better represent themselves at the Game Commission's annual public meetings.

In the latter days of employment, the Commission hired a new regional manager, Gwynn Kelley, who played such a major role in the Mercy Kill. By that time, some of the constituents in the conservation and hunt clubs had gotten totally frustrated and fed up with the way the Commission was dealing with wildlife and the hunters. At the meetings, they would raise holy hell if they didn't like the way the Commission was handling a project, which they had every right to do. However, their criticisms, some very sound, reflected directly on Regional Manager Kelley. Bob Brantley, the director of the Commission, got tired of this scenario (unfortunately from hearing Gwynn Kelley's side only) and simply disbanded the meetings. So we no longer held public meetings with the very groups that we were supposed to serve and who had supported our efforts for so many decades.

Then there were issues concerning the alligators. For years, of course, we'd been educating the public on how important the alligators were in keeping a healthy Everglades wetlands. But the new "revamped" Commission began educating the public on how beneficial the alligators would be to this Game Commission by making new regulations.

All of this was so disheartening. We had worked so hard, so long, so diligently to protect the alligators. All of those nights of stakeouts, constant vigilance, risking our very lives, always mindful of upholding the law, and especially to protect the endangered alligators, in the name of "Everglades conservation." And I had just caught some of my *own* wildlife officers poaching alligators . . .

By the 1980s, the Commission was hiring "hunters" to handle the alligator complaints. They sent out a notice that they wanted to hire people to contract as "alligator trappers."

So I was sitting in the Regional Office in West Palm Beach, and I was interviewing these people, crowds of people—crowds of alligator poachers. Here were these guys I'd been chasing for years, and now we were going to hire them to be part of "US," the Wildlife Commission, an organization that I truly had believed in!

It became extremely hard for me to accept this logic and the conflicting purpose of this new directive set forth by the Commission. It was hard for me personally to accept the fact that I had to interview rough-and-tough gator poachers at the Regional Office and put them on the Commission's payroll. You know how much I simply love the alligator, so these regulations in the hands of former poachers appeared to me more a case of "organized crime" than of conservation!

And further, due to those new regulations, when these trappers handled our alligator complaints, they could no longer turn the gators loose in the wild. New Commission regulations said that they'd have to kill them! The meat was sold and the hides were turned over to the Commission, who received 33 percent of sales when the hides were bid off each year.

Next, the Commission created even more latitude with permits, making it legal to go out into the Everglades and capture baby alligators, alligator eggs, allowing people to rob the nests for commercial sales. Gator hunters could go out and mark down the alligator nests on GPS so when the next year rolled around they could go directly to them and rob the eggs. That doesn't leave much future for the alligator, as it's still on the "threatened species" list!

Ironically, Arnold Brunell, a wildlife biologist with the Commission's alligator program, commented in a 1994 Associated Press article that the alligator-protection laws in the 1970s that ended poaching had allowed the alligator population to rebound.

So it looks like, inadvertently and ironically, I was actually an accessory to this "open hunting season" on alligators! By so influencing the New York Zoological Society that they pushed for bans on the sale and importation of alligator products that ended poaching, I had made it possible for the Everglades alligators to multiply to the point that they could be hunted as game animals!

My employment with the Game and Fresh Water Fish Commission was from 1955 to 1985. In that time, the Commission went through many changes in policies, procedures, priorities, credibility, and spirit. Many good battles were once fought for conservation.

During most of those years I felt that my employment with the Game and Fresh Water Fish Commission was for a worthy cause, dedicated to the protection, conservation, and preservation of our wildlife. I had attempted to help keep America's traditional heritage of hunting and fishing rights for our future generations. I worked for these causes and for the Everglades wetlands. However, my dedication to what the Commission had become could not continue for another thirty years. I took my retirement.

I left everything behind me. I tried real hard to not be so involved in water and wetlands issues. I especially tried to not get involved with what was taking place with Water Management on the Everglades Restoration Project!

I opened a business, "Tom Shirley's Everglades Travel Tours, Inc.," I specialized in airboat tours, movie and television production services, photography, sightseeing, bird watching, bass fishing, and overnight camping. I gave people from all over the world an opportunity to really see what the Everglades wetlands looked like, but I didn't charge my clients. The business was my way of introducing interested individuals and groups, especially politicians, scientists, and the media to the Everglades wetlands and to have the opportunity to discuss its future preservation.

9

From Officer to Advocate

Deadly Toxins

Back in 1968, we were going through yet another deer crisis, another big fight between the Flood Control and the sportsmen. The director of the Game Commission, Earl Frye, and Palm Beach Circuit Court judge Thomas Sholts were with me in the Everglades to see the conditions and the dead deer firsthand.

I remember going to a particular area, and Dr. Frye looked down at the ground.

He said, "What's going on here, Tom? I've never seen this before. Look at all these dead turtles!"

Well, that was the beginning of the herbicide flow into the Everglades. The sugar people were back-pumping into Lake Okeechobee. That was the beginning of the end for the turtles. It was also when I noticed the snakes disappearing. The ribbon snake, garter snake, the water snakes had all been killed off. The last to go were the cottonmouth and the blue racer.

I have witnessed the spraying of herbicides and insecticides, which are still being used in the Everglades wetlands. I have watched snakes, turtles, and rabbits die moments after the spray entered the water. I often thought that if the State of Florida was really interested in saving the Florida panther, they should conduct a simple study showing the drastic effects that toxic water in the Everglades wetlands has had on the marsh rabbit. If they can save the rabbit, they can certainly save the panther.

I reported some of my own findings to the Game Commission. For instance, I told them that as the water first comes up, young water moccasins are healthy. But six weeks later they are dead. Well, I watched this happen for around three years. I tried my best to get the Commission involved, but my concern fell on deaf ears, as usual, because of politics.

After I retired, though, I thought I'd get on this project myself. So I collected several dozen moccasins, brought them home, and kept them in a big cage and fed them better than they would have been in the wild, to keep them healthy.

Meanwhile, I went to the University of Miami to try to contact a biologist, someone who would be willing to do a tissue study to see what was killing the reptiles.

Finally, I came across an individual who said, "Tom, I'll help you. As a federal government official, I'm on the payroll to determine such studies, to find out the problem and conditions, and give an annual report."

That was great news to me!

But despite feeding these cottonmouth moccasins healthy diets, they began to die. I took the snakes to the biologist's home and asked him to do a tissue study.

But instead of helping me as promised, he said, "Tom, what you said is, no doubt, the truth, but if I rebuild this I will be blackballed out of the State of Florida. I will never get another federal grant. I just can't help you with this project."

Then one evening, my friend Gus Graser and I were going across the Everglades in my airboat, and I saw this alligator in the shallow water of a marsh. So I stopped and I looked at it, and he was way too thin. It looked like it was sick.

So I decided I would go ahead and catch it and take it in to Game Management and let them do a tissue study to see what was killing it. I got out with a rope and caught that alligator with my bare hands. I caught him and ran him up to the airboat. But he started twisting. Next thing you know, I was up against the airboat and he got his tail wrapped around my leg.

Well, when an alligator starts to twisting, he's going into the "death roll" as if he's killing game. And when they go into a death roll, they have so much strength, that it's best just to turn them loose, which usually I do. Because you just can't overcome their strength.

Then, before I knew it . . . Bam! That alligator had turned and grabbed me by the hand!

There I was . . . It was a nightmare coming true. Here's the alligator with my hand in his mouth, and he was biting pretty hard—teeth to bone. I knew that he could twist my arm right out of my shoulder socket. So I turned, I let the alligator drop, but he still had my hand in the water.

Then he went into the roll again, rolling across the marsh. Since my hand was still in his mouth, I rolled along with him. I knew that if he shook, he could take my hand right off. And if I didn't keep up with his rolls, I knew he'd twist my arm off. So every time he rolled, I rolled.

Finally, I guess he got tired and he quit rolling. So I lay there in the marsh beside the alligator with my hand still in his mouth. After lying there for about five minutes, he just turned me loose!!! And there I was . . . bleeding all over the place. But I proceeded to go ahead and tie the gator up, and I took him in to the Game Management people. I told them they might want to do a tissue sample on this sick gator. But they weren't concerned. They didn't care.

They said, "Tom, you've got to take that alligator back out there and turn him loose."

Well, I didn't. I took him home, and he died two days later.

I'm sure they were afraid the study would reveal there was mercury in the water, and the levels were so high, it was killing the alligators. They would have been concerned that it would affect their new "alligator season."

Well, that gator had bitten up my hand pretty good. What's worse, sometimes more than the lacerations, it's the resulting infection. Every time an alligator bites you, it gets badly infected. So, knowing that, when I went home, I wrapped my hand up and went right to the emergency room at Hollywood Memorial Hospital.

They took my name and personal info and asked, "What happened?"

I said, "Well, I got bit by an alligator."

The nurse looked at me skeptically and said, "Go sit over there then."

So I went and sat down and I waited, and I waited, and I waited. Everybody was getting waited on except me.

My wife, Naomi, was in a room in that hospital with an ailment of her own. So after waiting a couple of hours, I got tired of waiting. I left the emergency room and went on up to see my wife. I visited with her quite a while, then I left to go home.

My wife later told me that after I left, a nurse came running in all excited, "Where's that man? Where's that gentleman who says he got bit by an alligator?"

"Well," my wife said, "he was here for a while but got disgusted with you guys and left."

The nurse said, "Well I'm sorry. We thought he was just joking. People don't get bitten by an alligator very often!"

So I went on back to the house and doctored myself with antibiotics and so forth. My hands and fingers were lacerated, but I felt extremely lucky to have my hand.

An alligator has 2,500 pounds of pressure in his bite—and it sure felt like it! I learned my lesson that time—don't ever try to hold on to an alligator when he goes into a death roll. He's going to win every time!

Snake Bite

For the 1987 Thanksgiving holiday, the family wanted to go to the Sawgrass Camp that I leased by permit on the Miccosukee Indian Reservation and have a joyful time. Well, I had a Labrador who was always anxious to go to the Glades with us, but for some reason, I was hesitant about taking him for fear he might get bitten by a poisonous snake.

So I pondered on it for several days. I decided to take him. We all loaded up in the airboat and off to the camp we go.

Well, we got there, and right away I got out and walked over to where recently I had planted a little palm tree. A raccoon had torn the palm out of the ground. So I went right to work trying to replant the palm and pack the soil back over the roots.

There was a leaf on the ground. All in one motion, I picked up the leaf and rolled and pushed the soil underneath the palm tree. Well, I didn't realize it, but there was a baby water moccasin underneath that leaf, and I pushed him into the ground with the dirt. No doubt I ticked him off pretty bad—and he bit my index finger.

I figured, "Uh, oh, the party's over!"

Well, I anxiously looked at my finger and yep, there were two fang marks.

It wasn't hurting, but two seconds later, it *was* hurting. Five seconds later, boy it was *really* hurting, so I walked to the camp.

I said, "Boys, pick up. We've got to head back in. Dad's been bitten by a moccasin. So we picked up, loaded up the boat, and off we went back across the Everglades to the landing.

Boy, that bite was really hurting. First, I took some black electrical tape and put it around my finger tight, thinking it would help to stop the poison from traveling and reduce the pain. But the pain was too strong. I couldn't do it.

We got back to the vehicle and my younger son, Barney, drove. Boy, we were going full blast all the way through the east gate on Alligator Alley. I called ahead to Hollywood Memorial Hospital and told them I was on my way.

"I've been snake bit! I'm coming in, so get things ready for me!"

I got there, and it seemed like everybody in the hospital had to gather around and to look at the man that got snake bit! Is he some sort of a monster or something? One by one they came sticking their heads in the door to take a look at me. They were all excited!

They put a cuff on my arm, took my blood pressure, and all that.

Half an hour later, they came back. By mistake, they had left the cuff on my arm! Then they put a name tag on my wrist, but by mistake the name tag was also strapped to the bed post.

And it sure took a long time to get antivenin. It took so long I could have caught a taxi and gotten it myself!

So in frustration, I got on the phone and called Bill Hass at the Miami Serpentarium. He was an expert on snakes, snake bites, and venoms. I told him what had happened and about the antivenin I was waiting to receive.

Bill said, "Well, Tom, so much time has elapsed, that it isn't the stuff that they should give you. Too much time has passed; it's not gonna do you any good anyway."

So then five doctors came in for a discussion on what to do.

I was really aggravated by then, and I said, "I have my old Boy Scout Book if you guys need it!"

One doctor said, "Tom, if you don't elevate your arm and keep it elevated, I'm gonna have to slice your arm open from the wrist all the way up to your shoulder. So be sure to keep it elevated."

So I did.

He was the only doctor who made any improvement in my condition.

It was my wife, Naomi, who finally found out that the Arizona Poison Institute is on standby twenty-four hours a day.

By then the platelets in my blood, which should have been around 300,000, had dropped way below 10,000.

I was in a very dangerous position. The Arizona Poison Control said I was a "time bomb."

And I had found out the hard way a fact that I didn't know before: baby snakes are six to ten times more potent than adult venomous snakes!

So they were giving me platelets, trying to bring up my blood condition, but I wasn't holding my own. They kept putting in more platelets, more platelets. It was a long period before my blood began to build back up. The doctors said they weren't going to release me unless it was well over 100,000 platelets.

Well, the next day was Thanksgiving. I really wanted to get out of there real bad. So reluctantly, the doctors released me with only 50,000 platelets, but I was very careful, like I told them I would be—for a day!

The day after Thanksgiving, I went back out to the Sawgrass Camp, found that nest of baby moccasins, and disposed of them! And remember! If you're ever bitten by a poisonous snake, call the Arizona Poison Control ASAP!

Everglades Advocate—1999

Knowing the water levels in the Everglades wetlands was most important to us Gladesmen who derived livelihood and pleasure out of riding the Everglades in our vehicles, whether skiff, airboat, swamp buggy, half-track, or full-track. Since I had traveled Dade, Broward, Palm Beach, Monroe, and Collier Counties in my airboats for decades, I saw all of the changes.

In the early years before the Everglades wetlands were affected by all of the man-made structures of levees and locks, it was especially important that my officers and I knew the depth of the water table throughout the various areas. If we made a mistake in judgment, it could result in a very serious situation for us, possibly in our being stranded in some remote area for several days. If an airboat driver took a shortcut to save fuel, he had better know what the water conditions were in that area. Spending nights in the Everglades with the mosquitoes is pretty rough. In an emergency, walking is sometimes impossible because of thick, 10-foot-high strands of saw grass. The closest airboat put-in might be 50 to 60 miles away. But, after years, decades of experience, we learned that by knowing the water table in one area, we would know what it was going to be in other areas as well.

The following "Schedule of Seasons" regarding water in the Everglades wetlands is "insider" information. This is what all of us Gladesmen familiar with the Everglades wetlands knew as fact. This is what the water managers and scientists have never taken the time to understand:

In an average year, in May, the water is approximately 6 inches under the ground. The ground has dried up on the surface, which is part of the ecology in the Everglades wetlands. The sun then is able to thoroughly kill the harmful fungus and bacteria in the river silt that would affect the fish. And, after being too wet to support seedlings and other plants, the ground is now dry enough to support seasonal plant life.

In June and July, the season changes: The water table begins to rise, and the ground becomes wet once more. The fish begin to move from the ocean into the cleansed marsh lands to spawn. The summer lightning storms arrive and start many grass fires in prairies across the Everglades. The fires burn the dried cattails and destroy them, which is very necessary, as too many cattails rob the water of oxygen. And, as you now know, meter readings in cattail thickets read "o." But by being burned over seasonally, the cattail stands are replaced by beneficial saw grass. This is the natural ecology of the Everglades wetlands.

In August, September, and October, the water table will rise to its [normally] highest point of 15 inches. This is adequate for the fish, the crawdads, and shrimp to move deeper into the upper marshes to propagate. The early migrations of waterfowl from the north arrive to feed on the new growth in the marshes. [A higher] water table of 18 inches or more [will begin] . . . to stress the hammock islands and the animals that they support. The roots of the large trees begin to rot. If the water does not go down, the huge trees actually lose their footing and fall. The mammals (the deer, raccoons, bobcats, otters, the endangered Everglades mink and Florida panthers), the fowl (the herons, ibis, egrets), and others are in jeopardy. If the water table does not drop very soon, within six weeks, the mammals will begin dying off; and the water table [will] now [be] over the heads of most wading birds, so they also cannot feed.

This [higher-than-usual water level] was a *natural* phenomenon that happened infrequently, as the natural runoff into South Florida's rivers was usually rapid, so there was seldom a long-term flood crisis in the Everglades wetlands. It was certainly *not* a controlled and contained man-made flood!

In November, December, January, and February, the water table continues to recede. Now the mammals could leave the island hammocks where they were stranded and begin to feed in their normal patterns. The surge of migratory birds from Canada to South America stops in the Everglades annually to feed on a vast quantity of fish, crayfish, shrimp, insects, snakes, frogs, and much more. The Everglades wetlands in the fall is like a breadbasket of plenty that the thousands of migratory birds depend upon.

In March and April, the water table continues to recede. Fish and other aquatics are becoming stranded in shallow bodies of water in the sloughs and in the large ponds made by the alligators. Now the food is abundant for the birds, raccoons, otters, panthers, and the alligators. Food is so abundant that the alligators have enough to build up fat to last until the next drought. The birds concentrate on their rookeries around the alligator ponds where they will make their nests and bear their young. The insects, reptiles, and turtles have dry ground to lay their eggs. And alligators begin looking for an area to make their nests. The food chain for the plants and animals has now been completed. We must never lose sight of the fact that the Everglades wetlands depends on this seasonal cycle of water, drought, and fire for its survival. (Shirley 2000)

This is what I related to the folks I took out on my airboat tours. I told them that I do not believe that the best computer has better knowledge than can be gained by hands-on experience in the Everglades. But it does have a great advantage. If something turns out wrong, the computer can always be blamed. But will it then be too late to breathe life back into the Everglades? There is too much water in many areas, flooding is rampant, huge trees are falling, and the inundated tree islands are no longer able to support wildlife at all.

In my tour business, I had several accounts with scientists. Most of the time I would take them out to do water sampling. One day we were in the wetlands and an important biologist said, "Tom, this area that we're going through now has one of the highest mercury contents . . . probably within the United States!"

I just couldn't believe it! That was really disturbing news.

But that was what got me back into the fray. Now I could fight as an Everglades advocate with no fear of losing my job!

I wanted to get all of the information I could from the Tallahassee Office on the company that was doing the research on the mercury. They had heard of me.

It seems that they had first blamed the highest concentration on the agricultural interests, but by the time I got involved, they had changed their minds and said that they know it's *not* coming from agriculture. It looked to me as if all studies get thrown aside by politics.

Next they began blaming the mercury content in the Everglades on the incinerators.

So there I was, back in the Everglades again. This time I was conducting water studies, taking samples and readings, taking photos, collecting all of the evidence and information that I could on the total destruction of these Everglades wetlands. I was literally up to my neck in Everglades politics again.

In 2006, Stanley Kern and Gus Grazer helped me conduct surveys of the water levels in Conservation Area 3. In this manner I proved that the height of the levels proposed by Water Management would be well over the height of the Everglades islands. While some of the islands contained vital archaeological evidence from as early as five thousand years ago, the islands were, as noted, the important habitations for the Everglades animals during natural seasons of high water. They were an integral part of the Everglades wetlands ecology and should not have been destroyed. I utilized this photo in my advocacy mailings to former governor Jeb Bush. He never replied. (Photo by Tom Shirley.)

I made a great contact with the conservationist Jack Moller in 1998. I gave him statistics on water depths that I had collected, accounts of the changes I had seen in the Everglades wetlands. He sent my data out to individuals and organizations via the Internet.

In 1999, I reviewed the Restudy Team and the Army Corps of Engineers Draft Comprehensive Plan Alt D13R concerning the water table duration curves within Conservation Area 3. I found that it far exceeded the water table conditions that were in place before the manmade structures were put in the Everglades. But it does not come anywhere close to representing the Everglades ecosystem on a seasonal basis! And money, *big* money, was still being spent on this project!

It was obvious that the water schedule would still keep levels entirely too high within the Everglades. It would result in the further destruction of the island hammocks throughout Conservation Area 3.

Jack Moller continued to send out e-mail updates of my reports and concerns. Meanwhile, my associate, Stan Kern, and I took a transit and made surveys across many Everglades islands, recording water depths over the islands in Conservation Area 3 to see what impact the new proposed water schedule would have on the islands in that area. Seven islands were surveyed from north to south. Our findings, published in a 2000 booklet by the Everglades Coordinating Council, showed the following results under seasonal high water conditions:

Island No. 1: 13 inches underwater at high periods.
Island No. 2: 14 inches underwater at high periods.
Island No. 3: The highest island in the area would be only ½ inch above water.
Island No. 4: 4 ½ inches underwater at high periods.
Island No. 5: 5 inches underwater at high periods.
Island No. 6: 8 inches underwater at high periods.
Island No. 7: 10 inches underwater at high periods.

By December 1998, these conditions were produced in Conservation Area 3. The approval of 30 inches in Area 3 was completely devastating, destroying the Everglades north of the Tamami Trail. It was frightening to think that our own government would ignore facts and proceed with such a plan.

With facts in hand, I wrote a letter in January 1999 to Governor Jeb Bush. I included copies of hydrographs of water levels in Conservation Areas 2 and 3 with my graphs of the destructive water levels dating from 1965 to 1995.

Not receiving a reply, I again wrote him in March 1999:

There is much debate as to what the Everglades water table, wildlife, and plant life was like in the early years. We highly recommend that we take advantage of the more direct experience that we still have available. The elder men who have spent most all of their lives and livelihood within the Everglades have much direct knowledge of this ecosystem that would prove to be very beneficial to the natural restoration.

We recommend that a special effort be put forth to locate some of these men who can relate and forward such vital information that may otherwise be overlooked by the study team.

It would be advantageous to appoint a special board of these qualified men to act as advisors to the study team. We are not against spending the 8.4 billion dollars to save the Everglades, not destroy it.

I noted the strong political clout of the South Florida Water Management District and the U.S. Army Corps of Engineers. I contrasted that clout with the deficit in wildlife from the Game Commission's statistics showing currently only 59 deer in Conservation Area 3, where in the 1960s the deer herd was estimated at 10,000!

I again wrote to the governor in August 1999 reiterating that the water depth should never exceed 15 inches. I closed the letter:

In 1955 when I became employed by the Game and Fresh Water Fish Commission, I was requested to take an oath to protect the State of Florida's natural resources, which included birds, fish, mammals, reptiles, plant life, the whole ecosystem. I cannot turn my head or ignore the procedures which are taking place. Governor Bush, without your leadership to truly save the Everglades, it will be lost forever.

cc: Frank R. Fitch, South Florida Water Management District; Christ McVoy, South Florida Water Management District; Col. M. Robson, Florida Federation of Wildlife Coordinating Council; Lorraine Heisler, Florida Federation of Wildlife Coordinating Council; and Steve Coughlin, Florida Federation of Wildlife Coordinating Council

But I never received a reply to any of my Bush correspondence.

Meanwhile, the Game and Fresh Water Fish Commission combined with the Florida Marine Patrol to create what was expected to be a great force in the movement to protect Florida's fish and wildlife. But that new agency turned an about face and recommended 30 inches or more of water in the Everglades! That is twice what the Everglades animals can withstand!

I took this photo of a Florida panther (*Felis concolor coryii*) in 1967 in the Big Cypress. This was in an area that was going to be flooded to 3 feet by Flood Control. Obviously that depth would destroy the habitat of this "endangered species." I used this photo in 2000 for my advocacy project for the Everglades Coordinating Council, the booklet *Will You Help?* (Photo by Tom Shirley.)

In 2006, I illustrated another excessively flooded area, also habitat of the endangered Florida panther that Water Management ignored and flooded out at will. (Photo by Tom Shirley.)

And the next year, I visited a section in this area that was designated Florida panther habitat. The federal and state governments approved millions of dollars for studies on the panther. One section was over 36 inches below water. Panthers will not survive under such conditions. They, like other vertebrates, require dry ground on which to live, feed, and bear their young.

In short, the Restudy Team was requesting $8.4 billion to destroy a large and valuable wildlife habitat in the Everglades by continuing to flood out all of the dry ground within its borders!

Mercury Poisoning—2000

Then, in 2000, Lee Chamberlain of the Everglades Coordinating Council (ECC), Jack Moller, and I compiled a booklet under the auspices of the Council that we entitled: *Will You Help? This Is Our Last Chance to Get It Right!* This booklet discussed the Everglades under the Comprehensive Everglades Restoration Plan (CERP), a plan to improve water conditions. For that reason alone, we wanted the ECC to be a contributor to the process, to reiterate our concerns, to again present my statistics on water issues and the health of the Everglades. That was all we could do. We were shouting into the wind, beating a dead horse, while hoping that someone would really *read* the material and start asking questions.

Our booklet was sent by the ECC to congressmen, senators, and representatives in Washington, as well as to top Florida politicians and environmentalists. It contained forty pages of statistics, graphs, and photographic evidence concerning the alteration of the Everglades wetlands by Flood Control, Water Management, and other interests over decades. It included letters to politicians. We asked the recipients to "Please approve an Everglades plan with necessary protection language that will provide proper seasonal water depths that will replenish life and natural habitats to the entire remaining Everglades ecosystem."

Wayne Jenkins, president of the Everglades Coordinating Council, noted in the cover letter:

Tom Shirley supplied a lot of the letters, documents, and actual real-time photographs. Tom has spent most of his lifetime in the Water Conservation Areas of South Florida and can be considered an expert in the opinion of ECC. He has become active during these past two years because he knows firsthand what is happening in the Everglades. Please take the time to read his enclosed input about the existing problems and his recommendations to make the right decision. The most important document in our report is Tom's seasonal water depth chart. This chart shows the proper water depth to be maintained on a monthly basis to ensure a healthy Everglades ecosystem. This is the key to restoring life or bringing final death to the Everglades.

Looking back, our booklet was such a futile attempt to get Washington's support and secure their acknowledgment of what was really taking place down here in the Everglades. We wanted them to look at the situation not from their marble halls, but from the grassroots of plant and animal survival . . . knowing all along that all they wanted to deal with was water, water, water!

But we desperately needed to try, and we desperately needed their help. We wanted them to approve money to save the Everglades, not just use the name "Everglades" to get money! Realistically, the booklet probably went to an aide, and then into a receptacle.

But my advocacy soon came to a screeching halt! Very soon after we completed the booklet I became very ill, very weak. I lost 22 pounds in eleven days. Every test known to man was run on me trying to find out what was wrong. They found nothing.

But my wife's cousin was a cardiologist in West Virginia. When he heard about my condition, he advised the physicians to run a test on me to see if I had something called "giant cell arteritis." So, in an operation, they cut two veins on either side of my head and tested them. It was indeed giant cell arteritis, a condition where the body's own immune system attacks itself.

A drove of doctors came in questioning me. They said, "This is a very rare disease that you have. We don't know for sure where it comes from, but we highly suspect it comes from herbicides or insecticides of some sort."

Well, in compiling the data for the ECC's booklet, I *had* spent weeks wading around in the Everglades, where all of the toxic levels were high.

I was barely alive when I finally was allowed to exit the hospital. When I looked in the mirror, I thought I was already dead.

But I was put in contact with one of the most effective doctors in the Southeast. She gave me a horribly large dose of steroids. I was on them for a long time. They swelled up my body, and I have never gotten my strength back. But I'm alive! My illness appears to have been a result of the toxins or the mercury in the Everglades.

I recalled what had happened to a crew out at Ron Bergeron's Camp in the saw grass in Conservation Area 3. That camp is located 4 miles west of Alligator Alley and 6 miles west of the Miami Canal. Some of the guys out there had a habit of catching a few alligators to eat. One night after dinner, they all ended up in the hospital! Obviously, there are some very harmful additives in certain waters in the Everglades.

But, back to the health of the Everglades wetlands. For me, being a Gladesman since my youth in the 1940s, the most telling marker to illustrate the plight of the Everglades wetlands is the absence of the insects. On my early morning Everglades patrol, I would pull in at various gas stations that were on the border of the Everglades. They would have their employees out there with huge brooms sweeping up big heaps of dead bugs, thousands of large and small insects that had been attracted by the station's lights during the night. Where are those bugs today? Even out Alligator Alley at the Miccosukee Truck Stop, you won't see so much as a moth flying around . . . and that's in the middle of the wetlands!

That simple fact should be a strong wake-up call to show that we have altered the ecological system enough . . .

And, we should use caution because there is something very toxic is in the water. I know this firsthand. Death is all around us, and we haven't the slightest idea.

It's like the well-known Everglades National Park champion Art Marshall Jr. told the media when I had him out in my airboat one day, "When Tom Shirley says the Everglades is dying . . . then it *is!*"

Epilogue

Gladesmen, Then and Now

I really enjoyed the people I met in the Everglades wetlands while I was on patrol. They were unique. Many were the offspring of the original Gladesmen's families.

Uncle Steve Roberts stands out. Without a doubt, he was the best-known of all the Roberts settlers and acted as the unofficial historian for the clan. I interviewed Uncle Steve on several occasions. And it was some of his younger kin that I chased after when I was on patrol.

Uncle Steve remembered the old days, when the living was harder, but the Everglades was full of life. He and his wife, Dora Jane, left Orlando in 1895 and migrated southwest to White Water Bay. They arrived to settle in Flamingo in 1901. Life at the Cape of Florida was pleasant enough, although, of course, there was the slight matter of insects.

Uncle Steve said:

People nowadays can't realize what insects used to be like here in the tip end of Florida. According to the seasons, localities, and several natural factors, we'd have sand flies along the beach, horseflies in the spring. All summer long, we had deer flies, and of course, the gnats in your eyes, nose, and ears.

The experience of the mosquitoes bein' so thick . . . they'd get on ya, coat ya all black! You couldn't breathe without getting them in your nose. You opened up your mouth, and they'd go down your throat. It was a horrible experience. I don't think there's any other place in the world that had such a heavy mosquito population.

We was lucky that only the females bite ya. Males do not bite; they feed on the plants, lucky for us. At times, even high noon out in the middle of a gigantic prairie, 12 noon, mosquitoes would still be eatin' you up. I've come up on deer that were just beside themselves, just goin' crazy with the mosquitoes. They'd be so messed up mentally that you could walk up within 10 feet of 'em and they didn't care. And I'm sure many of the young deer, the fawns, died in the heavy mosquito seasons.

By the 1950s, the Gladesmen were of a different breed. They were hardworking individuals who usually held down jobs during the week. They were active in designing and building airboats, swamp buggies, half-tracks, full-tracks, whatever it took to better travel through the Everglades terrain that they loved. Most of their spare time they would be working, often till 2400 hours on their equipment. Then on the weekend, they would get up at 4:00 a.m. to pull that equipment 50 to 60 miles to the Everglades where they would launch it. Let me tell you, they had to be tough and possess a true love for the Everglades wetlands to put out that much effort!

It breaks my heart to see this breed of Gladesmen being pushed out of their environment because of politics and policy. These men were my friends, supporters, allies, and . . . yes, even adversaries. Many policies have regulated them right out of the Everglades. As the old saying goes, "It was time to get out of Dodge!" And they left for the freedom of the wilderness areas in Georgia, North Carolina, and even Colorado!

A person is now required to attend school to learn how to drive an ATV, even though he or she has been driving that vehicle for twenty or thirty years. If a father wishes to take his young child out on an ATV, it's against the law! No child under the age of sixteen is allowed to be on an ATV.

For a hunter, owning and keeping Everglades equipment in running order requires a major outlay of time and money. It also takes several men to keep a full-track operating. The full-track carries at least three to five hunters. Yet each hunter is required to pay for a permit to enter a hunting or game management area, and each hunter is required to purchase a hunting license. This gives the hunter license to take only

Here is a modern full-track that sportsmen and hunters like my son Ray Parks take out into the Everglades today. (Photo by Tom Shirley.)

two deer a season, but the Game Commission further regulates that three hunters on a full-track can only shoot *one* deer.

The hunters would have to divide that deer up three ways . . . and that's not much game to take home for all of the permits and time and expense on the vehicle. This regulation is only in the Everglades District.

Then there's your Everglades camp. To add to hunting expenses, camp permits also have to be paid. No sooner did the National Park Service come into Big Cypress than they began to enforce restrictions. Camp owners now have to have a permit before they can enter lands where they have their camp. I am not allowed to drive off the road but must go straight to my camp. Now there are even restrictions on *who* I can take to my camp. My own family, my own sons and grandchildren, can't go to the camp without permission for *each* entry from the Big Cypress Management, yet one of my baby granddaughter's first words was "Camp!"

Also, Everglade camps now have to have approved plumbing (no outhouses) and carry insurance. I own my home, "my camp," but the regulations we have to follow just to journey out to it in a car,

I invited a group of the old Gladesmen and their friends to a barbecue in 1986 on Island 23, which is 10 miles north of Alligator Alley, in order to discuss the present state of the Everglades wetlands and to talk about old times. *Left to right, back row:* Al Henschel, Tom Shirley, unknown, unknown, Pete Gonzalez, Tommy Lanier. *Front row:* Paul Ledbetter, Freddy Fisikelli, unknown. (Photo by Timmy Nemith.)

much less to take family members or friends out to it, are unbelievably strenuous. It makes it more of an ordeal than a "fun" experience. Again, our freedom is very infringed upon at this juncture.

The federal government wants the public to know that this area is federal property that is "POSTED! FEDERAL LANDS!" Now we cannot see or touch our own land. They have not lived up to the "traditional use" agreement, which was a federal regulation. There is no respect shown for our constitutional rights. And, as I have mentioned, I actually approved the federal transfer in the first place!

And we who live in the western Everglades live under the threat of the federal government. There is talk of making Big Cypress a Wilderness Area. All it takes to create a "Wilderness Area" is the signature of a presidential pen. Then everyone who has invested in the Gladesmen's way of life; those who have upgraded their camps to meet regulations, codes; families who have had that camp for generations, will have to leave. It's a real shame because these camps were by law "traditional use" properties, properties on which families were raised, where holidays were celebrated and generations passed. We Gladesmen will have lost more of our heritage and rights.

Then, when Alligator Alley became Interstate I-75, the government fenced the road, which has become a part of the usual highway infrastructure. But in doing so on this roadway, it shut the fishermen, boaters, and sportsmen from our former access to the Everglades wetlands, except in a very few designated entry areas along that trans-Everglades highway.

The Miccosukee Tribe has a reservation in the Big Cypress where camps were leased by permit decades ago. Now, the Tribe has begun breaking many leases on old established camps that were initiated back in the days when the impoverished Tribe badly needed tribal revenues. This happened to one of my close friends recently.

This is all sad because we can't enjoy the freedom that we once experienced in the Everglades wetlands. Now, I lie awake at night, angry, thinking of our soldiers who have died to protect our freedom, while our freedom in Big Cypress is being taken away in the loss of our "traditional use" ownership. This is not the kind of "freedom" that Americans have fought and died for. Today, politics and policymaking show little regard for the Gladesmen's culture, heritage, and right to "traditional use" of the land. First, government policies supported the destruction of our wildlife. Now they are pushing Gladesmen, sportsmen, and the recreational public off the public lands.

We all bemoan the loss of the freedom of the earlier days in the Everglades wetlands and hope that younger generations will pick up the banner of advocacy that we have had to carry since the 1960s, when the threats to the Everglades wetlands first became apparent—apparent to us Gladesmen, my friends, especially Calvin Stone, John Fritchie, Freddy Fisikelli, Lee Chamberlain, Pete Gonzalez, Jack Moller, who have all aided so greatly in protecting the Everglades wetlands and wildlife, who all have lived as Gladesmen.

Calvin Stone wrote about it in *Forty Years in the Everglades* (1979). John Fritchie, who hails from a pioneer Gladesmen family, published *Everglades Journal* in 1992. Also by Gladesmen are *Totch: A Life in the*

My infrared motion-detector camera at my Big Cypress camp caught this very large panther passing through one night in 2010.

Everglades by Loren G. Brown (1993) and *Gladesmen: Gator Hunters, Moonshiners, and Skiffers* by Glen Simmons and Laura Ogden (1998).

Although I could go on and on about the downside of the Gladesmen's lack of freedom in the Everglades today, I do wish to close on a happy note.

It is summer of 2010 as I conclude this narrative, and I am comfortable in my Big Cypress camp. In the past few weeks, a large panther was documented right in my front yard by my infrared motion detector camera. And we have had a total of nine bear cubs born near the camp this season! One sow bear chose my front yard to bear her babes at night. The infrareds show her in labor and chronicle the delivery of her four cubs. The camera was only 11 feet away at the time. And one of the other moms ambles in frequently with her three cubs to visit.

I've always gotten along with the bears. I realized long ago that if I just talked with a soft tone, or sang a tune like "Mary Had a Little Lamb," they seemed to immediately realize that I was nonaggressive and they would remain quite near with their cubs, even feeling comfortable enough to turn their backs on me. Several generations of bears, doubtless this mom's parents and grandparents, have been as

In a rare series of photos from July 2010, the infrared motion-detector camera chronicled one of my Big Cypress bears delivering her four cubs right in my front yard! In all the Big Cypress swamp, this bear chose to have her cubs right in *my* front yard, obviously feeling that this was a safe place. The bears there are as common as squirrels in a city park and almost as tame.

This was the first litter of bears born near my Big Cypress camp on Father's Day, 2010. (Photo by Tom Shirley.)

much a part of the landscape in my Big Cypress home as squirrels in a city park! And should the bears begin to walk off, I just say, "You get back here!" They almost always turn around and come back. The same goes even for large buck deer. They seem to know a true friend when they see one!

Many of the old Gladesmen are fighting to save their culture and their heritage, and we're not getting any younger. Over the last one hundred years, we have been beaten, stabbed, kicked, cut, burned, bitten, drowned, and even killed while trying to save the Everglades wetlands and its wildlife. It has been our home, our life. Many of us are advocates, and we all realize that even when we lose, we must get up, dust off, and keep fighting for the Everglades wetlands in order to save it. I challenge everyone who reads this book to do your part to see that the Everglades wetlands is restored *to the ecosystem that it once was*, a natural wonder of this world, and to keep it safe and available for "traditional use" for generations as yet to come.

Sources

Interviews and phone conversations

Ed Dale, telephone conversation with Tom Shirley, 1966.
Brantley Goodson, telephone conversation with Tom Shirley, 1972.
Victor Heller, telephone interview by Patsy West, June 9, 2010.
Johnny Jones, telephone interview by Patsy West, June 9, 2010.
Ray Kramer, interview by Tom Shirley, 1962.
Joxey Redding, interview by Tom Shirley, Blue Shanty Canal, Tamiami Trail, 1970.
"Uncle" Steve Roberts, interview by Tom Shirley, Florida City, after 1985.
"Uncle" Steve Roberts, interview by Tom Shirley, Camp Hoot Owl, Everglades, 2005.
Sig Walter, telephone conversation with Tom Shirley, 1963.
Tommy Williams, interview by Tom Shirley, 1964.

Published and unpublished resources

Algar, James. *Jungle Cat*. Directed by James Algar. Walt Disney Productions, 1959.
Aldrich, A. D. Annual Report of the Florida Game and Fresh Water Fish Commission. *Florida Wildlife*, October 1957, 5, 42.
Askew, Reuben. Introductory remarks to the Governor's Conference on Water Management in South Florida. *Water Management Bulletin* 5, no. 3 (December–January 1971–72). Excerpted online, *Everglades Digital Library*, Arthur R. Marshall Jr. Collection. http://everglades.fiu.edu/marshall/FI06011112/index.htm.
Associated Press. "Hunters by Hundreds Will Gang up on Alligators." 1994.
Brown, Loren G. *Totch: A Life in the Everglades*. Gainesville: University Press of Florida, 1993.
Carr, Archie. "Alligators: Dragons in Distress." *National Geographic*, January 1967, 132–48.
Caulfield, Patricia. *Everglades: Selections from the Writings of Peter Matthiessen*. Edited and introduced by Paul Brooks. San Francisco: Sierra Club, 1970.
Dahne, Robert A. "What's a Wildlife Officer?" *Florida Wildlife*, March 1961, 16–19.
Daytona Beach News-Journal. "Shots Fired at Fishermen: Two Facing Charge at Palatka." March 1956.

Dineen, Walter J. Letter to Marjory Stoneman Douglas, August 3, 1982. Marjory Stoneman Douglas Papers. Florida Collection, University of Miami Richter Library.

Douglas, Marjorie Stoneman. *The Everglades: River of Grass*. 60th anniversary edition, with an update by Michael Grunwald. Sarasota, Fla.: Pineapple Press, 2007.

Everglades Coordinating Council (ECC). *Will You Help? This Is Our Last Chance To Get It Right!* Booklet. Cover letter by Wayne Jenkins. February 10, 2000.

Fitzgerald, Randy. "Sugar's Sweet Deal." *Reader's Digest*, February 1998, 91–95.

Florida Game and Fresh Water Fish Commission (FGFFC). "Everglades Wildlife Management Area." *Florida Wildlife*, December 1955, 29.

———. "Florida Hunting and Fishing Licenses." *Florida Wildlife*, December 1958, 41.

———. "Everglades Larger than Rhode Island." *Florida Wildlife*, January 1959, 33.

Florida Times-Union. "Judge Denies Jury Probe in Fishing Feud." March 17, 1956.

Fritchie, John. *Everglades Journal*. Miami: Florida Heritage Press, 1992.

Grunwald, Michael. *The Swamp: The Everglades, Florida, and the Politics of Paradise*. New York: Simon and Schuster, 2006.

Hardie, Jim. "Islands Could Be Alternative to Killing off Helpless Deer." *Miami Herald*, July 11, 1982.

Kersey, Harry A., Jr. *Pelts, Plumes, and Hides: White Traders among the Seminole Indians 1870–1930*. Gainesville: University Press of Florida, 1975.

Krause, Renee. "Panther Killing Charge Reinstated Against Leader." *Fort Lauderdale News and Sun-Sentinel*, October 4, 1986.

Ledbetter, Paul. Letter to Tom Shirley, 1963.

Loftin, Horace. "Classroom in the Everglades." *Florida Wildlife*, March 1960, 12–15, 41.

Loveless, Charles M. *The Everglades Deer Herd Life History and Management*. Florida Game and Fresh Water Fish Commission Technical Bulletin No. 6. Tallahassee, Fla., 1959.

Massey, Howard T. ("Toby"). "Tusker Tug of War." *Florida Wildlife*, June 1956, 21.

McIver, Stuart B. *Death in the Everglades*. Gainesville: University Press of Florida, 2003.

Miami Daily News. "Game Violation: Policeman Sentenced over Gun." May 14, 1956.

Moeser, Bill. "Drought Lingers, Disaster Is Near." *Miami Daily News*, February 24, 1959.

Perkins, Marlin, Jim Fowler, and Stanley E. Brock. "Swampwater Safari" (1967). Rereleased on Mutual of Omaha's *Mammals of North America*, vol. 2, disc 1. Brentwood Home Video, 2006.

Philip, Kenneth R. 1977. "Turmoil at Big Cypress: Seminole Deer and the Florida Cattle Tick Controversy." *Florida Historical Quarterly* 56 (July 1977): 28–44.

Saling, Vic. "Sink or Swim . . . The Fight for Survival in Conservation Area Three." *Gator Tales*. Newsletter of the Everglades Conservation and Sportsmen's Club. N.p.: Everglades/Poinsettia Press, 1966.

Scaggs, Chad. "Eyewitness: Fishermen Balk Game Wardens." *Daytona Beach News-Journal* Bureau, March 1956.

Shabecoff, Phillip. "Tribal Chief Acquitted in Killing of a Panther." *New York Times*, October 9, 1987.

Shirley, Tom. Letter to Earl Frye, Asst. Director, Game and Fresh Water Fish Commission, September 7, 1963.

———. Letter to Florida Gov. Jeb Bush, January 21, 1999. Reprinted in ECC booklet, February 10, 2000.

———. Letter to Florida Gov. Jeb Bush, March 2, 1999. Reprinted in ECC booklet, February 10, 2000.

———. Letter to Florida Gov. Jeb Bush, August 26, 1999. Reprinted in ECC booklet, February 10, 2000.

———. "Schedule of Seasons." Typescript printed in ECC booklet, February 10, 2000.

———. "What Happened to the Everglades?" August 1986. Typescript in possession of author.

Simmons, Glen, and Laura Ogden. *Gladesmen: Gator Hunters, Moonshiners, and Skiffers*. Gainesville: University Press of Florida, 1998.

St. Petersburg Times. "Judge Allows Deer Kill to Begin Today." July 18, 1982.

Stone, Calvin R. *Forty Years in the Everglades*. Tabor City, N.C.: Atlantic, 1979.

Taylor, Tommy. "Tom Shirley: Myth or Legend?" Typescript in possession of author. N.d.

Tolpin, James H. "Billie Won't Be Retried, U.S. Drops Its Case in Panther Shooting." *Fort Lauderdale News and Sun-Sentinel*, October 10, 1987.

U.S. Army Corps of Engineers and South Florida Water Management District. South Florida Everglades Restoration Restudy Plan AltD13R. *Central and Southern Florida Project Comprehensive Review Study*. April 1999.

Van Dresser, Cleveland. "Florida's Hunting and Fishing Picture, The Everglades." *Florida Wildlife*, July 1955, 18–20.

Walker, Sig. Letter to Bob Aldrich, director, Game and Fresh Water Fish Commission, 1963. In possession of author.

Wayman, Stan. "A Battle to Aid Ailing Deer." *Life*, September 30, 1957, 14–20.

West, Patsy. "Pre–Second Seminole War Settlements in Lowlands Florida." Typescript. 2010. In possession of author.

Wickstrom, Karl. "Airboat Fight: Roberts Boys Lose in Court." *Miami Herald*, 1964.

Index

Jordan, Jimmy, 56, 105, 143–46, 180
Jungle Cat (film), 107
Justice Department, U.S., 217

Kamikaze flight, 77
Kannington, Fred, 97
Karado, 181, 225
Kelley, Gwynn, 212–13, 232
Kennedy assassination, 157–58
Kern, Stan, 76, *244*, 245
Kersey, Harry, 109
Key West, 67, 171
Kinder, David, 125
King, Vern, 35, 36
Kramer, Ray, 159

L-4 Levee, 117, 130
L-5 Levee, 130, 225
L-28 Levee, 81, 210
L-31 Levee (and canal), 205
L-67 Levee, 203
Labor Day Storm of 1935, 6–7
Lacey Act, 206, 222
Lake Okeechobee, 1, 25, 27, 199, 200, 235
Lanier, Tommy, *254*
Lawless, Bruce, *190, 193*
Lawrence, Dick, 132
Ledbetter, Paul, 154, 189, *254*
Lee, Tommy, 173
Life (magazine), 64
Ligas, Frank, 63, 70
Lily Slough, 60
Lincoln Vail of the Everglades (television series), *146*, 152
Little River, 5
Lone Palm Slough, 74
Looney, Rory, 196
Loop Road, 81, 86, 94; Capone and, 17; fishing near, 18, 35; Homestead Outlaws and, 53, 77–78, 83; mangroves near, 56; in 1930s, 17–18; Redding, Bobo, and, 141; Roberts family and, 95, *101*; Walker and, 143–45
Lopez, Virgil, 88, 89, 90, 181

Lord's Hammocks, 59
Lost City, *22*, 23
Lott, Elliott, 155
Loveless, Charles, 63, 65, 68, 201, 202
Lowe, M. C., 144
Loxahatchee, xiii
Loxahatchee National Wildlife Refuge, 30

Mack's Fishing Camp, 12, 17, *219*; as airboat put in, 47, 136; Grapefruit Head and, 84, 138; Harris and, 47, 49, 51; recreation areas near, 35, *35*, 137; robbery threat against, 219–20; Sawgrass Camp construction and, 124, *125*
Manard, Archie, *169*
Manatees, 14, 94
Mann, Chuck, 222
Mansfield, Jane, 34
Maples, John, 97–98
Marathon, 177
Marcus, Bud, *169*
Marine and Wildlife Resources Office, 217
Marshall, Art, 200, 250
Martinez, Roy, 226–28
Marvonious, Hellen, 100
Mason Smith Act, 206
Massey, Toby, 60, 73, 107, *108*, *110*, 189, *190*, 191
Matthews, Dave, 220
Matthews, George, 220
Matthiessen, Peter, 206
McBroom, W. Thomas, 152, 194, 195, 196
McCloud, John, 81–82
McCullough, Bill, 161, 179
McDonald, Bob, 195
McIver, Stuart, 221
McNamara, Robert, 80
McVoy, Christ, 246
Medley, 133
Melaleuca, xv, *xvi*
Mercury levels, 243
Mercury poisoning, 237, 248–50

Born in Kennedy, Texas, in 1930 and raised in Miami since 1931, Tom Shirley joined the Florida Game and Fresh Water Fish Commission in 1955, where he served in Law Enforcement for the Everglades Division. Making lieutenant in 1960, he had twenty-eight wildlife officers under his supervision. As area supervisor, he was in charge of the vast Everglades in Dade and Broward, as well as parts of Collier and Munroe Counties. He retired in 1985 after a career of thirty years. Since retirement, he has been an active advocate for the protection and restoration of the Everglades wetlands to its *original* ecosystem and for acknowledgment of the Gladesmen's "traditional use" rights.

The University Press of Florida is the scholarly publishing agency for the State University System of Florida, comprising Florida A&M University, Florida Atlantic University, Florida Gulf Coast University, Florida International University, Florida State University, New College of Florida, University of Central Florida, University of Florida, University of North Florida, University of South Florida, and University of West Florida.